HIROHITO

The
War
Years

HIROHITO

The War Years

Paul Manning

BANTAM BOOKS

NEW YORK · TORONTO · LONDON · SYDNEY · AUCKLAND

HIROHITO: THE WAR YEARS

*A Bantam Book / published by arrangement with
the author*

Bantam edition / December 1989

Library of Congress Cataloging-in-Publication Data

Manning, Paul.
    Hirohito : the war years / Paul Manning.
    p.   cm.
    Reprint. with new intro. Originally published: New York, N.Y.:
Dodd, Mead, c1986.
    Includes index.
    ISBN 0-553-34795-0
    1. World War, 1939–1945—Japan.   2. Japan—Politics and
government—1926–1945.   3. Hirohito, Emperor of Japan,
1901–1989.
I. Title.
[D767.2.M265   1989]
940.53'52--dc20   89-14860
                                                              CIP

Published simultaneously in the United States and Canada

PRINTED IN THE UNITED STATES OF AMERICA

CW   0 9 8 7 6 5 4 3 2 1

Contents

Introduction

Two days after Emperor Hirohito broadcast his surrender statement on August 15, 1945, to Japan and to the world, I went ashore at Yokohama and drove to Tokyo in a jeep with two U.S. Coast Guard officers. On the docks where they had unloaded the jeep from a Coast Guard vessel, I had struck up a conversation with them, and they asked me where I would like to go. I, too, had just stepped off a ship, as the first war correspondent ashore in Japan, and I replied, "Tokyo, and the Imperial Palace." This fit in with their assignment to take pictures of the damage to Tokyo as part of a U.S. naval history of World War II.

When we reached the Imperial Palace, we walked toward the entrance at Nijubashi, where citizens of the city had been praying for forgiveness by the Emperor for having failed to win the war for him. It was now August 17, and the civilians who had first gathered had largely been replaced by military men, in civvies now, each with small kit bags, making their final bows of apology. Once their bows and prayers were made, they would depart, misty-eyed but stern-faced as they began the long walks across Japan back to their homes.

I was in the uniform of a U.S. war correspondent, and I walked across the bridge over the moat and onto the grounds of the Imperial Palace. It was beautifully quiet and tranquil. The armed Imperial Household guards who watched me as I passed assumed this unaccompanied American was an official of the surrender situation, perhaps an advance officer surveying the damage to the Imperial Palace and its grounds. There were areas of untidiness, not unlike Berchtesgaden or the Fuehrerbunker in Berlin after the final Allied air raids. I approached the outer entrance to the Imperial bomb shelter, which had been constructed hurriedly after Colonel Jimmy Doolittle and his sixteen B-25s had bombed Tokyo, on April 18, 1942. There I saw Emperor Hirohito, no longer in military uniform, dressed now in a business suit. As one journalist put it later, General Douglas MacArthur, the Supreme Allied Commander, helped Hirohito off with his cape of invincibility and into the Western-style suit of a constitutional monarch.

When I came upon him, Hirohito was assessing the bomb damage to his palace. I stepped toward him and he acknowledged me with a nod. "The damage is very considerable," I remarked. He agreed, but added, "With peace and time it will return to its former grandeur, like the nation itself, which will also change." I asked him if he was glad that the war had come to an end, and he answered, "Yes, I want my officers and men not to do anything heroic now." This was the "Voice of the Crane," the Emperor of Japan, who had closed his surrender broadcast with these words: "My subjects, let us carry forward the glory of our national structure and let us not lag behind the progress of the world. Submit, ye, to our Will!" I quoted his closing words back to the Emperor, and he made another remark to me: "My people are hardworking. Japan will recover." His Majesty then nodded politely to me, turned away, and walked toward the Gobunko, the building on the palace grounds where the affairs of state were administered and the war's progress had been planned and directed by him.

Introduction

The Emperor is dead now, and his burial site alongside his father, Emperor Taisho, in Hachioji City, a suburb of metropolitan Tokyo, is a national shrine. Yet there continues to be controversy over his role in shaping six decades of Japanese history, particularly his military leadership before and during World War II.

I stand by my statement to *The Wall Street Journal* at the time of Hirohito's passing. They were assessing the man who embodied so much Japanese history—the Pacific war, the defeat of his country, the occupation, followed by the postwar economic success, and I commented on his wartime participation. "He plotted with his advisors the invasions of Manchuria and China, and the attack on Pearl Harbor, which thrust the United States into the Pacific war. He listened to his army and navy leaders, and once the details had been worked out, approved their recommendations for aggression and war."

The image of the late Emperor as a gentle lover of peace who may have opposed these aggressions but did not know how to or have the power to stop them goes against recorded history. Following the ceremony of surrender aboard the *USS Missouri*, on September 2, 1945, Hirohito was the object of the greatest public relations campaign in history. Lord Privy Seal Kido, his number one civilian assistant and advisor, directed it with the financial backing of powerful Japanese banking and business leaders known as the twelve-family Zaibatsu. It was a national and international campaign to convince people everywhere that the Emperor was not to blame for the invasions of the Pacific war.

General MacArthur helped along this Japanese campaign of disinformation when he recommended and promoted the policy that Hirohito continue to reign as a constitutional monarch and not be tried as a war criminal. MacArthur, against the popular wishes of Australia,

Britain, and many in the U.S. Congress, stated he needed Hirohito's continued presence on the Throne to stabilize Japan and establish the nation as an American ally against Soviet communism.

Many war correspondents who covered the Pacific war and the early occupation years knew that the Emperor was guilty of misdeeds as grave as those attributed to Hitler. But the momentum in favor of "Hirohito the Meek" was too great for them to overcome. American reporters at MacArthur's headquarters had their dispatches altered by censors, or by their editors back in the States, many of whom had never ventured into Pacific war zones. Too many editors were taken in by the Japanese message that Hirohito had sat idly by in the Palace, praying to his ancestors, powerless against the wishes and decisions of his military advisors.

Network commentators were misled, and such news authorities as H. V. Kaltenborn dutifully echoed the peacetime message that Hirohito had been an unknowing innocent all through his country's aggressions in Southeast Asia, which culminated in the attack on Pearl Harbor.

The campaign of disinformation in support of the rehabilitated Hirohito accelerated when General Hideki Tojo, who also served as Premier during the war, agreed to be the Imperial scapegoat for all war crimes. He agreed as well to acknowledge that he had triggered the attack on Pearl Harbor, which brought America into the war. He accepted this role at the request of the Emperor and at the urging of Lord Privy Seal Kido and the Zaibatsu leadership, who early on had backed him to command Japan's armies. Tojo was a brilliant and energetic man, totally committed to his country's destiny to conquer half the world. He had promised a "Strike South" that would deliver vast and needed raw materials and territories into the hands of Japanese industrialists.

When he was presented to Emperor Hirohito with the backing of Lord Privy Seal Kido and the Zaibatsu leadership, he was accepted by the Emperor as the man who would carry out the military orders of the Emperor as well as the wishes of Japan's business leaders. But in 1946, as he languished in Sugamo Prison awaiting trial, Tojo agreed to assume all wartime blame, simply because by so doing his wife and family were provided food, coal, and good treatment by the Zaibatsu leaders, who in better times had presented him with a fine mansion following victory at Pearl Harbor. By assuming blame for Japanese aggression and misdeeds, Tojo paid the supreme penalty: execution by hanging.

To General MacArthur it was all charade, even though Tojo was guilty of many military sins and should pay the penalty for the transgressions of his armies. As for Emperor Hirohito, he stated to MacArthur, in their first meeting, in the American embassy, on September 27, 1945: "I bear sole responsibility for every political and military decision made and action taken by my people in the conduct of the war."

This statement, which a MacArthur aide repeated to me personally at the time, was confirmed by me many years later as I searched through the military intelligence files of the Pacific war kept by the U.S. government in Suitland, Maryland. And I came across an additional revelation in a letter that Admiral Yamamoto had written following his surprise attack on Pearl Harbor: "It is my wish to dictate surrender terms to the United States in the White House." During this period, following a meeting at the Imperial Palace, Lord Privy Seal Kido recorded in his diary a conversation between Emperor Hirohito and Yamamoto, in which the Emperor asked his admiral how he thought the war would go now, after Pearl Harbor. Yamamoto answered: "I will run wild for the next eighteen months, and after that it will be all downhill if we have not achieved victory by that time." To this, the Emperor replied: "Well, by that time Hitler will have won his war against Russia, and I can make an accommodation with President Roosevelt. We will keep much of the territory we have conquered."

Yamamoto did run wild in the Pacific for a time, and his victory in the Battle of the Java Sea gave Japan control of the Dutch East Indies, with their rich resources of oil, tin, and tungsten. Prime Minister General Tojo, as well, enjoyed his military successes, with the invasions of the Philippines, Hong Kong, Malaya, Singapore, Siam, Burma, Sumatra, Borneo, the Celebes, Timor, the Bismarcks, the Gilberts, Wake Island, Guam, most of the Solomons, and a part of New Guinea.

Admiral Yamamoto wanted to land an expeditionary force in Australia, but General Tojo objected, feeling the risk was too great. According to the Emperor's chief of staff Sugiyama (as noted in the "Sugiyama Memorandum"), the matter was settled in the Imperial Palace when Hirohito decided that any invasion of Australia should be postponed. In Hirohito's opinion, and in line with his global strategy of intending to divide the world with Hitler, an advance into India and the Middle East took precedence over an attack on Australia. Hirohito urged caution to his generals and admirals too. He told a meeting of his military and naval leaders that while the war must be prosecuted aggressively, Japan must not overextend herself nor must she neglect the consolidation of the great territories she had already conquered.

In the glory year of 1941–42, Hirohito was filled with euphoria, thanks to the successes of his armed forces, which he had directed hands-on much like his European partner, Adolf Hitler. The Emperor could scarcely believe his good fortune in Japan's conquests. Lord Privy Seal Kido recorded the following in his diary regarding one meeting he had with Hirohito while the war was going exceedingly well for Japan and for His Majesty:

> The Emperor was beaming like a child. "The fruits of war," he said, "are tumbling into our mouth almost too quickly. The enemy at Bandung on the Java front announced their surrender on the seventh, and now our Army is negotiating for the surrender of all forces in the Netherlands East Indies. The enemy has surrendered at Surabaja and also on the Burma front has given up Rangoon." He was so pleased.

The Emperor's generals and admirals had accomplished all that had been promised Hirohito, and one month short of his forty-second birthday the goals held since his youth were realized. But, as he told Kido, "My ancestors still require more of me."

It had been a well-planned war, beginning in 1931 when Japanese troops invaded Manchuria and China. These armies had been preceded by Japanese secret agents who had drawn up the battle plans and strategies for Emperor Hirohito. Once the plans were approved by him, all field commanders met with the Emperor at his summer beach villa and received the imperial blessing for success in the field.

The espionage factor was important in the fine-tuning of Hirohito's military machine, from Manchuria to Pearl Harbor. When the Japanese were making their moves along the Siberian border into Manchuria, Joseph Stalin became alarmed. He thought this might be a prelude for a "Strike North" into Russia, which many Japanese politicians and military men were urging the Emperor to do. Hirohito allayed Soviet suspicions by having his Lord Privy Seal Kido meet with the Japanese links to the Red Army intelligence network and inform them of His Majesty's real intentions. Kido met with Saionji Kinkazu, who listened carefully and then arranged a meeting with Ozaki Hotsumi, a Japanese journalist who fed top secret information to Richard Sorge, Stalin's premier spy in Japan. The information was sent along the Red Army intelligence channel and reached the Soviet dictator; it was accepted and believed, which kept Japan out of a war with Russia at a delicate moment. Hirohito's intent was that when Japan was ready for a large war it would launch a "Strike South," not north, and he was pragmatic enough not to get into an unwarranted clash with Soviet troops.

To be sure, the Emperor could have communicated all this to Stalin in the normal way of diplomacy, through his foreign minister, but Hirohito recognized that Stalin believed only the information his agents stole and relayed through secret channels. Winston Churchill learned this early on, during the Soviet-German war. When Churchill warned Stalin through the British ambassador in Moscow that Hitler was planning an attack on the Soviet Union in June 1941, Stalin paid no attention to the warning simply because it came to him in a proper diplomatic manner, open and aboveboard.

Prime Minister Prince Konoye imitated Hirohito's strategy with the United States. His foreign office statements to his embassy in Washington that were routinely given to our State Department were always suspect. He used an American agent in the U.S. embassy in Tokyo to transmit his messages to the White House.

When I started to write this book, which is based on seven hundred documents I researched in the military files in the U.S. Archives in Suitland, Maryland, including the Kido diaries, as well as on my own on-the-scene records and observations of those war days, I felt it necessary to add the input of an American spy, one who had been on the scene, underground, in Japan throughout the war. I telephoned my friend John H. Taylor, of the Military Documents Section in the National Archives. He is a veteran of the OSS, was a special researcher for the late William J. Casey of the CIA, and was the man who could pinpoint such an American agent. Taylor said he knew of such a man and would call him and see if he was agreeable to an interview. Taylor subsequently called me back and said I could have my interview. I went to Washington with my son John and a film company executive, Marsha Heath. We met with the wartime agent. The initial interview lasted for an hour, with Marsha Heath taking extensive notes, as did I. As we left the agent's apartment, Marsha declared she was absolutely satisfied that we had our spy and that his information would provide fascinating sidelights to my central account of Hirohito's and General Douglas MacArthur's roles in the war.

Days later in New York, Kobi Jaeger, an executive more senior than Marsha, told us he wanted the wartime spy to come to New York and meet with him. Jaeger is a very savvy man, and he did not want any factual slip-ups. He told me to make reservations for the agent and his wife at the Marriott, and he would pay their expenses.

The conference took place in an office. Once again the agent told his story of espionage in Japan, which I relate in this book. Every word he uttered was openly recorded on tape by Marsha. When the office conference was over, we left together for lunch, and as we ordered, Marsha placed her tape recorder on the table and recorded further statements by the agent. After lunch we returned to the office and still more data was taped. It was an all-day session, after which the agent and his wife returned to the hotel.

A pseudonym is used in this book to identify this American spy. We will call him Ralph M. for purposes of identification, because he is still alive and the Japanese secret service has long arms, even these days. People I have spoken with in the covert world say "Ralph" was indeed MacArthur's best agent in Japan throughout the war.

I also wanted to document the information I had obtained that Japan had worked hard in the midst of the war to develop an atomic bomb. I needed a corroborating source but could not find documentation in the military archives at Suitland, Maryland. As it turned out, however, the whole story of Japan's race to perfect atomic fission came to me unexpectedly from a source in Europe. From Strasbourg, France, I received a letter written by a Dr. Leon Grunbaum, a man I didn't know. In the letter he explained that he was a nuclear scientist who had worked in the West German nuclear center at Karlsruhe. He had read my book *Martin Bormann, Nazi in Exile,* which a friend of his in New York had mailed to him. "This is a great book," he wrote, "and it reveals hidden history which is absolutely true." Grunbaum had been doing research on the same subject for a long time. His own book about Bormann focused on the nuclear fission activities of the German expatriates in Argentina working under the direction of Nazi-in-exile Party Minister Bormann. Bormann had promised Argentina's leaders he would bring Argentina into the thermonuclear age, and Dr. Grunbaum referred to this program as "The resurgence of Nazism in the nuclear age." He asked to meet with me in New York City, and I wrote in answer that I would be glad to talk with him. Only days later I received a telephone call from Grunbaum, who was in New York City. Never having met him—it is my nature to be cautious with strangers—I suggested we meet the next day at 3 P.M. in the lobby of the Waldorf-Astoria, opposite the Peacock Alley restaurant. I arrived on time and, after a brief wait, saw a short, muscular man carrying a briefcase step from behind a pillar. He was being cautious too. But as my photograph had covered the back jacket of my book, he recognized and identified me without trouble. We shook hands, and I suggested we step across the lobby and have drinks while we discussed what was on his mind.

We both ordered tomato juice, not trusting each other on such short notice. However, Grunbaum was direct. He said he had absolute evidence that Martin Bormann was still alive in South America. He suggested we both go to South America and interview the Nazi leader. This had been on my mind in the past months, but I had not considered having a partner for such a venture.

In the first place, who was Dr. Leon Grunbaum? Was he KGB, using me as an entry to Bormann? Or was he an Israeli Mossad agent? Either way, we would both be terminated if Grunbaum was unacceptable to General Heinrich Mueller. I had been told of the Israeli agent who had successfully tracked the Vice Fuehrer to his Argentine ranch. The agent's grave there is a memorial to an Israeli who got too close to his target and became one himself.

At a later date I would decide to go to Argentina to follow several leads that could not be confirmed except by a face-to-face meeting with Bormann. But that's another story.

Grunbaum and I ordered sandwiches, and he asked how my book on Hirohito was coming along, for I had told him of my current project. "It's about finished," I replied. I asked him, in turn, how well the Germans and Japanese had worked together during World War II in the field of developing nuclear power, and further, "Did the Japanese have an ongoing program of developing an atomic bomb?"

"Yes, they did," he told me. "They carried on their research in university laboratories. They had a small amount of uranium, for experimental purposes. But as they pushed ahead they needed more. And after their defeat at Midway, the importance of an A-bomb loomed large on their priorities list. They called on their German allies for assistance."

"Did the Germans respond?" I asked.

"Very quickly. They sent a shipment of heavy water and uranium oxide aboard a submarine from Norway. It was the U-boat 234. They also duplicated the shipment by Japanese submarine of the I-52 class. They included in this shipment to Tokyo precise data on their experiments to date. It was incomplete, because the Germans had yet to make an A-bomb. Still, it was a large beginning. Japanese scientists took this data and pushed forward on their own. But they made the same two fundamental mistakes the Germans made."

"And they were?" I pressed him.

"First, in trying to separate uranium, they used heavy water instead of graphite, and second, they utilized thermal diffusion instead of ultracentrifuge. The scientists working for General Groves, on the other hand, on the Manhattan Project in Los Alamos, went the graphite and ultracentrifuge route and won for America the race for the atomic bomb."

I now had my confirmation that Japanese scientists had worked desperately hard to discover the secret of nuclear fission for their Emperor and Japan.

In 1943 Hirohito looked again to the Germans for additional help and suffered another disappointment. Because he was facing a general of immense capabilities and Allied armed forces of great numbers, he knew he had to do something to hinder the onslaught of General MacArthur, who, in his drive toward Japan, would make eighty-seven amphibious landings, all of them successful, cutting Japanese escape routes and lines of communication. By 1945 he was in Manila, and planning moves to the Japanese mainland. The Emperor turned to Adolf Hitler and, through his ambassador in Berlin, General Hiroshi Baron Oshima, asked the Fuehrer to send him some V-2 rocket weapons. He had already received blueprints and some parts for the V-1 flying bomb, by freight-carrying submarines. Yet now he wanted the fifteen-hundred-mile-an-hour weapon so he could wipe out MacArthur at his headquarters in the Philippines. Hitler turned him down, explaining, "I need all the V-2s I have for London. When my scientists have solved the secret of making an atomic bomb, I will use other V-2s with atomic nose cones to bomb Moscow."

When Hirohito was turned down by Hitler, he knew there was nothing more he could do except instruct his commanders of the army and navy to fight on. He waited for some manifestation that would point the way for his next move, and it came when President Harry Truman ordered atomic bombs dropped on the cities of Hiroshima and Nagasaki. These were shocking enough disasters to warrant a face-saving surrender, and that is just what Hirohito ordered when he presided over a midnight meeting of the Supreme Council for the Direction of the War, a conference held in the bomb shelter beneath the Imperial Palace, on August 9, 1945.

This was the second time Hirohito had wanted to come to terms with the United States. In 1942, when he was winning big, he thought it an opportune moment to make peace with President Roosevelt and so began directing feelers toward the White House through Geneva and Lisbon. What he did not understand, however, was the Western mind, that the atrocities committed by his troops in the field threatened any peace overtures. There had been the Rape of Nanking in 1937, in which twenty thousand Chinese, after surrendering, had been massacred by Japanese soldiers who raped more than twenty-five thousand Chinese women as well. The Fall of Singapore on February 15, 1942, saw more mass executions, and a shipload of wounded Australian soldiers with nurses was sunk off Banka Island on the Sumatra coast. Wounded soldiers and nurses who managed to swim ashore were bayoneted or machine-gunned by Japanese soldiers. In London, in the House of Commons, British Foreign Secretary Anthony Eden revealed to the entire world that Japan had also committed abominable atrocities on a wide scale following their seizure of Hong Kong in January of 1942. Thousands of British, Australian, and New Zealand troops died from neglect and starvation as prisoners of war in Japanese concentration camps. The Bataan Death March, in 1942, went down in history as another major Japanese atrocity. Of the seventy thousand American and Filipino soldiers who surrendered, only fifty-four thousand managed to walk to San Fernando, the terminus of the march. The sixteen thousand who never arrived had been bayoneted and shot en route for their inability to keep up.

Lord Privy Seal Kido spoke to Hirohito regarding Eden's speech and the atrocities, but the Emperor was not concerned about them or about preventing a recurrence of such dreadful deeds, which by now were the trademark of Japanese invasion forces.

But Colonel Jimmy Doolittle's raid of April 18, 1942—one day after the Bataan Death March ended—did anger Hirohito. When those sixteen B-25s had dropped their bombs on Tokyo and then flown on to the Chinese mainland, the Emperor's rage was unbridled. He ordered General Okamura Yasuji, the senior Japanese commander in China, to prepare a reprisal expedition against the Chinese province of Chekiang, where many of Doolittle's airmen had found refuge. When the Japanese forces had accomplished their devastation and withdrawn from Chekiang in mid-August of 1942, they had killed two hundred fifty thousand Chinese, most of them civilians. The villages where the American fliers had been given sanctuary were reduced to cinders. In Japan's brutal eight-year war with China the vengeance on Chekiang was unrivaled, except for the march on Nanking in 1937.

Hirohito's anger against Colonel Doolittle and his airmen was directed, really, at President Roosevelt. To Hirohito the Doolittle raid demonstrated that the United States had no intention of settling with him or backing down and that Roosevelt continued to insist on "self-determination" and "freedom of opportunity" throughout Asia. It was clear now that this was to be a long war.

Emperor Hirohito's death marked the end of an era for Japan and the world. They have all passed away now, those leaders of World War II: Franklin D. Roosevelt, Winston Churchill, Adolf Hitler, Benito Mussolini, Joseph Stalin, and Hirohito—the 124th direct descendant of the Emperor Jimmu Tenno, who ruled in the seventh century before Christ.

HIROHITO

The
War
Years

One

"Voice of the Crane," Emperor Hirohito

Every year since the end of World War II, Emperor Hirohito led his nation in prayer for the two and a half million Japanese servicemen who died in that conflict. Dressed in black, this leader of Shinto remembered vividly the war years and remarked softly that "The past forty years have passed so quickly that we still feel close to those who died during the war. Even today, my heart aches," the Emperor added.

The announcement of Japan's surrender took place at noon on August 15, 1945. It was broadcast by Hirohito himself over the Japanese national network, NHK, the first radio broadcast ever made by the Emperor of Japan to his people.

The night before, Hirohito had held one last meeting of the Supreme Council for the Direction of the War. For the last time they had gathered in the bomb shelter beneath the Imperial Palace. The army was opposed to surrender. They wanted to die defending the homeland, and take with them a million or more invading Ameri-

1

cans. They would have, too, if General MacArthur had been forced to invade Japan. MacArthur had read the invasion plan prepared by the War Department in Washington, called "Operation Olympic," with the actual landing code designated as "Downfall." He knew that the War Department had grossly underestimated the defensive forces under Hirohito's command. They had estimated Japan's ground forces at seven hundred and fifty thousand. The actual figure was 2,350,000 regular soldiers for ground defense and two hundred and fifty thousand garrison troops with a backup of thirty-two million civilian militiamen, all prepared to die for the Emperor and Japan. Behind the beaches where Allied troops would land, tunnels were packed with enormous quantities of ammunition and food to assist in the long and bloody fight. Backstopping all of this were ten thousand kamikaze pilots and their planes, along with the regular homeland air-defense force of trained pilots, who had been held back from Okinawa and were ready for air battles over Kyushu and Honshu. There were the batteries of V-1 flying rocket bombs, which had been manufactured by the army and navy from designs and samples sent by submarine from Germany. These V-1s would take their toll on Admiral Nimitz's battleships and landing fleets as they made their slow way through minefields. Japanese air force commanders in Korea, Formosa, and China could also be counted on to fly their squadrons to Japanese homeland airfields and take part in *Ketsu-Go,* Japan's "Operation Decision." The Japanese navy, notwithstanding its heavy losses at Leyte and Okinawa, remained a formidable defense.

MacArthur, who did not know whether the United States would perfect the atomic bomb, was proceeding with his invasion plans, which called for the Downfall landings on November 1, 1945. He told Secretary of War

Stimson that the cost of the invasion would be "one million American casualties alone."

But an atomic bomb was test-exploded in the New Mexico desert in July 1945, and counterparts were shipped to Tinian Island. President Harry Truman, impatient over Japan's slowness in accepting surrender and the terms of the Potsdam Declaration, ordered two bombs dropped on Japan; the Air Force sent one B-29 from Tinian, the *Enola Gay*, with Hiroshima as its target city; two days later Nagasaki was hit.

President Truman, who had read MacArthur's estimate of predicted casualties and was determined to prevent such a toll, declared that the awesome death and destruction of Hiroshima and Nagasaki could be laid at the doorstep of the Emperor and the Japanese military establishment for their failure to comply promptly with American surrender terms.

In a broadcast from the White House Truman stated: "We have spent two billion dollars on the greatest scientific gamble in history and won. If the Japanese do not now accept our terms, they may expect a rain of ruin from the air, the like of which has not been seen on this earth . . ." The President added, for Emperor Hirohito's benefit: "The source from which the sun draws its power could now totally eclipse the Land of the Rising Sun, on whose throne sits a direct descendant of Amaterasu O-Mikami, the Goddess of the Sun."

Hirohito wanted total agreement—Group Harmony— on the question of surrender. If he could not achieve agreement he would order surrender. The meeting in the bomb shelter went on for several hours, with all present expressing their opinions, including army leaders who wanted a fight to the finish. With all opinions expressed, Hirohito, in army uniform, made his views crystal clear with the following statement:

3

I have listened carefully to all the arguments opposing Japan's acceptance of the Allied reply as it stands. My own opinion, however, has not changed. I shall now restate it. I have examined the conditions prevailing in Japan and in the rest of the world, and I believe that a continuation offers nothing but continued destruction. I have studied the terms of the Allied reply, and I have come to the conclusion that they represent a virtually complete acknowledgment of our position as we outlined it in the note dispatched a few days ago. In short, I consider the reply to be acceptable . . .

Although some of you are apprehensive about the preservation of the national structure, I believe that the Allied reply is evidence of the good intentions of the enemy. The conviction and resolution of the Japanese people are, therefore, the most important consideration. That is why I favor acceptance of the reply. I fully understand how difficult it will be for the officers of the army and navy to submit to being disarmed and to see their country occupied. I am aware also of the willingness of the people to sacrifice themselves for their nation and their Emperor. But I am not concerned with what may happen to me. I want to preserve the lives of our people. I do not want them subjected to further destruction. It is indeed hard for me to see my loyal soldiers disarmed and my faithful ministers punished as war criminals.

If we continue the war, Japan will be altogether destroyed. Although some of you are of the opinion that we cannot completely

4

trust the Allies, I believe an immediate and peaceful end to the war is preferable to seeing Japan annihilated. As things stand now, the nation still has a chance to recover.

I desire the Cabinet to prepare as soon as possible an Imperial Rescript announcing the termination of the war.

The Emperor rose and left the bomb shelter. His ministers and councillors stayed respectfully behind, in a state of shock, some in tears.

It was morning now of the same day, August 14, and engineers and producers of NHK were setting up recording equipment in the Imperial Library. The Emperor was about to record his surrender statement, which would be aired at noon the next day. With everything in readiness, Hirohito entered the library and sat down before the microphone, his Imperial Rescript in hand. When he had recorded the statement and left the library, the engineers wrapped up their equipment, the senior producer carefully carried the record to the truck outside, and the unit drove off to NHK. The record was deposited safely in a vault belowground.

That night rumors of the Emperor's recorded surrender swept though army circles. A horde of firebrands marched on the Palace, where they were joined by rebels of the Imperial Guard. Following a rousing speech on the grounds of the Palace they rushed inside, going from room to room. Some were searching for the recording; others were looking for Lord Privy Seal Kido, the Emperor's advisor, and for Prime Minister Suzuki. These two were traitors to Japan and the Emperor, they shouted; they wanted blood. But Marquis Kido and the Prime Minister, alerted, fled. Kido descended belowground, locking himself in the bomb shelter; the Prime

5

Minister hurried out a back exit and went to his residence. The Emperor was aroused by his household minister, and as he quickly dressed he asked: "A coup d'etat?" The minister replied: "No, they want the surrender recording destroyed and Lord Privy Seal and the Prime Minister killed." But Kido was safe, and the Prime Minister at his residence was warned by telephone of an army group on their way. He left the house immediately by car for the countryside. As he drove away he looked back and saw his house go up in flames. Prime Minister Suzuki had escaped a lynch mob.

At the Japanese Broadcasting Corporation another dissident army unit marched into the newsroom. The unit's leader ordered the news producer to put him on the air so he could tell all Japan what was going on. The producer stalled, said he would have to clear all stations around the country and that this would take some time. As they waited, an army squad loyal to the Emperor broke into the newsroom and overwhelmed the dissidents. Other loyal troops regained control of the Imperial Palace and formed a safety cordon around the Emperor.

At noon on August 15, life in Tokyo stopped as everyone waited for the Emperor to speak. All radios were tuned to receive this historic broadcast. Hirohito in the Palace also had his radio tuned to NHK.

Then, on cue, the national anthem, "Kimigayo," came over the air. The announcer intoned, "His Majesty the Emperor will now read the Imperial Rescript to the people of Japan." Speaking in the Imperial Third Person as the "Voice of the Crane" (the Emperor), Hirohito proclaimed:

> We, the Emperor, in view of world conditions and the present situation of Japan, I

6

hereby announce to you, our loyal subjects, that in our profound anxiety to bring an end to this state of affairs by some extraordinary measure we have instructed the Japanese government to accept the Joint Declaration of the United States, Great Britain, the Soviet Union and China.

In conformity with the precepts handed down by our Imperial ancestors we have always striven for the welfare of our subjects and for the happiness and welfare of all nations. This is precisely why we declared war against Great Britain and the United States. It was out of our anxiety to preserve the confidence of the Empire and maintain the stability of East Asia that we took this step. It was not our intention to infringe on the sovereignty of other nations or to carry out acts of aggression against their soil.

However, the war now has lasted for four years and despite the valor of our land and naval forces, despite the valor of our heroic dead and despite the continued efforts the situation has not taken a turn for the better and neither has the aspect of the world situation taken a more favorable turn.

What is more, the enemy has employed its outrageous bomb and slaughtered untold numbers of innocent people. The damage is incalculable.

Accordingly, to continue the war under these circumstances would ultimately mean the extinction of our people and the utter destruction of human civilization.

Under these circumstances, how were we to save the millions of our subjects or justify

7

ourselves to save the spirits of our Imperial ancestors?

It was this which led us to have the Imperial Government comply with the Joint Declaration.

We must express our regrets to our Allies who have fought alongside us for the emancipation of East Asia.

We are now thinking of our subjects who met an untimely death and our brave warriors, and of those they have left behind. We also feel deeply for the welfare of those who have suffered great losses in the pursuit of victory and those who have lost their livelihood.

We are aware that the Empire is now confronted with unparalleled distress and fully know how you, our subjects, feel. However, by patiently enduring the tide of events, however difficult it may be, we will open the way for peace for generations to come.

By maintaining our national structure, we shall encourage you our loyal subjects in your singleness of purpose. We are ever with you. If you should now become agitated and create needless complications, thus making difficulties with each other, you would only infringe the principles of morality and lose the respect of the world. We therefore earnestly warn you against such agitation.

Let us therefore face the long road ahead of us as one united nation in firm fidelity to the Throne and in full confidence in the indestructibility of our Divine Land, and let us resolve to bend all our energies to future reconstruction, let us be strong in our moral principles and firm in our ideals.

"Voice of the Crane," Emperor Hirohito

My subjects, let us carry forward the glory
of our national structure and let us not lag
behind the progress of the world.
Submit, ye, to Our Will!

The Emperor's surrender broadcast was listened to
with relief by most of Japan, although it was emotionally
upsetting to everyone. There were tears by those who
kneeled together in the midst of rubble as they listened
to their Emperor speaking on the radio. Among the
fanatics of the armed forces there was a wave of suicides.

At the Atogoyama army base, some officers and
soldiers blew themselves up with their own grenades. At
the Atsugi air base, kamikaze pilots, who had sworn
to die for their Emperor when MacArthur invaded,
dropped leaflets over Tokyo declaring that the Emperor
had been tricked. They threatened to bomb the American fleet when it arrived offshore. They were persuaded
to obey the Emperor's surrender order only by a personal plea from Hirohito's brother. At the Imperial
Palace, the Emperor himself witnessed the suicide of ten
young soldiers. They stood beyond the moat, bowed to
the Palace, then ripped open their stomachs as an "act of
sorrow and of penance for having failed our divine
Emperor."

Vice Admiral Takijiro Onishi, Vice Chief of the
Naval General Staff and organizer of the kamikaze units,
took his life. His last message was addressed to "the
spirits of the Special Attack (Kamikaze) Units." He
declared his death was an effort to "make atonement to
the souls of my former subordinates and to their be-
reaved families." He urged the survivors to do their
utmost "for the revival of the Japanese race and for world
peace."

War Minister General Korechika Anami committed

his final act of *seppuku* like a samurai, with a dagger. After drinking sake he put on his most prized possession, a white shirt given to him by the Emperor, then with the dagger slit his stomach. As he died, an aide covered his body with his bemedaled uniform. His last wish was that the soldiers who went on living—"and they must"— would work to rebuild Japan for the Emperor.

The widespread sorrow, the shock of total defeat, was summed up by General MacArthur as he drove to his headquarters in Yokohama. He commented, "Their whole world has crumbled. It is not merely the disintegration of everything they believed in and lived by and fought for, but they were left a complete vacuum, morally, mentally, and physically." Better than anyone, MacArthur knew that whatever filled this vacuum would determine the future of Japan and the entire Pacific basin. If the United States failed to bring Japan back to normality, Soviet communism would surely move in. United States intelligence officers had already informed the Supreme Commander that Japan's Communist Party was working hard to move Japan into the Soviet orbit.

The same thought was going through the mind of Emperor Hirohito. He spoke to Lord Privy Seal Kido, his close advisor, about the dangers of Russia and the wisdom of cooperating with the United States now that the war was over. He knew that the history of the world for the next thousand years would be written in the Pacific, despite the present setback of military defeat, and he was determined that Japan would never become a Russian subject-nation. Japan's future was with the United States, and when the occupation period ended he wanted his nation to take its place with dignity alongside America and Great Britain in shaping the future of Asia. When General MacArthur stepped to the microphones as part of the surrender ceremony aboard the USS *Missouri* on September 2, Hirohito was listening on his radio in the Imperial Library. One significant passage in MacArthur's statement on that occasion appealed to the Emperor. The General declared:

> The energy of the Japanese race, if properly directed, will enable expansion vertically rather than horizontally. If the talents of the race are turned into constructive channels, the country can lift itself from the present deplorable state into a position of dignity. To the Pacific basin has come the vista of a new, emancipated world. Today, freedom is on the offensive, democracy is on the march. Today, in Asia as well as in Europe, unshackled peoples are tasting the full sweetness of liberty, the relief from fear.

The surrender ceremony was MacArthur's greatest moment. I watched it from a vantage point on the deck of the USS *Missouri*. The day was clear and sunny, yet brisk for September in Japan. It was a totally different scene from Reims, France, where the German delegation had surrendered, which I also witnessed and broadcast to the United States as a war correspondent. Here in Tokyo Bay warships of all classes and types and nations rode at anchor clear to the horizon. Overhead an armada of aircraft passed to celebrate the coming of victory and peace. It was symbolic of the war in the Pacific, the most expansive battleground in all history, in which MacArthur and Hirohito as the prime protagonists had directed vast armies and navies and aircraft over distances exceeding by many times the size of the United States.

The surrender ceremony itself took but eighteen

minutes. The delegation from Japan, representing Hirohito, lined up before the table where the articles of surrender lay. As General MacArthur walked from the Admiral's cabin to the microphones behind this table, the Japanese stood at attention. MacArthur then beckoned to the leader of the delegation, Mamori Shigemitsu, to step to the table and sign for his country. Shigemitsu, in formal morning dress, hobbled forward, handicapped by his artificial leg, the result of a terrorist attack in Singapore. He managed his silk hat and cane with difficulty, and as he seated himself it was apparent he could not readily see where he should sign. MacArthur, noticing Shigemitsu's embarrassment, snapped an order to his chief of staff: "Sutherland, show him where to sign. He can't make out the correct line." The signature accomplished, Shigemitsu stepped back with the other members of his delegation. Then Yoshijiro Umezu, Chief of the Imperial General Staff, walked to the table. Not bothering to seat himself, he wrote his signature. After the Japanese the victors signed, with MacArthur the last signatory.

MacArthur then rose, stepped to the microphone, and spoke. "I speak for the thousands of silent lips, forever stilled among the jungles and the beaches and in the deep waters of the Pacific which marked the way. . . ."

In the Imperial Library Emperor Hirohito listened. He was deeply moved by the sentiments expressed by the American general, and it was then that he decided to instruct his foreign minister to arrange for a meeting with the Supreme Commander. He knew the Japanese code that covered victory and defeat held that once defeat has been acknowledged the only "manly thing is to leave everything to the victor and to trust the enemy commander."

He was buttressed in this belief by the confidential report brought to him by his personal informer, Toshikazu Kase, who had attended the surrender on the USS *Missouri*. Kase told the Emperor in the Palace: "It was a piece of rare good fortune that a man of such caliber and character should have been designated as the Supreme Commander to shape the destiny of Japan." Kase also expressed sad thoughts to the Emperor. "When I looked up at the bulkhead of the *Missouri* and saw small Rising Suns, our flag, painted on steel, indicating the number of Japanese ships, submarines, and planes that had been destroyed by this American battleship, a lump rose in my throat and tears quickly gathered in my eyes. I could hardly bear the sight. These were young boys who defied death gaily and gallantly . . . they were like cherry blossoms, emblems of our national character, swiftly blooming into riotous beauty and falling just as quickly."

The Emperor listened carefully and sadly replied, *"Ah so, ah so, deska"* ("It is so"). He remarked later to the Empress about this and she too was moved and saddened by Kase's observation.

General MacArthur transferred his headquarters from Yokohama to Tokyo on September 18. He moved into the Dai Ichi building, which had been a Japanese army headquarters, and designated the American Embassy for his living quarters. On September 27, Hirohito dispatched his foreign minister to the Dai Ichi building to ask permission to make a formal call on the Supreme Commander. Colonel Courtney Whitney, MacArthur's new chief of staff, looked up with astonishment when he saw Shigemitsu, the foreign minister who had signed the surrender document for Hirohito, standing before him, requesting a meeting with MacArthur for the Emperor. Whitney rushed into MacArthur's office to tell him. The

General was surprised and pleased, but recognized he could not go to the palace, nor could Hirohito come to the Dai Ichi building. It would look to the Japanese as if he had summoned the Emperor. He told Whitney to arrange the meeting for that afternoon in the U.S. Embassy, and instructed that Brigadier General Bonner Fellers should be on hand to greet and escort the Emperor to the Embassy drawing room. He also instructed Whitney: "Only an interpreter and a Signal Corps photographer will be present for this meeting. The photographer will take one picture and leave." Whitney walked out of the office and told Shigemitsu that the Supreme Commander had acceded to the Emperor's request. They would meet that afternoon in the American Embassy at two o'clock. Shigemitsu bowed and left.

Early that afternoon the old-fashioned high-topped Daimler limousine, bearing the Emperor, the Lord Privy Seal, Shigemitsu, the Lord Grand Chamberlain, and Terasaki, the interpreter, bumped across the moat headed for the American Embassy. At the entranceway the Imperial group climbed out and walked up the steps to the entrance. Kido, Shigemitsu, and the Lord Chamberlain were not allowed beyond the entranceway. (Kido in particular was distressed by this precaution because he had always served as a buffer in such situations.) General Bonner Fellers, a born diplomat, stepped forward and introduced himself to Hirohito, saying, "Welcome, it is a pleasure to meet you, sir." He extended his hand, which Hirohito took. Together they walked to the elevator and ascended to the drawing room floor. Hirohito, attired in formal morning dress, was then escorted into the drawing room. MacArthur wore army fatigues without tie. The Signal Corps photographer took one picture (which illustrates this book) and withdrew, along with Fellers. The Emperor and his interpreter remained.

Hirohito was hesitant at first. MacArthur, to ease the strain of the moment, offered a cigarette, which the Emperor took. But the Emperor was so nervous his hands shook, and MacArthur leaned toward him with a cigarette lighter. Together they smoked and relaxed before an open fire at one end of the long reception room. General MacArthur later described this moment: "I tried to make it as easy for him as I could, but I knew how deep and dreadful must be his agony and humiliation."

The Emperor then explained why he had asked for this meeting. "I come to you, General MacArthur, to offer myself to the judgment of the two powers you represent as the one to bear sole responsibility for every political and military decision made and action taken by my people in the conduct of the war."

Hirohito was perfectly willing to be labeled the commander in chief of the Japanese forces. Hirohito had been no godlike figurehead hiding in the Imperial Palace and removed from the shot and shell of events. He had followed every battle with intense interest, and had intervened when his field commanders failed to follow the battle strategy that had been worked out in the Imperial war room. In the South Pacific, when General MacArthur congratulated his two field commanders, Eichelberger and Krueger, for dealing the first major setbacks to the Japanese at Buna, Papua, and Guadalcanal, Hirohito in Tokyo told his War Minister, Hajime Sugiyama: "The fall of Buna is regrettable, but the officers and men fought well." He added, "Now give enough thought to your plans so that Lae and Salamaua don't become another Guadalcanal."

MacArthur and Hirohito sized each other up as they talked in a relaxed atmosphere and discussed in general terms the war both had waged and the future of Japan.

MacArthur had met Hirohito's father once, years before, upon the General's return from observing the Russian-Japanese war in Port Arthur. Hirohito had been seven years old at the time, the Crown Prince. Now, in 1945, he appreciated the gracious remarks made by Mac-Arthur about his father. He especially enjoyed one anecdote related by MacArthur that attested to the almost mystical power of the Emperor over his people. In 1906, cholera was sweeping the Japanese army; the soldiers had been issued medicine to prevent it but had refused to take the capsules. The general in charge did not know what to do. On MacArthur's advice to the Emperor, each soldier was given the medication in a little box labeled "The Emperor requests that each soldier take one capsule every four hours." They did, and that was the end of the problem. MacArthur and Hirohito laughed together over this. They knew now they were to be partners in the task of occupation that lay ahead, and both knew some laughter was necessary to the success of their relationship and the awesome objectives to be accomplished together. It was like a classic Kabuki play, in which an anecdote provides a light and insightful touch to a serious and tragic situation: a nation on its knees, two and a half million Japanese servicemen killed in action, and six hundred and seventy thousand civilians killed during the bombings. MacArthur was also well aware of his own battle casualties on land, air, and sea; while they did not approach those of the Japanese, they were a severe loss to America.

They talked for thirty-five minutes, and when they concluded both knew they could work together to rehabilitate Japan and its people. Their respect was mutual, their courtesy and empathy marked. They agreed to have many other talks in the time ahead in order to set

Japan on the course best for her and for all the peoples of the Far East. At the end of their conversation, Hirohito bowed ceremoniously and left the drawing room. As he walked from the Embassy and stepped into his Daimler, he asked Lord Privy Seal Kido to get the name of the American officer who had greeted him in such a gracious fashion when he arrived. Later, he wrote a personal note to Bonner Fellers, thanking him.

Upstairs in the drawing room there was a relaxing of tension. The General's wife, Jean MacArthur, who had been listening, fascinated, in an adjoining room, came bouncing out and hugged her husband. General MacArthur observed to her, "That indeed is the first gentleman of Japan."

It may be true that Hirohito was the first gentleman of Japan, but it also is true that he plotted with his advisors the invasions of China and Manchuria and the attack on Pearl Harbor, which thrust the United States into the Pacific war. He listened to his army and navy leaders and, once the details had been worked out, approved their recommendations for aggression and war. He paid attention, too, to the persuasive arguments put forth by the Zaibatsu, who held that economic expansion was the way to proceed for Japan. The Zaibatsu, the twelve big-business and big-money families of Japan, had shaped Japan's economy into a ready instrument for war. (The Imperial Household economic structure was also Zaibatsu, so Imperial wealth increased if the nation prospered under Zaibatsu leadership.)

When the Emperor declared, in his surrender address to his nation, "We have always striven for the welfare of our subjects and for the happiness and welfare of all nations," he was stretching the truth. If Japan's prosperity spread somewhat into its subject lands, it was incidental to the expansionist adventure embarked upon

17

by Hirohito in the 1930s. The statement made to his people asserting that "it was not our intention to infringe on the sovereignty of other nations or to carry out acts of aggression against their soil" was directly contrary to the facts. Japanese soldiers in their conquest of Manchuria and China had marched with the idea that the Emperor was divine and that the Japanese people were superior to other races and fated to rule the world. It was hard-headed commercialism and the need for oil, rubber, and other natural resources that had sparked Japan's expansion in those years.

In the Thirties the Zaibatsu had shifted Nipponese economic development from light to heavy industry, with emphasis on machine tools, chemicals, trucks, and all the equipment an army would need for war. The Prime Minister, the Foreign Affairs Minister, and the War and Navy Ministers all had approved a document on August 11, 1936, titled "The Fundamentals of Our National Policy," which ordered the continued economic expansion in Japan and on the mainland of war industries. The Zaibatsu and military leaders envisioned China and Manchuria as a great manufacturing supply source. Their grand plan targeted Singapore as the center of Japan's future aviation industry, rich as it was in rubber plantations and ores of bauxite, iron, and tin to be smelted in Malaya and in the Philippines with coal shipped from Indochina. By refining oil in Sumatra they would save tankers.

So the planning went; but for the present, in the Thirties, Japan concentrated on her five-year plan for the development of Manchoukuo, the state established within Manchuria that was controlled by Japan's Kwang-tung army. Following Japanese military victories in Manchuria and China in 1931 and 1932, including the "Rape of Nanking," control was absolute. A puppet ruler named Pu-Yi signed a Japanese-conceived letter which said that hereafter the national defense of Manchuria, and also control of all railroads, harbors, water routes, air routes, and industries, would be entrusted to Japan. As time went on the telephone and telegraph services were also drawn under Japanese control. The cost to China: fifty million dead.

The oil that was being pumped in Manchuria exclusively for Japanese use became a diplomatic issue with the United States in 1934. U.S. Ambassador Grew in Tokyo protested that Japan had assumed an oil monopoly position in Manchuria that was unsettling to American interests. Japan replied that control of the oil industry in Manchuria was not a concern of the Japanese government, which was falsification of the boldest order. Japan could say this because, militarily and economically, she was riding high at that time.

Japanese financial investment in Manchuria had risen to 2,210,000,000 yen, and the production of trucks, warplanes, tanks, and ammunition and artillery was exceeding that put forth in the Japanese five-year plan. Nippon Industrial Company, Ltd., a giant conglomerate with fifty thousand shareholders in Japan, moved its headquarters to Manchuria and changed its corporate name to "Manchuria Industrial Development Corporation." Businessmen and bankers were now at the helm of this profitable war industry, and as their ace card they had the Kwangtung army to provide muscle. Directives streamed from Tokyo guiding the destinies of other industries, which were expanding and filling Japan's need for increased war material production on "the Continent." Similar plans were going forward in Korea, yet another recent territorial conquest of Japan.

In 1945, investigators and lawyers on General MacArthur's staff put together a legal brief detailing how Japan had employed economic aggression in China. The brief, which was presented to the Allied prosecution in Tokyo, stated:

> The exploitation of Manchurian industries and control of economic affairs was so complete the Chinese were not permitted to enter into businesses competitive with those sponsored by the Japanese. About 64 special companies were formed in Manchuria and large capital sums were involved. The object was to make China bankrupt and to expand Japanese influence "outwards." The banks were controlled by Japanese. Loans were not made to Chinese. Monopolies were in the hands of the Japanese. The Bureau of Monopolies was under control of the Japanese, as was the cotton industry. The best quality rice was controlled by the Japanese, and all steel, iron, cotton cloth and other commodities were under their monopoly control. Money was printed or minted in Japan and the control of the national currency was in the hands of the Japanese-controlled Bureau of General Affairs. All Chinese were required by law to deposit moneys in the banks as a way of exercising economic control over individuals. Japanese immigrants were able to acquire land on favorable terms, the Chinese owners being forced to sell at low prices. Under a Labor and Civil Service Law Manchurians between the ages of 18 and 45 were required to render labor services to the Japanese Army under the supervision of Japanese companies and foremen. The conditions of labor were harsh. The Japanese used Manchurian labor and resources to make Manchuria the basis of their arsenal. There was no equality of treatment; the Japa-

nese ranked first, then the Koreans, then the Manchurians. The courts were controlled by the Kwangtung Army and the General Affairs Bureau.

To Japanese leaders, the conquest of Manchuria and China had been logical expansion. Japan in the Thirties had an economy that was growing faster than any other economy in the world, bursting with surplus talent, energy, and ideas, but in need of the raw materials and space to expand. Emperor Hirohito was pleased about the successful inroads into Manchuria and China and the economic strength it gave his nation. It was the growth he had visualized in 1921, when he assumed the regency.

At that time Hirohito had taken over a Japan of fifty-six million people. It had increased its population by 25 percent and its gross national product by more than 100 percent since Hirohito's birth in 1900. Now he and his military advisors made their long-range plans for Japan's new army. There were to be new mechanized transport groups, machine-gun squads for every infantry company, and research teams to study modern weapons of France, Britain, and Germany. Increased attention was to be paid to intelligence matters in Europe, the United States, and the Asiatic countries coveted by Hirohito and his advisors. Two new air regiments were to be added to the army, as well as an antiaircraft regiment and a fifty-five-hundred-man tank corps. Special military schools were set up: a signal academy and a school for chemical and biological warfare. The plan called for an educational corps of twelve hundred drill masters to be assigned to high schools so every young man would be infused with the martial spirit and a knowledge of sword and rifle drill before even entering military service.

21

This planning was done with the collaboration of three trusted military officers: Nagata, Obata, and Okamura, Japanese military attachés in Europe who had returned to Tokyo to assist Hirohito in modernizing the armed forces. Known as "The Three Crows," they were absolutely dedicated to Emperor Hirohito. They had studied the weaponry produced by Britain, France, Germany, and Italy and planned to duplicate it from blueprints they either bought or stole. In Tokyo they established a secret staff college on the grounds of the Imperial Palace, where lectures were given to reliable young officers on the course of the new army. The Three Crows had all graduated in the military academy class of 1904–1905. Major Tojo, a graduate of the same academy, served as military aide to The Three Crows in Europe. They marked him for promotion in the new Japanese army. Tojo's rise to leadership of the army, as well as prime minister of his own cabinet following Pearl Harbor, was due to the influence of The Three Crows on Hirohito, a recommendation that also had the support of the Zaibatsu.

As part of his command changes, Hirohito was determined to eliminate from the army and the Imperial Palace all vestiges of the Choshu clan. This decision turned on a very human point: his relations with Yamagata, the army chief and leader of the Choshu clan. Yamagata wanted a princess of the Choshu clan to be Hirohito's bride for the influence it would give him within court circles, or so he thought. To block Hirohito's relationship with Princess Nagako, he circulated false rumors about her, hoping this would rally royal support to his side. Instead, it infuriated Hirohito, and following his marriage to Princess Nagako he eliminated Yamagata and the Choshu clan from the affairs of the army and the Throne.

Meanwhile, at the secret staff college on the Imperial Palace grounds, many of Japan's new military and naval leaders were familiar speakers. There was Admiral Yamamoto, the brilliant naval tactician who was to plan and direct the Japanese attack on Pearl Harbor, and Major Tojo, who rose to be Minister of War. Yamamoto lectured on his specialty, attack by carrier-borne aircraft. Tojo spoke about the economics of warfare. His theme was repeated often in his lectures:

> Economic strength is essential to military power . . . war springs from economic causes . . . the essential elements in the development of economic strength in any nation are Materials, Manpower, Machines (manufacturing and mining facilities), and Markets, compounded into an effective whole under competent Management.
>
> But economic strength alone does not make a nation a power for military aggression. To economic strength must be added specialized military organization, schooled in the development of war plans and in the effective orientation of civilian activities to war uses . . . It goes without saying that beneath this organization there must be true political unity— the existence of a common will among the people to promote and accept economic organization for war and the privation which it entails.

Such was the military philosophy guiding Japan as it moved to victory in Manchuria and China. From Emperor to lowliest commoner, this thrust, it was agreed, was the key to Empire. The Emperor congratulated and decorated his field commanders for any successes. But the prevailing feeling in the United States and Europe toward those invasions of 1931 and 1932 was tempered resentment. Both Britain and America were preoccupied with the Great Depression; whatever was going on in Asia was for the diplomats to handle. Still, Japan was not held in a favorable light by thinking people. Poet Ogden Nash summed up popular opinion in the West with the following verse, which appeared in *Life* magazine in 1932:

> *How courteous is the Japanese;*
> *He always says, "Excuse it, please."*
> *He climbs into his neighbor's garden,*
> *And smiles, and says, "I beg your pardon";*
> *He bows and grins a friendly grin,*
> *And calls his hungry family in;*
> *He grins, and bows a friendly bow;*
> *"So sorry, this is my garden now."*

The Thirties were passing. Hirohito and the Zaibatsu looked to the South Pacific as their next target for expansion. President Roosevelt sensed he was approaching a period of imminent war. President Chiang Kai-shek was pressuring him to do something about Japan and its control of Manchuria and other Chinese areas. It was a distraction not welcomed by Roosevelt. The threats facing Winston Churchill and Britain were his real concern, and he seemed to want to wish away the possibility of war with Japan. He did demand of Hirohito withdrawal from China, but ten years had passed since the first Japanese encroachment on these lands. By 1941, the conquests were generating enormous wealth for the Zaibatsu and the treasury of the Imperial Household. It was providing thriving Japanese factories with raw materials, to say nothing of the boon to the armament industries. Japan would lose not just face if it retreated from China and Manchuria, but also wealth and the economic strength that are essential to military power.

These economic matters were in Emperor Hirohito's mind as he met with his advisors in the Imperial Palace the night of July 2, 1941. Present were Prime Minister Prince Fumimaro Konoye, War Minister Hideki Tojo, Navy Chief of Staff Admiral Nagano, Army Chief of Staff General Suzuki, Field Marshal Sugiyama, military aides Generals Muto and Shimada, Ministers Toyada and Togo, and Japanese Ambassador to the United States Admiral Kichisaburo Nomura.

The July 2 conference, according to the sworn statement of Lord Privy Seal Kido, who monitored the meeting, was the first time that the Japanese government contemplated war with the United States. Prince Konoye had petitioned the Emperor for this conference. In addressing the Emperor he urged "that for the present there would be no movement against Soviet Russia"; instead he asked for a "Strike South" policy to the Philippines and the Dutch East Indies. Hirohito agreed. He was opposed to a "Strike North" against Russia, believing that a movement into the South Pacific would pay immense dividends to Japan in required commodities. Hirohito, who could be as tough and hardtalking as anyone present, said that if as a result the United States moved to enter the conflict, that decision would be met with force.

At the same time, according to Kido, "It was the Emperor's opinion that this matter of southern expansion must be handled very delicately. The Emperor was worried about this possible war . . . war with the United States was not to be taken lightly." Kido went on, "Interference on the part of the United States in Japan's move into the South Pacific was a subject for serious consideration by everyone present at this July 2 conference. If serious consideration was given to the matter and the group decision was war, then the Emperor would sanction this policy." Without his approval there would be no war.

When Hirohito gave his approval on July 2 for Japan to move toward war, the army and navy started serious preparations, and Zaibatsu industrialists stepped up their production of heavy armaments. An air-raid shelter was even built below the Imperial Palace in anticipation of an air strike by U.S. military aircraft. Aside from these preliminary moves, nothing decisive was done until the night of September 6, when the same group gathered again with the Emperor. This was a more far-reaching conference, and its outcome was threefold, according to statements made in Sugamo Prison, Tokyo, on March 8, 1946, by Lord Privy Seal Kido, the Emperor's close advisor and secretary:

> (1) Preparation for war against America and Britain will be started; (2) the negotiations with America will be vigorously continued; (3) if the negotiations are not successful by the 10th of October, war will be decided against Britain and America.

During this conference Hirohito questioned the readiness of the Japanese military forces. He was assured that the navy, army, and air forces were moving into top strike capabilities. Field Marshal Sugiyama, who had performed well in Manchuria and China although his victories had not been achieved as rapidly as he had promised, declared to the group that a strike south to the Dutch East Indies would be easily and quickly accomplished. Hirohito replied sharply, "That is what you said about China, and it was otherwise." Sugiyama remained silent throughout the rest of the meeting.

Tojo, however, assured Hirohito that Japanese forces

were indeed coming to a peak of efficiency, and that they would never be better prepared for a major war with America.

In Washington, at about the same time, President Roosevelt was meeting in the Oval Office on this same matter with Secretary of State Cordell Hull. He commented to Hull, "I've done everything possible to head off a war with Japan. I even offered to meet with Emperor Hirohito on a ship off the coast of Alaska to discuss what can be done to ensure peace in the Far East." Hull replied, "Insisting that Japan withdraw from Manchuria and China as Chiang Kai-shek wants is a strong position." Roosevelt said, "Well, it is my minimal demand. I believe the Emperor will agree to it."

But in the Imperial Palace on that September night in 1941, Hirohito had another opinion. He told members of the conference: "It is impossible for Japan to withdraw troops from China without losing face, at least. If Ambassador Nomura does not succeed in reaching an accord with America by October tenth, Japan will move toward war with the United States and Britain."

War was in the air, and President Roosevelt failed to comprehend the dynamism driving Japan toward battle. Japan's leadership—the Emperor, the army and navy chiefs of staff, and the young officers below them, as well as the Zaibatsu who visualized a new world of economic and industrial opportunities—felt their nation stood on the brink of great success. Force of arms, they held, was the key to world prestige and ownership of vast sources of raw materials and new markets throughout the East. They pointed to the fact that this was the means historically followed by America and Great Britain. The opening of the West, the acquisition of the territory of Alaska, and the conquest of other lands had guaranteed the United States vast and profitable markets, as had been the case with Britain in her colonial era of growth and prosperity. With Hitler holding Britain at bay on one front and attacking the Soviet Union on another, this was Japan's golden opportunity, and the leadership was determined to take it.

Both the Japanese army and the Emperor regarded with pride their remarkable military defeat of Russia in 1905; it had brought honor and prestige to the nation and to the Emperor. But it was this victory that, in a historical perspective, really started Japan on the road to war against the United States decades later.

The attack on the Russian Asiatic fleet at Port Arthur in 1905 was made without warning, a prologue to the attack to be made thirty-six years later at Pearl Harbor. Emperor Meiji, Hirohito's grandfather, sent his torpedo boats in a surprise attack. The ships they did not sink were bottled up inside the harbor, and two days later Meiji issued his Rescript declaring war on Russia. He accused Russia of threatening Japan's plans for expansion. (Similarly, in Hirohito's Imperial Rescript declaring war on the United States two days after the 1941 Pearl Harbor attack, he blamed the United States and China for imperiling the existence of the Japanese Empire.)

At Port Arthur the going was slow. Japanese troops were under heavy fire and bogged down in a field of land mines. Emperor Meiji from his command post in Japan sent an order to General Nogi to take at all costs the citadel that overlooked the battlefield. Against heavy artillery fire from the citadel Japanese troops made their charge, and, though losing twenty thousand men, stormed the heights and achieved a victory, raising their flag over the citadel. Remnants of the Russian fleet that had been at anchor within the harbor suddenly came under artillery shelling from the heights; at the same time, the

Russian vessels came under attack from the Japanese navy as they attempted to steam from the harbor and were sunk to the last ship. It was then that Japanese Admiral Togo turned his fleet around to meet the oncoming Russian Baltic fleet that had been steaming for a month from the Kattegat in the Baltic. When the Russian ships emerged from the narrows between Korea and Japan, Admiral Togo swung his battleships and began firing broadsides. When the naval action had ended, twenty Russian ships had been sunk, five more had been captured, and eighteen thousand Russian sailors had drowned. Japan had lost three torpedo boats and 116 seamen.

But after nine months of war, both Japan and Russia were looking for peace. President Theodore Roosevelt offered to mediate, and peace terms were arranged. Korea was given to Japan, as was Port Arthur, the Kwantung Peninsula, and all railroad rights in southern Manchuria. Because there were no war reparations to be paid by Russia, which the Japanese people had been expecting—they had put up with a great many privations to support this war—there were riots in all major industrial Japanese cities. Calm descended after Emperor Meiji assured his people that the benefits to Japan would, in time, be immense. "This was only the first step in the building of a vast Japanese empire," he declared.

Lieutenant Douglas MacArthur and his father, Major General Arthur MacArthur, were the U.S. Army observers of this war. When they returned by way of Tokyo, both observed that "the future and very existence of America is irrevocably intertwined with Asia and its island outposts." General Arthur MacArthur also made the observation that Japan's imperialistic ambitions posed "the central problem of the Pacific."

*   *   *

Emperors have come and gone since the establishment of the Imperial institution in 660 B.C. Some have been strong and some have died in poverty and obscurity. But it was not until the Meiji Restoration in 1868 that the Emperor became revered. The Throne itself was always the all-powerful instrument of power. But when Emperor Meiji ascended it, Throne and Emperor were perceived as one. Meiji was a strong man who understood the need for easygoing charm and careful subterfuge in dealing with those who initiated and carried out domestic and foreign policies. Once he was established as an Emperor with power, the leadership groups—the military, the aristocracy, and the Zaibatsu— all vied for his approval of their various ventures. The Shogun period that preceded Meiji marked a time in which military chieftains controlled the Throne. Such was no longer the case with Meiji; directives, Rescripts, and other official dicta now came directly from the top. And in 1889 a new constitution was written that made definitive the power of the Emperor. Article One of this constitution declared, "The Empire of Japan shall be reigned over and governed by a line of Emperors unbroken for ages eternal. The Emperor, who is Supreme Commander of the army and navy, declares war, makes peace, and concludes treaties." It was this power that Emperor Meiji used in his war on Russia. But in the spring of 1912 he was stricken with cancer. Knowing he was dying, he delegated his authority to the oligarchs of the court. As he lay ill tens of thousands of his people prayed for his recovery outside the Palace. When he died July 29, 1912, Emperor Meiji's funeral cortege rolled across the double bridge traversing the moat around the Palace and made its way to Tokyo Station— the end of his journey—to lie beside his ancestors in the ancient capital of Kyoto.

Meiji had more than a dozen sons, but only one

survived, the child of a concubine: Crown Prince Yoshi-hito, the father of Hirohito. Yoshihito assumed the Throne and took the name of Taisho ("Great Correctness").

The new Emperor decided to be an empire builder, but he did not have the grace and subterfuge to rule as did Meiji. He was blocked at every turn, even in the Diet. As for the people themselves, they wanted a reduction in the armed forces, fewer taxes, and a pause to Imperial ambitions. So Emperor Taisho for the time gave up his dreams of the conquest of Malaya, the East Indies, and the Philippines. He knew that the world was moving toward war and he told intimates he would back the Western nations in a war against Germany. "These are the countries," he said, "who have power in the Pacific: England holds Malaya, France governs Indo-china, and the United States controls the Philippines." In victory something would come Japan's way, he was sure, such as German possessions in the Pacific. Taisho admired Germany, but he was a realist.

War did break out in 1914, and Foreign Minister Kato respected the feelings of Taisho by aligning Japan with England and France. He told his colleagues in government that it was not so much to help Britain as to silence in advance any British objections to Japanese moves on China. Japan performed token duty for the Allies in the Pacific. She undertook to protect British interests in Hong Kong and Shanghai, and her navy convoyed British merchantmen through the Indian Ocean to the Mediterranean. But Japan flatly refused to contribute troops to the battlefields of Europe. Instead, she sent her Imperial Marines ashore on all German islands in the Pacific. Other Japanese divisions landed on the Shantung Peninsula, which juts out toward Korea from the North China coast, began a drive on the German-leased port of Tsingtao, and soon occupied this city and the entire Peninsula. After 1914, the president of the new Republic of China tried to persuade Japan to leave this territory, a demand that was refused. Japan then countered with twenty-one demands that would in effect bring China and Manchuria under the rule of Japan.

At the Versailles peace conference of January 1919, the Japanese delegation succeeded in keeping the lease-hold on Tsingtao and the German-mandated islands in the Pacific. They relinquished the areas of Siberia they had occupied, and also the Shantung Peninsula. All this territorial jockeying moved Japan into the Big Five of nations, alongside Britain, France, Italy, and the United States. It had been a prosperous war for Japan.

It fell to Hirohito to expand Japan's ambitions for empire, and he did so with invasions of Manchuria and China.

But in September of 1941, at an Imperial Conference in the throne room of the Palace, he faced his biggest decision. War Minister Tojo, who represented both the army and the Zaibatsu, was pressing for war against the United States. He said victory over America would be the apogee of Japanese military glory and would reflect on the Emperor even more brilliantly than victory over Russia had in 1905. He said that Hirohito's grandfather, Emperor Meiji, who was surely listening to this conference, would approve of such a decision. Furthermore, he said, "It will assure Japan of equality among world powers and will guarantee to Japan control of East Asia and its markets for generations to come."

Others who were present expressed their views. Admiral Nagano, the armed forces chief of staff, was not so convinced of the wisdom of war against America. He wanted oil for his ships but felt a sufficient quantity could be obtained from the United States by negotiation. If not, war became for him a distinct possibility. At the moment, they had enough oil on hand. Kido commented that that opinion "worried the Emperor quite a bit, as a rash statement with no thought behind it."

Hirohito asked Nagano if the navy thought they could win a war against the United States. The Admiral replied, "Yes, the navy thinks they can, but I am doubtful." This difference of opinion disturbed and perplexed the Emperor. The essence of Japanese leadership, whether in business, military service, or government, was Group Harmony, and Hirohito was sensing nothing but discord on this matter. He required total assurance of victory before he was willing to put his nation at war.

For the most part, the young officers of the navy advocated war. Among them was Admiral Nobumasay Suetsugu, whose belligerence toward the United States and Britain went back to the Washington Naval Conference of 1922, where, he felt, certain slights and indignities had placed Japan in an inferior position militarily. The Conference had placed a limit on the size of the navy that Japan could build; in addition, massive battleships had been ruled out. (Curiously enough, these restrictions would later work to Japan's advantage. The vessels they would build—aircraft carriers, pocket battleships, cruisers, and submarines—would be better suited to their means and the type of war that would evolve in the Pacific.)

Admiral Yamamoto, Japan's best naval tactician, was opposed to war against the United States, and was as a result summarily removed from his post as Vice Minister of the Navy, a position in which he had influenced policy, and relegated to commander in chief of the Imperial fleet. Hence, the last political deterrent to war was removed. Admiral Nagano and his vice chief of staff,

33

Admiral Ito, both of whom had opposed going to war, were finally swung around to the opposite camp.

Emperor Hirohito had his Group Harmony. The planning for the attack on Pearl Harbor would now move forward.

Two

Planning the Attack on Pearl Harbor

Planning for war against the United States now entered Phase Two: perfection of all details that would ensure a successful attack on Pearl Harbor; tightening of security within Japan to prevent intelligence leaks; positioning of troops and transports for the coming land invasions; and diplomatic maneuvers calculated to confuse President Roosevelt.

Admiral Yamamoto, now commander in chief of the Imperial fleet and the brightest naval officer in Japan, had conceived the attack plan for Pearl Harbor. He now moved ahead in his training program for the naval airmen who would take part in the attack. During the summer of 1941 he had watched with satisfaction as his naval airmen swept in from the sea in repeated simulated attacks on ships in the harbors of Sukomo, Saeki, Kagoshima, and Kanoya. Aircraft of the first assault unit, led by Commander Misuo Shibuta of the Akago Air Unit of Torpedo and Horizontal Bombers, and the second assault unit, led by Lt. Commander Shigekazu Shimazaki of the Suikoku Air Unit of Dive Bombers, all performed brilliantly. The ships they hit with dummy torpedoes and bombs were all positioned in the exact battle order of the U.S. warships in Pearl Harbor. Japanese spies and German agents had been sending information on American defenses at Pearl since June 1941.

After the September 6 meeting in the Imperial Palace, this training period came to an end. Admiral Yamamoto brought his fleet commanders and air assault leaders to the naval war college in Tokyo for specialized war games. When the naval officers entered the auditorium they saw a massive plaster model of Pearl Harbor on a center table. Toy American battleships and aircraft carriers nestled in their berths around the blue-painted harbor. Nearby on model airfields were B-17s, hangars, and fighter planes, all wingtip to wingtip on the toy-sized air bases of Hickam, Bellows, and Wheeler. CINCPAC, the nerve center of the U.S. Navy command, had its place, as did army barracks, roadways, radar warning installations, and antiaircraft positions.

Naval Team A was to be the attacking force. The carriers of the battle fleet were instructed to approach a line designated as two hundred miles off Hawaii, at which point the bombers of the First Navy Air Fleet would take off from their flight decks. The submarines at periscope level and much closer to land would feel their way past the coral reef and into Pearl Harbor, where they were instructed to surface and torpedo every American ship in sight.

As he laid out this plan with other details of action, Admiral Yamamoto lectured his fleet commanders on the importance of destroying all U.S. aircraft carriers within the harbor. "If the American carriers are not destroyed in the first strike," he warned, "and they escape to sea, it will be a long war indeed. They must be annihilated for this to be a successful operation. Otherwise, there will be other sea battles between our forces and those of America during the coming year." The battles of Coral Sea and Midway would later substantiate his point.

Opposing Naval Team A was Japanese Naval Team B, the simulated defenders of Pearl Harbor. All spoke English. They manned the miniature radar installations, intercepted U.S. naval and air force messages from the mainland to Hawaii, and played recordings of actual GI music broadcast to the U.S. forces in Hawaii. Japanese airmen would be hearing music on their attack run, and would use it as a veritable beacon.

Team A and Team B squared off, both sides putting on a realistic show that had men shouting and sometimes laughing. Team B demonstrated how the American defenses would react under attack pressure—with surprise, disbelief, slow reaction, and chaos in the harbor and airfields. Yamamoto had selected a Sunday for his attack. As a former Harvard man himself, he knew that Saturday nights were given over to dancing and merrymaking on most U.S. military bases and that Sunday mornings usually brought hangovers and lethargy—ideal conditions for the Japanese strategy.

As the war games drew to a close the senior officers were satisfied with the planning. Navy General Staff officers not familiar with the plan of attack had been present in the background, as had Marquis Komatsu and Prince Takamatsu, who would later report to Hirohito that Yamamoto's Pearl Harbor plan was well thought out and had a good chance of success.

As important as Pearl Harbor was to the coming war, it was only a sideshow to the entire battle plan. Later in September, Admiral Yamamoto gathered with other senior naval officers at the naval staff college to demonstrate for the army's Unit-82 Strike South leaders how they were going to coordinate troop landings in Malaya, the Philippines, Wake, Guam, Borneo, and Java. This was an important session for Yamamoto, for unless he could demonstrate tactical skills and sufficient ships to handle troop movements and landings, he would not receive the battle fleet he needed for Pearl Harbor. The war games went on for six days; it was a demonstration in depth that the navy could shoulder its responsibilities for the army. Thirty-nine of the best officers in the Japanese army watched the production put on by Yamamoto, and when it was finished they nodded approval. Likewise, naval leadership was agreeable to diverting the ships needed for the hazardous enterprise at Pearl Harbor. Hirohito was informed, and Japan had moved a step further toward war.

President Roosevelt had meanwhile returned to Washington from a meeting with Winston Churchill, where the two leaders had signed the historic Atlantic Charter. Now Ambassador Nomura went to the White House and asked that the President consider an American-Japanese summit meeting in the Pacific. Roosevelt was surprised, but pleased. Nomura suggested a meeting like the Atlantic Charter conference with Churchill, this time with Hirohito and his Prime Minister, Prince Konoye. Roosevelt consulted with Cordell Hull, who expressed little enthusiasm; and in the Imperial Palace Hirohito talked with War Minister Tojo about such a conference off the coast of Alaska, but Tojo was equally negative. He thought Roosevelt's charm and charisma might soften Hirohito and derail the war plan. So on the advice of two subordinates, the leaders of the United States and Japan let this opportunity for conciliation slip from their grasp.

Admiral Yamamoto was riding high by now, and rightly so. He possessed the vision of General Billy

Mitchell of the United States, who had also believed in and demonstrated the superiority of air power over battleships and proved that a new dimension of warfare had arrived on the world scene. In 1923, Yamamoto had taken over the planning and development of air power for the Japanese General Staff. He had graduated first in his class at the naval staff college, then gone on to two years at Harvard in the United States, where he specialized in the manufacture of petroleum and aviation gas. (He once hitchhiked to Mexico during a summer vacation, spending some valuable time in the Texas oil fields.)

Back in Japan in 1924, he had assumed charge of the navy's top-secret Air Development Station on the banks of Kasumigo-Ura, "the Misty Lagoon," a lake approximately the size of Lake George in New York State. There he taught a generation of navy pilots to land on simulated flight decks of wharves and barges as they practiced torpedo-bombing techniques. When he acquired a task force of four aircraft carriers, Yamamoto was ready to display Japanese naval power. In October 1930, Emperor Hirohito steamed north to the Inland Sea to watch the demonstration. Rear Admiral Yamamoto and his pilots of carrier-borne torpedo planes of "Fleet White" theoretically sunk the battleships of "Fleet Blue." The naval General Staff and the Emperor were given a new perspective on the future of naval warfare.

The second preparation for war was the elimination of spy rings in Japan. In September 1941, the "Thought Police," the *Kempei-tai*, began to disband the Richard Sorge ring, which had been under surveillance for more than a year. First they pulled in Ito Tadasu, then Miyagi Yatoku, who had been sent by the American Communist

Party to assist Sorge, and finally the major Japanese connection, Ozaki Hotsumi, who was a close friend and confidant of Prince Konoye. Hotsumi had learned of the arrest of Yatoku and sensed he would be next. He had a dinner engagement with Sorge but did not keep it; instead he stayed home all that day, waiting for the Thought Police. When finally they came to his house he left with them for police headquarters, bidding his wife and daughter good-bye. He would never return. When Hotsumi had failed to appear for dinner Sorge had known something was wrong. For some time he had been under close watch, and he knew now the *Kempeitai* were closing in. He returned to his house and waited in fear.

It had been a long run for Richard Sorge. He had been a Communist agent in Japan since 1931, the personal selection of Lavrenti Beria, who was his mentor in Moscow. Born in Germany, Sorge had gone to Moscow for his indoctrination and training, then returned to Germany, where Communist connections secured him an editorial position on the *Frankfurter Zeitung*, a conservative newspaper that supported Hitler. After a time he was posted to Tokyo as Germany's chief correspondent in Japan and became a friend to everyone in the German Embassy. He had access there to an Enigma code machine and as a matter of course received top-secret information from Berlin. He also became friendly with the military attaché and even wrote many of the military reports that went to Berlin on the Enigma machine. The feeling toward Sorge in the Embassy, as in the various Japanese government bureaus where Sorge was a familiar figure, was that he was a very friendly and accommodating journalist. But as war approached he was under increasing pressure to send more secret information to Beria at the Center in Moscow. Through Ozaki

The firebombing of Tokyo by three hundred B-29 bombers on the night of May 25, 1945. This was the most destructive raid ever made on Japan, even greater than the devastation of Hiroshima and Nagasaki. (U.S. Air Force photo)

At noon on August 15, 1945, life in Japan stopped as people listened to Emperor Hirohito announce over national radio that he had accepted surrender. The street scene pictured here indicates the reaction of the Japanese people to this Imperial announcement.

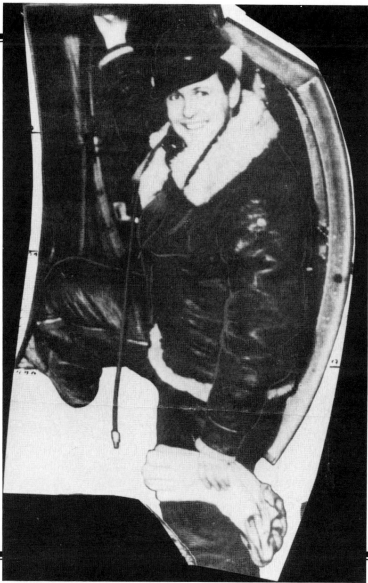

Paul Manning flew as a nose gunner and war correspondent over Germany and Japan. He is shown here as he climbs into a U.S. bomber for the 2000-mile round-trip from Guam to Tokyo on the May 25-26 mission of 1945.

Emperor Hirohito paid close attention to all aspects of Japan's military machine. Here he leads a review of his Imperial Cavalry in 1939. (Imperial Household Agency photo)

Emperor Hirohito inspects bomb damage in Tokyo following U.S. firebombing raid of May 25-26, 1945. Over 100,000 perished in Tokyo, while Japan radio estimated 2,725,000 were left homeless. (Imperial Household Agency photo)

Emperor Hirohito in full military uniform presiding over a midnight meeting of the Supreme Council for the Direction of the War. This conference was held in a bomb shelter beneath the Imperial Palace on August 9, 1945, to discuss the Potsdam Declaration and surrender to the Allies. (Imperial Household Agency photo)

Crown Prince Hirohito as Regent of Japan with his fiancée, Princess Nagako. They announced their engagement in 1917 and were married on January 26, 1924, following Hirohito's celebrated tour of Europe in 1921. (Imperial Household Agency photo)

The Japanese Emperor Hirohito (on white horse) reviews Japanese troops prior to the outbreak of war. (Photo courtesy National Archives)

Supreme Commander General Douglas MacArthur and Emperor Hirohito meet in the American Embassy in Tokyo on September 27, 1945. (U.S. Army Signal Corps photo)

Emperor Hirohito is shown delivering a message to the then Japanese War Minister, Lieutenant General Hideki Tojo, following a military review held in Tokyo, October 21, 1941, to mark the 2,600th anniversary of the founding of the Japanese Empire. (Photo courtesy National Archives)

Emperor Hirohito atop his favorite horse, Shirayuki. (*New York Times* photos)

Emperor Hirohito reviews the Japanese troops in 1932. *(New York Times* photos)

A corridor in the underground bomb shelter of the Imperial Palace. (Imperial Household Agency photo)

Hotsumi he had access to Prince Konoye, so information he could uncover was valued by Beria. His workload was impressive—he sent thirty thousand coded reports by radio to Moscow.

At the same time the United States Embassy was under watch by the Thought Police. Ralph M., the American spy, an embassy aide and career official for the State Department, had no ring the likes of Sorge's, but he was just as effective a spy. He traveled throughout Japan by third-class transportation, "where you learn the temper of the people and their thoughts." On some occasions, he walked many hundreds of miles through the countryside, from Tokyo to Kyoto and back. He was a friendly, gregarious young man of twenty-two at the time, and spoke Japanese fluently. He was welcomed at the army bases and naval ports; the Japanese officials wanted to show off their military capabilities to this American from the U.S. Embassy who would surely inform Washington that the Japanese war machine was not to be lightly regarded. Ralph M. also knew Prince Konoye, and regarded this Prime Minister as a good source of confidential information.

However, Lord Privy Seal Kido was playing a complex game with both Richard Sorge and Ralph M., the American spy. He knew Prince Konoye would soon be deposed as Prime Minister (Konoye was succeeded by War Minister General Hideki Tojo two weeks after the Pearl Harbor attack). The spot that Kido had in mind for Konoye was as leader of a "Peace Faction," which would grow in strength if the war did not go well. Meanwhile, for this prewar period, he had the Prime Minister pump information to Sorge through Hotsumi, which gave the Throne and Hirohito a pipeline to the Kremlin. Kido knew the Russian mentality; whatever reached them through secret sources was more apt to be believed than an official foreign-office message. Likewise, Ralph M., the American agent, received information from Konoye with the same taint, and this went on to Washington. So Kido had channels to both the Kremlin and the White House, a circumstance that pleased the Emperor.

Richard Sorge and Ralph M. were no fools, of course. They had sensed the Palace strategy. And the information they received in bits and pieces was generally accurate, which it had to be at this stage of the game if they were to continue their relationship with Prince Konoye. It was a game of Oriental intrigue with which both men were familiar, and the only fool was the one who allowed himself to be fooled, who mistook information for misinformation, or vice versa.

When talking about this years later with Ralph M. in Virginia, I asked him if he had met Richard Sorge while he was stationed in Tokyo. "Only once," was his reply. "It was in a German bar-restaurant, Das Reingold. The place was crowded with German sailors from their U-boats, and with merchantmen just arrived with a supply of war equipment for the Japanese military. The brass band was loud. But I heard the sound of a motorcycle coming to a halt outside. Then in walked Sorge. He ordered drinks for the sailors, took one himself, looked around, and then walked over to my table. I was sitting alone. He was friendly, outspoken certainly. As he sat down he remarked, 'A German and an American can exchange views in a neutral capital. No?' He laughed.

"'Tell me,' he asked, 'how do you find the Japanese?' Without waiting for my reply he provided his own. 'These are deep and strange people. As a journalist I find truth here is unknown. The purpose of conversation in Japan is to be polite, not to convey information.'

"Sorge then quoted Upton Close, the American socialist author who had spent considerable time in Japan. 'The Japanese are a race who hate tremendously, who can give themselves to unspeakable savageries, and yet when the fury passes are the most gentle-mannered people in the world.'"

Ralph M. said Sorge then sat back in his chair, took a drink, looked around the room and, pointing at two Japanese men, said, "Those are *Kempei-tai*, the Thought Police—the Japanese Gestapo." Sorge suddenly got up and went over to them and sat down and began talking, Ralph M. continued.

Ralph M. knew it was time for him to leave. He did not like the spotlight that Sorge always attracted to him, he said. He left and returned to the U.S. Embassy. In his modest office, he began going over the financial accounts of U.S. missionaries in Japan. Among his other duties, Ralph M. was paymaster for the modest sums contributed from church groups in the United States. He passed on this money to the churchmen. "These were very poor men of God who were trying their best to bring Christianity to Japan and were finding it hard going in a land of Shinto," he said.

On this evening, after Ralph M. met Sorge for the first and only time, he turned off his office lights and left the Embassy, walking to his billet. As he walked he thought how fine it would be to be back in Washington. He was due to leave in one week.

Sorge was not so lucky. He had done a tremendous job for the Russians; among the thirty thousand transmissions he had sent were such priceless bits of information as the warning to Moscow that Hitler would attack Russia with three million men on June 22, 1941. Sorge learned this from the code specialist in the German Embassy who operated the Enigma machine.

The data on the impending attack had come from Berlin to the German ambassador, but Stalin ignored the warning, just as he had brushed aside one from Winston Churchill. (Churchill had learned of the attack from Ultra, the British codebreaking machine that had tapped into Enigma, the coding machine of the Supreme Command of the German armed forces, which transmitted the same information from Berchtesgaden to Wehrmacht headquarters in Berlin.)

Like Sorge's, Ralph M.'s intelligence discoveries were also top-grade during the years he spent in Japan. As war approached they were increasingly important to Washington. U.S. Secretary of the Navy Frank Knox, in particular, valued the reports Ralph M. sent.

Now, in the fall of 1941, Richard Sorge knew he was about finished. He sent a request to the Center to be transferred to Shanghai, and then tried to book passage on a ship to this China port. He was rebuffed in both instances. So he waited and drank a case of sake with Brando de Voukelitch, his photographic expert. Max Klausen, his radio technician, came by and left after only ten minutes. At 5 A.M. the Thought Police knocked on the door. He opened it, and they filled the room. They asked him to come with them, and he was taken to Sugamo Prison. He went through three years of examination, trial, judgment, and appeal. At one point he asked for someone from the Russian Embassy to visit him. The Russian attaché who came had no words of encouragement; he simply said, "Comrade Beria thanks you but says you are on your own." The Russian left, and Sorge was returned to his cell. On November 7, 1944, Osaki Hotsumi and Richard Sorge mounted the gallows and were hanged.

In July of that same year, Ralph M., who had made it safely back to Washington before the Pearl Harbor attack, was parachuted into Japan. He had been recruited from the State Department by William J. Donovan, director of the new Office of Strategic Services (OSS). Saipan had recently been taken, which brought Japan into range of the new American B-29 bombers. In early July, the first B-29 took to the air. Part of a bombing mission, this B-29 carried Ralph M. and five other OSS agents who were to be dropped at night into Japan, where they would operate transmitting intelligence information back to General MacArthur's headquarters. Each man carried a suitcase transmitter for this purpose, as well as Japanese currency, guns, a knife, and emergency rations to hold them until they became settled in areas where members of the Japanese Fifth Column would provide food.

Unlike the other five agents, Ralph M. knew the countryside well. He picked his own drop point, and was first out of the aircraft as it flew over Honshu. As the plane flew on, the other five went out the side at widely dispersed drop points.

Ralph M. landed safely and made his way through the countryside to his destination. He carried his suitcase transmitter and the parachute, fearing that if he buried the parachute some sharp-eyed peasant would spot the turned earth and go running to the local police station. After all, this was not Normandy, with enormous hedgerows; this was poor country, every unit of acreage under cultivation.

As Ralph M. tells what happened then: "I reached my destination before daybreak. It was a church run by missionaries. I had decided long ago that this mission and the other churches across Japan made ideal collection points for strategic information. All I had to do was to organize them into such an operation. They all knew me from the earlier years. I had brought them money to keep going for many years and all were my friends. While they liked the Japanese, they liked Americans more. It was their birthright. I now asked them to provide me with protection. The church I went to first on this night of the drop I planned to use as my field headquarters."

The missionaries agreed, and they became his field agents. They made their way to strategic areas as they conducted their missionary activities. Some went to Yokohama to inspect the warships in the harbor and count them; others went to air bases and reported on the aircraft. They collected information from American businessmen who, strange as it may seem today, were still doing business in Japan. (There had been no effort by the Japanese government to round up and imprison Americans who had been living in Japan, unlike President Roosevelt's strategy to move Japanese from the Pacific Coast to camps inland in the hope of preventing espionage against U.S. military installations.) Ralph M. had accomplished in Japan what Japanese military intelligence agents had tried to do for their own country on the West Coast of America: soliciting of information. Japanese agents, trained in Kyoto for just this purpose and sent to the United States to establish spy rings along the West Coast, failed because the move had been anticipated by the FBI. Ralph M. in one of his reports of 1940, following a visit to Kyoto, told Washington this was to be one Japanese tactic and to watch for it.

During the remainder of 1944 and into 1945, Ralph M. transmitted his information at 10:00 P.M. twice weekly. He gave MacArthur shipping and troop movements that helped to produce heavy ship losses for the Japanese. The Japanese soon became alarmed, as a military message intercepted by Magic, the U.S. decoding intercept unit at MacArthur's headquarters and in Washington, indicates:

The enemy is clearly spying upon the activities of our convoys. Submarine attacks against the "Take" convoy, which was carrying a major part of the 32nd and 35th divisions from China, resulted in the sinking of 4 out of the 9 troop transports—one off NW Luzon and three off Mindanao. About 4,000 of the estimated 21,000 troops aboard the convoy appear to have been lost in the sinkings. It also appears that spy information resulted in the 23 April air attacks in which B-24s sank 5 ships of a convoy off Cap St. Jacques. Utmost caution must be taken to preserve ship movement information. We urge investigation in your areas.

MacArthur, incidentally, read this intercept and commented to his aide, "They're hurting."

But in Japan secret police and trained military units had alerted the country to this danger. They scoured the countryside. Eventually they uncovered, one by one, the five agents who had parachuted with Ralph M. The five were taken to Sugamo Prison and interrogated. They were executed in the same month and on the same gallows where Richard Sorge had died.

Only Ralph M. survived. He became a colonel of intelligence on General MacArthur's staff once Japan was occupied and he could surface. The missionaries continued to receive their stipends and went on doing their good work for the people of Japan.

The last part of Phase Two in Japan's preparation for war—diplomatic approaches to the United States—continued through September and October of 1941. Nomura, the Japanese ambassador to Washington, met with

Secretary of State Cordell Hull on October 1 and was told that Japan must withdraw from China if relations between Japan and the United States were to stay on a good footing. When this hard line was reported to Tokyo many influential Japanese sent messages to the Emperor stating that war with the United States would be a disaster. On October 10 Hirohito dismissed Navy Minister Oikawa because of the latter's doubts about the wisdom of war with America. Admiral Shimada Shigetaro replaced Oikawa and was told it would be his task to persuade the elderly naval admirals that such a war could be won by the navy.

Next, Hirohito approved Kido's suggestion that Tojo should replace Prince Konoye as Prime Minister. Konoye knew what moves were taking place. He sent a last desperate message to President Roosevelt to the effect that unless a dramatic peace gesture was made, meaning a softening of the U.S. hard line, the Konoye Cabinet would have to resign, leaving the field free for the war leaders. But there was no softening by President Roosevelt, and Tojo was summoned to the Imperial Palace, where Hirohito, calling him a "man for the times," told him he would be the next Prime Minister.

Diplomatic moves continued into November. Tojo was upset about delays that he said were handicapping military preparations, and he almost wept in the Imperial Presence. "The Supreme Command needs orders from the Emperor to begin their final exercises," he stated. But the Emperor was still cautious about war with the United States. Some of his advisors were telling him not to take on America but instead to go for the Dutch East Indies, a wiser move, they said, because there would be no direct confrontation with the United States. In retrospect, had this advice been heeded, Japan may have fared better, for President Roosevelt might not have been able to rally the United States as he was able to after the attack on Pearl Harbor. (Indeed, Prime Minister Churchill believed that without a direct Japanese attack on U.S. territory Roosevelt could not go to war, and England, he feared, would continue to be alone against Hitler and the Third Reich.) But in the Imperial Palace Hirohito at last gave his approval to Tojo and the final military exercises that would bring the Japanese army to a state of readiness.

At the same time Admiral Yamamoto was also moving with all due haste to wartime preparedness. He issued to a select few—among them the Emperor and Navy Chief of Staff Nagano—his Order Number One. It incorporated the Pearl Harbor attack plan as the opening salvo in a complete order of battle for the Strike South. The main point in Order Number One: "The Japanese Empire will declare war on the United States, Great Britain, and the Netherlands. War will be declared on X-day. The order will become effective on Y-day." His order described the units to be used in the various operations.

When Navy Chief of Staff Nagano received his copy he went to the Imperial Palace for a meeting with the Emperor. Also present was Army Chief of Staff Sugiyama. Hirohito asked about the projected weather conditions in Malaya and the Pacific during the attack periods. He also inquired as to the target date for the attack on Pearl Harbor. Navy Chief of Staff Nagano replied: "December 8 is the target date."

"Isn't that a Monday?" asked Hirohito.

"Monday in Tokyo, Sunday in Hawaii," Nagano clarified. "We chose it because everyone there will be tired and slow to awake."

In his memorandum on this meeting, published in 1967, Army Chief of Staff General Sugiyama states that

Yamamoto's Order Number One was approved at this time. The message of approval was forwarded immediately to Admiral Yamamoto, and that night, aboard the flagship *Nagato,* there was a solemn ceremonial drinking of sake for the battles ahead.

The Supreme War Council then met with Hirohito in the Imperial Palace. Order Number One was discussed in detail, each Council member expressing his opinion. Finally, when Group Harmony had been achieved and all were agreed that "the time to activate our military forces is set for early December," the Emperor converted Order Number One into Great Order. Tojo declared to the Emperor, "We await only your mandate to move."

An Imperial Rescript was written, scheduled for release the day after the attack on Pearl Harbor, and announcing war on the United States, England, and Holland as well as the establishment of a New Order in Greater East Asia. With the Rescript ready and Great Order signed, Tojo had his mandate.

Tojo gave the order to the first and second submarine squadrons of the Combined Fleet to set sail at night from the Kure naval base. Their destination, the first anchorage, was Kwajalein in the Marshall Islands.

After the war I spoke with a Japanese submarine officer who was aboard one of these submarines the night they left Kure. He recalled, "It was a departure for war without fanfare. There was no one to send us off, only the mountains of our native land which rose beyond the curtain of night like a painting in black and white, and the flickers of lights from homes sleeping peacefully without any knowledge of the battle storm brewing in the Pacific."

He said the submarine squadrons reached the Inner South Seas and advanced to Kwajalein, far below the

Equator. As they slipped into port, they saw that the flagship of the Sixth Fleet, *Katori*, was already riding at anchor. The squadrons dispersed; some proceeded to nearby Notje and others to Maloelap. All waited for the signal to advance. Commander Naoji Iwasa, remembering that moment, said the signal from Tokyo came on November 11. It said: "Proceed to Hawaii." On the same day other submarines of the first and third squadrons left the Yokosuka naval base and bore straight for Hawaii. When all submarine squadrons had reached the waters off Hawaii they all stood by, "a net of readiness," as one Japanese officer recalled. "We were not to prepare for action until November 20, the turning point of the Washington conferences. If Japanese-American negotiations were still deadlocked on that day, the submarines were to become operational."

In Washington the fourth formal conference was taking place. Cordell Hull, as spokesman for President Roosevelt, gave Japan his ultimatum: a multilateral nonaggression treaty calling for the withdrawal of all Japanese troops from China and French Indochina. "This is the only basis for negotiation," Hull declared.

In the Imperial Palace another Supreme War Council conference was taking place. It was agreed on the night of November 20 that the war would go forward. There would be no treaty with the United States on terms laid down by Hull.

The following day an order was issued to the Japanese battleship and carrier force to proceed to assembly point Tankan-wan in the Kurile Islands, far to the north. The First Navy Air Fleet, Vice Admiral Nagumo commanding, followed in his flagship and sped to join the naval forces moving toward their anchorage in Tennei harbor at Tankan-wan. The attack fleet arrived on December 1. They were to await the signal to proceed that would come from the Imperial Palace on December 2, following one last Imperial Conference. There was now at Tankan-wan a total of forty-six ships, including six standard aircraft carriers, the *Akagi* and the *Kaga* of the First Air Attack Force, the *Soryu* and the *Hiryu* of the Second Attack Force, and the *Zaukaku* and the *Shokaku* of the Fifth Air Attack Force. Also part of the assembled forces were four high-speed battleships of the Third Battleship Division: the *Kongo*, the *Haruna*, the *Hier,* and the *Kirishima*. There were crack air defense cruisers of the Eighth Cruiser Division, the *Chikuma* and the *Tone;* and the First Destroyer Squadron, with the *Sendai* as its flagship. All were accompanied by flotillas of tankers and supply ships for refueling at sea.

The night of December 2, the final prewar conference was held in the Imperial Palace, the Emperor presiding. When the discussions had ended, all agreed the attack on the United States should be launched. The Emperor gave his sanction with a nod of agreement. The signal was sent, in the new naval code, XB, prepared for this attack only, to the waiting fleet at Tankan-wan to commence war. The submarines waiting off Hawaii also received a brief message that the war was on.

On the morning of December 3, the townspeople of this harbor town in the Kuriles awoke to find the harbor empty and the battle fleet gone. The task force had disappeared over the horizon and was making its way through the stormy northern Pacific for Hawaii.

On December 5, the Foreign Office in Tokyo sent a signal in Purple Code to Nomura and Kurusu, the Japanese envoys in Washington, to sever diplomatic relations with the United States at "0300 the morning of December 8." But faulty wireless relays due to Pacific atmospheric interference delayed transmission of the message's significant fourteenth paragraph. Decoding the message in the Japanese Embassy was also slow. The code clerks and diplomats were suffering from hangovers from a Japanese party the previous evening. The full message was not handed to Cordell Hull until forty minutes after the attack on Pearl Harbor had begun, though both the President and Secretary of State had been reading the intercepts and knew that war was imminent.

Three

Hirohito: The Glory Year

The Japanese assault on Pearl Harbor began Sunday morning at eight o'clock, December 7. The attacking aircraft had been launched from aircraft carriers two hundred miles off Oahu, a point decided upon after the Japanese passenger ship *Taiyo Maru*, making a practice run from the Kurile Islands to Honolulu on November 1, had determined that U.S. aerial reconnaissance reached only to the one-hundred-mile line offshore. The *Taiyo Maru*, whose run had followed the northern course that the attack force would take on December 2, had also compiled weather, sea, and iceberg data, which would likely be needed by Admiral Yamamoto's battle fleet. Yamamoto was directing all operations from a control point at naval headquarters in Tokyo. Vice Admiral Nagumo Chu-ichi, aboard his flagship carrier *Akagi*, commented to his captain that the *Taiyo Maru* had performed well, that its information had been accurate. When this passenger liner had reached Honolulu on November 1, Japanese Consul General Kita had come aboard with detailed answers to one hundred questions he had been ordered to answer by Japanese naval intelligence. FBI and DIO (Department of Intelligence Operations, U.S. Naval Intelligence) agents noted that Kita had spent little time aboard. The Japanese passengers who had debarked for sightseeing had returned quickly and the ship had left its berth the same day it had arrived, followed closely by U.S. naval patrol boats. The Japanese vessel had disappeared from view over the horizon, bound for Tokyo with all the information Japanese naval headquarters would need to launch their attack on Pearl Harbor.

Once launched from their carriers, the pilots of the torpedo and horizontal bombers, the dive bombers, and the escorting Zero fighter planes cruised at varying altitudes up to eleven thousand feet. As they headed toward land they listened to music being broadcast over the Hawaiian GI station on Oahu. The music served as a beam for the navigators and lead planes, just as had been predicted during the tabletop war games at naval staff college in Tokyo. The initial launch completed, Vice Admiral Nagumo also listened to the GI music as he sat in the officers' ward room. As Japanese planes came down the valley, the white clouds over Pearl Harbor suddenly opened and brilliant sunshine bathed the entire target area. The pilots began their bombing and torpedo runs. Ninety-four warships, including eight battleships, were at anchor, and the *Pennsylvania* was sitting in drydock. But there was disappointment for the flight leader who circled the harbor directing the attack. Admiral Yamamoto had predicted a long war if the American carrier fleet was not destroyed in Pearl Harbor. And there were no aircraft carriers below.

At a conference in the White House on November 27, President Roosevelt, Secretary of War Stimson, and Secretary of the Navy Knox had decided it would be prudent to order all carriers and half of the army aircraft from Pearl Harbor. Everyone in top authority knew the Japanese were going to attack somewhere. General Marshall thought it might be the Panama Canal; others predicted the Philippines, or Malay. None pinpointed Pearl Harbor. The President, at his advisors' urging, told Stimson and Chief of Naval Operations Stark to issue a war warning. The statement declared in part: "This dispatch is to be considered a war warning . . . An aggressive move by Japan is expected within the next few days." The warning added that the move would probably be an "amphibious expedition against either the Philippines, Thai or Kra Peninsula in Malaya, or possibly Borneo."

When Admiral Kimmel and army commander Lt. General Walter Short received this warning in Hawaii, they agreed to activate a plan to send all carriers and fifty percent of the aircraft from the island. Vice Admiral Halsey was ordered to Wake Island with the carrier *Enterprise*, three heavy cruisers, nine destroyers, twelve marine Wildcat fighters, and some army bombers. Vice Admiral J. H. Newton received orders to leave for Midway with the carrier *Lexington*, three cruisers, five destroyers, and eighteen marine fighters. The third aircraft carrier under Admiral Kimmel's command, the *Saratoga*, was in San Diego being refitted and would remain there until events were resolved.

The conference that produced this repositioning of America's vital aircraft carriers from Pearl Harbor just days before the attack had followed an earlier critical meeting in the White House. Among the officials present was Colonel Rufus Bratton of Army G-2, one of the Magic group that was routinely intercepting and decoding Japanese messages. Although the Japanese navy had switched to a new code for the Pearl Harbor attack, the XB code, it was deciphered by U.S. Navy cryptographers by December 4. And Colonel Bratton had sufficient intercept material as early as November 29 to predict war.

The presumably unforeseen attack on Pearl Harbor stunned many, including Colonel William F. Friedman, Chief of the U.S. Army Signal Corps Intelligence Service. Friedman was the man who broke Japan's Purple Code, and his Magic intercepts telling of an impending attack on Pearl Harbor had been sent by special Signal Corps messengers to the White House. Hearing the news of Pearl Harbor on December 7, Friedman was convinced his information had simply been ignored. His wife, Elizabeth, a brilliant cryptographer who had set up the OSS code system in World War II for General William Donovan, spoke of Pearl Harbor day with her husband in their home: "He could do no more than pace back and forth across the room, muttering to himself over and over again, 'But they knew, they knew, they knew.'"

There is no doubt that President Roosevelt wanted to provoke the Japanese into a first attack on the United States. He had instructed Cordell Hull to draft a final statement of the American moral position which he knew Hirohito could not accept. Roosevelt held it was apparent that Hirohito and Hitler had grand designs to conquer the world, despite what they might say officially.

A November 25 entry in Secretary of War Stimson's diary credited Roosevelt with making the following statement during a Cabinet meeting:

> We are likely to be attacked next Monday, for the Japanese are notorious for making an attack without warning, and the question is what should we do. The question is how we should maneuver them into the position of firing the first shot without allowing too much danger to ourselves. It is a difficult proposition.

Winston Churchill was to comment later that U.S. leaders "regarded the actual form of the attack, or even its scale, as incomparably less important than the fact that the whole American nation would be united for its own safety in a righteous cause as never before."

President Roosevelt, in one of his conversations on the scrambled telephone line between the White House and 10 Downing Street, had commented to Churchill that "I cannot get too far out in front of the voters in peacetime. But I am most anxious to come to grips with Hitler." Yet he had not envisioned the magnitude of death and destruction the well-planned and ruthless Japanese attack would produce:

Eight battleships, three light cruisers, three destroyers, and four auxiliary craft were either sunk, capsized, or heavily damaged. Naval aircraft casualties were likewise heavy: thirteen fighters, twenty-one scout bombers, forty-six patrol bombers, three utility planes, two air transports, two observation-scout aircraft. The army lost four B-17s, twelve B-18s, two A-20s, thirty-two P-40s, twenty P-36s, four P-26s, two OA-9s, one P-49, eighty-eight pursuit planes, and six reconnaissance aircraft; thirty-four bombers were damaged. Hickam and Wheeler Fields, Ford Island, and the Kaneoche and Ewa installations were heavily damaged.

The United States dead and missing totaled 2,402, and 1,178 were wounded. When these figures were placed on the President's desk, a presidential aide overheard Roosevelt exclaim, "Oh, God, I never thought it would be so great."

When the Japanese had completed their destruction, the air fleet flew back to their carriers and the code signal of success, "Tora, Tora, Tora!" was issued to Admiral Yamamoto at naval headquarters in Tokyo and Hirohito in the Imperial Palace. The submarines, however, had been less successful. The harbor was too small for maneuvering, and the submarine flotillas that had remained in the ocean outside to torpedo any U.S. aircraft carriers fleeing the naval base had none to attack.

Much later, when General MacArthur was beginning his long haul back from Australia to the Philippines, he met with General Marshall at his staff headquarters on Goodenough Island off New Guinea. It was their only meeting during World War II. At a luncheon, Marshall was waspish and downgraded MacArthur's ego and his staff. At one point he snapped at this military leader who had been his superior for many years in Washington and said, "You don't have a staff, you have a court." MacArthur, whose brilliance as a strategist was considered awesome by his peers, asked Marshall why he had been horseback riding instead of tending to business the morning of December 7. He asked Marshall why he had sent a warning message to General Short at Pearl Harbor, a message that arrived forty-five minutes after the Japanese attack, by commercial telegraph instead of through the Signal Corps. General Marshall, who was dedicated to President Roosevelt as commander in chief, declined to answer.

Following the attack on Pearl Harbor, Lord Privy Seal Kido had released the Imperial Rescript declaring war on the United States and Great Britain. In the tenor of that day, it contained all the reasons why Japan thought she should go to war, including the supposed threat by the United States and England to Japan's desire to lead the peaceful conduct of commerce in Asia and the entire Far East.

News of the attack on Pearl Harbor, with all the details of Nipponese bravery and concurrent disaster to the United States, turned Tokyo into a festival of jubilation. The people could not get enough of the facts concerning this assault on a mammoth power. All compared the victory to the one achieved over Russia in

1905. But a single well-planned battle does not a war make, and despite the gleeful hysteria raging in the streets and in the bars and cafés, there was a soberness among the elder statesmen. Prince Konoye, who had served as Prime Minister through three Cabinets, had no doubts that Japan had pursued the wrong course; in another week he was to resign and be succeeded in office by General Tojo. Every time the name of Admiral Yamamoto was mentioned over national radio he was cheered in the bars of Tokyo by the sake- and whiskey-drinking Japanese.

But Yamamoto, at Imperial naval headquarters, was also filled with doubt. Not one American aircraft carrier had been damaged. Yamamoto had urged Tojo to follow the Pearl Harbor attack with an army landing, but Tojo had replied that it was too risky. Yet if Tojo had listened to Yamamoto and seized this great American island bastion, which he could have done with reasonable ease, the naval battles of Coral Sea and Midway would have been forestalled and General MacArthur would have been cut off from the troops and supplies that eventually made possible his seizures and containments from New Guinea to the Philippines. The U.S. Carrier Fleet would also have been isolated from supply lines.

A correspondent for the Japanese news service JiJi talked with Yamamoto at his advance headquarters in January 1943. Yamamoto said he was bitterly disappointed when Tojo and other generals rejected his proposal to follow up the surprise attack on Pearl Harbor. Yamamoto still held in 1943 that "only by occupying Hawaii could Japan have any chance of success in the subsequent war operations in the Pacific." Yamamoto added, "The navy was subsequently obliged to fight the losing battle of Midway despite obvious disadvantages to the Japanese."

But following the attack on Pearl Harbor, Tojo was

achieving a string of military successes that staggered the United States, Britain, and Australia. (Few Western leaders suspected that the Japanese would follow up the attack on Hawaii with invasions of the Philippines, Hong Kong, Malaya, and the Dutch East Indies, all in quick succession.) Tojo's divisions then moved on Guam and Wake Island. In the southwest Pacific, General Tomojuki Yamashito's Twenty-first Army moved onto Malaya and forty-three thousand men of General Honma's Fourteenth Army boarded transports at Formosa and the Pescadores for Luzon and an attack on the Philippines.

On the Malayan peninsula Yamashito's soldiers came on bicycles toward Singapore. The British never envisioned such a land attack through swamp and jungle; their naval guns were all pointed seaward, leaving the land route free of heavy artillery fire. During this period of heavy fighting, Japanese torpedo bombers spotted the two British cruisers *Prince of Wales* and *Repulse* steaming at high speed down the Malayan coast en route to the defense of Singapore. Japanese bombers came in at deck height, launching their torpedoes with accuracy. The two British warships went down. On land, the Singapore garrison crumbled and ninety-five thousand British Commonwealth troops surrendered. In London, Winston Churchill was shaken by the loss, calling it "the worst disaster and the largest capitulation in British history."

Days later, seventy-four Japanese warships sunk a fleet of American, British, Dutch, and Australian ships in the Battle of Java Sea, giving Japan control of the Dutch East Indies and its oil, tin, and tungsten resources.

The Japanese went on conquering in other places: Siam, Burma, Sumatra, Borneo, the Celebes, Timor, the Bismarcks, the Gilberts, Wake, Guam, most of the Solomons, and part of New Guinea. Vice Admiral Nagumo's task force sunk two British heavy cruisers and the aircraft carrier *Hermes* off Ceylon. It was then that General "Vinegar Joe" Stilwell came limping out of Burma into India with the remnants of his tattered forces and told reporters, "We took a hell of a beating and it was humiliating." Attu and Kiska, two of the Aleutian Islands off Alaska, were taken by the Japanese in June 1942. One of their submarines even surfaced off the state of Oregon and shelled that coast.

Admiral Yamamoto was the strategy genius in all the sea attacks. After his warships won the Battle of Java Sea on March 1, 1942, he again urged Tojo to be bold and invade Australia. "Five divisions will do the job," he told Tojo. General Richard L. Eichelberger, field commander of MacArthur's Eighth Army, recalled at the time: "Our fighter planes began arriving by ship, but it was already evident that the Japanese Zeros were superior in maneuverability and that the Japanese pilots of that time were well trained and highly skilled . . . we were outnumbered five to one."

General Tojo, although he had rejected Yamamoto's earlier suggestion for the land invasion of Hawaii, was agreeable to the idea of invading Australia. He had lost considerable face over General MacArthur's personal escape from the Philippines, and he knew that MacArthur would use Australia as a springboard for his announced "I shall return" to the Philippines. Tojo was now just as determined to deny the American general this military launching site.

Following Japan's sinking of three British warships off Ceylon, Admiral Yamamoto was calling for an invasion of India. In truth, everything had gone so fast that the Japanese were actually uncertain about their next moves. They had been so well prepared for war and the United States so unprepared that they had achieved initial victories beyond their wildest expectations. Yamamoto had expected to lose one quarter of his naval strength at Pearl Harbor; instead he lost one destroyer. Yamamoto and the Japanese navy felt, for now at least, as though they ruled the seas. Hence, Japanese military headquarters in Tokyo gave serious thought to Yamamoto's proposal to invade India. Japan was already in control of Burma, and a pincer movement from Burma and India would envelop and destroy British forces. Japanese leaders believed they could then pair up with their German allies and together control all of Asia.

In Calcutta, British General Headquarters were thinking along the same lines. German Field Marshal Erwin Rommel was racing toward Cairo and Suez, and the belief among the British military was that if Rommel took Cairo he would then swing north and link up in a pincer movement with German divisions that were annihilating a Soviet army of two hundred and fifty thousand in the Caucasus Mountains. If these two formidable German forces were to pair up with a Japanese army invading India, the entire area would be turned into an Axis-controlled region before the end of 1942.

In Cairo, the British Embassy was already burning secret documents. One Wednesday in particular, when the burning was at its peak with ashes and smoke emanating from English chimneys, was called Ash Wednesday.

In India, rumors of a Japanese invasion sent thousands of people fleeing north, jamming every train traveling from Calcutta to New Delhi.

But Rommel failed to reach Cairo. Australian and British defenders at Tobruk held like a rock. Rommel bypassed it and kept moving. Then the Australian government, fearful of a Japanese invasion of their own country, demanded that Winston Churchill release Australian divisions from the Middle East and return them to their homeland for defense duties there. Churchill did so, reluctantly. With the Australians gone, the vacuum was filled with twenty-five thousand South African troops. The Afrika Korps attacked and broke through the defenses and captured Tobruk. The German general was off and running again with his desert divisions, but his supply lines were stretched too far, and under attack he had to retreat from his last and final drive to Cairo. This was his high-water mark; following a defeat at El Alamein at the hands of British Field Marshal Montgomery, he had his forces surrender to General Eisenhower's troops in Tunisia. (Rommel himself had earlier been ordered back to Germany by Hitler, where he had received hospital treatment and then assumed the role of field commander on the Western Front in anticipation of Allied landings.)

German divisions also had to retreat in the Caucasus Mountains, but not until they had virtually annihilated Russian divisions in that region.

I had covered the fighting at Tobruk as a war correspondent, and had walked from there to Cairo with the Aussies. We took flights southward to Cape Town, but at Durban I received a cable from my New York news service to reverse my direction and go to India, where the action, it seemed to them, was more imminent and newsworthy.

From India I went on to Chungking, where I met Chiang Kai-shek. It was a grim, mountainous region, the last redoubt of Chinese forces that had been driven back by Japanese invaders. The collapse of Nationalist China had been apparent for quite some time. First came the Japanese in 1942. Later, in 1948, would come a massive Communist drive of a million of Mao Tse-tung's troops, who would cross the north bank of the Yangtze River in a drive that would move forces loyal to Chiang to Shanghai, whence they were to flee to Formosa. With U.S. critics on Capitol Hill decrying the corruption of

Chiang and his warlords, MacArthur would reply, "For the first time in our relations with Asia we have endangered the paramount interests of the United States by confusing them with an internal purification problem in Asia."

But in 1942, in Chungking, when it was apparent that Chiang was losing China village by village to the Japanese, an observer could not help but feel sorrow for the Chinese and their leaders of that day.

By this time the Japanese Empire stretched five thousand miles, from Tokyo to China, down the Pacific Basin to the Dutch East Indies, to Wake Island, to the seacoast of India, to the Kurile Islands off the coast of Siberia, and to the Coral Sea in the South Pacific. Emperor Hirohito now ruled almost a seventh of the world, much of it water but nevertheless under Japanese control.

It had been a good ten-year run for Japan. These were glory years for Hirohito, and when he would visit the Imperial family shrine in the palace forest and report to his ancestors and his grandfather Meiji in particular, he would tell them he had carried forward the expansion of Japan as they had wished.

As for War Minister General Tojo, India had begun to fade among the priorities that interested him. At the War Ministry in Tokyo, General Tojo continued to plan for the invasion of Australia. He was determined to settle accounts with General MacArthur. The last Filipino and American troops—totaling seventy-six thousand, ten thousand of whom would die during the infamous death march from Bataan to prison camps on the island—had surrendered on April 8, 1942. But what rankled Tojo and General Honma, who had been charged with the taking of the Philippines, was MacArthur's defense strategy. During five months of war there, MacArthur's tactics, with limited forces at his command, had been excellent.

General Honma had been forced to ask Tojo for more troops, a development upsetting to both Honma and Tojo. Fighting there was now over, but Tojo was determined to land five divisions in Australia and bring MacArthur to Tokyo a captive, to be paraded through the streets of the Japanese capital. The first step toward this fanciful objective was to send Vice Admiral Takagi, victor in the Battle of the Java Sea, southward with his fleet and troops to New Guinea with orders to take Port Moresby, only three hundred miles across the Coral Sea from Australia. Port Moresby was to be Tojo's launching port for the invasion. But MacArthur, sensing the strategy, met Takagi's fleet with U.S. naval and air forces. The Japanese fleet, whose progress south had been plotted by the Magic codebreakers, was intercepted on May 7 in the Coral Sea. A U.S. bomber squadron sunk the *Ryukaku*, a light carrier. Two more enemy carriers were badly damaged. In retaliation, Japanese bombers sunk the battleship *Lexington*, a tanker, and a destroyer before Takagi broke off the battle and returned his forces to Rabaul.

Three weeks later, Admiral Yamamoto, determined to take Midway Island, took his battle fleet out into the Pacific. The battle for Midway was not an isolated attempt at seizure of a Pacific island, but part of a grand naval strategy. Yamamoto planned to use Wake, Midway, and Johnson islands as a bridge across the Pacific to Hawaii. He still held hopes he could convince Tojo and Hirohito that the capture of Hawaii was necessary, that it would deny General MacArthur a vital base and supply center.

Magic intercepts located the position of the Japanese battle fleet on its approach to Midway, enabling Admiral Nimitz to position his carriers strategically. The *Yorktown* (damages suffered in the Coral Sea battle the previous month having been repaired), the *Hornet*, and the *Enterprise* moved quickly to a point 325 miles north of Midway to await Yamamoto's fleet. On June 4, 1942, bombers and fighters from the Japanese First Carrier Strike Force attacked Midway, killing twenty-four of the defenders, but failing to knock out the island's defenses for their planned invasion.

U.S. aircraft from Midway had located the Japanese naval force and carried out five futile air strikes. Admiral Raymond Spruance then launched every plane aboard the *Enterprise* and *Hornet*, as did Admiral Frank Fletcher of the *Yorktown*, but the bombers failed to score and were themselves badly decimated by Zeros flying from their own flattops. Then, as Vice Admiral Nagumo was about to launch a second raid on Midway, along with another strike at U.S. warships, American dive bombers found their targets: in six minutes three of Japan's most formidable carriers had been reduced to flaming wrecks. The Japanese counterattacked, crippling the *Yorktown*, which was to be torpedoed and sunk three days later by a Japanese submarine. But American pilots kept attacking; the Japanese carrier *Hiryu* was badly damaged.

In this climactic struggle, Japan also lost a heavy cruiser and 332 planes. Twenty-five hundred men, including some of their finest pilots, were killed. Nagumo then ordered his fleet to withdraw to Rabaul. He talked to Admiral Yamamoto about the defeat and asked what he would tell the Emperor. Yamamoto said, "It is my responsibility to inform the Emperor."

Hirohito considered the Battle of Midway the turning point in the naval struggle for control of the Pacific. His high-frequency radio was tuned continuously to channels that reported all naval and air action at Midway back to Imperial naval headquarters in Tokyo. Lord Privy Seal Kido tells in his diary about the moment he entered the Imperial library and saw Hirohito tuned to reports on Midway, listening intently. "I dared not interrupt him," Kido wrote, "so I just stood there in the darkened library. When the losses came over the air the Emperor sighed with a great sadness. He knew at that time that there now existed no hope of victory in the Pacific, but only a process of attrition and the hope that by continuing to fight a strong defensive war the United States could be induced to pay a price for peace." Hirohito withdrew to his private quarters for two days, then summoned Kido. In his diary Kido wrote of that June 8 meeting:

> We talked about the Midway battle. I had supposed that news of our terrible losses would have caused him untold anguish. However, his countenance showed no trace of change. He said that the setback received had been severe and regrettable, but that notwithstanding he had told Navy Chief of Staff Nagano to carry on and to make sure that naval morale did not deteriorate. He emphasized that he did not wish the future policy of the navy to become inactive and passive. I was very much impressed by the courage displayed by His Majesty today and I was thankful that our country is blessed with such a good sovereign.

Few civilians in Japan were allowed to hear of the losses at Midway. Hirohito appointed General Ando Kisaburo as head of propaganda and controller of civilian thought. He was to serve in the Cabinet as a minister without portfolio. Following his appointment, the news service and national radio announced to the people that Japan had won a great victory, that two American aircraft carriers had been sunk at Midway and 120 U.S. planes shot down with only one Japanese carrier and thirty-five aircraft lost.

The Navy General Staff then was told that the wounded from Midway should be brought back to Japan and placed in Yokosuka Naval Hospital under tight security. Once they were well, they were to be reassigned to other duties. The public cover-up was complete.

Japanese high command now ordered a two-month halt to naval activities. Time was needed to reassess future plans.

But by midsummer of that year, the Japanese were preparing air bases in the lower Solomons and moving onto New Guinea in a land drive toward Port Moresby. A repulse in the naval and air battles of the Coral Sea and a punishing defeat at Midway had failed to dampen Tojo's determination to invade Australia and destroy MacArthur's troops in an attempt to control all of Asia.

Four

Guadalcanal: Starting the Long Haul Back

In Australia General MacArthur knew the peril his forces faced if the Japanese landed in great numbers. He remembered how easy it had been for Japanese forces to invade Indonesia following their victory in the Battle of the Java Sea the previous February. The Japanese Second and Thirty-eighth Divisions had landed in western Java and quickly defeated fifteen thousand Allied regular troops and some forty thousand reserves and volunteers. One week later, on March 8, the Dutch Governor General signed a formal document of surrender, the same day Rangoon, the capital of Burma, fell to Japanese divisions at the northern end of the Pacific battle scene. The fall of Bataan occurred at about the same time. On March 11, 1942, General and Mrs. MacArthur, with their four-year-old son Arthur, had boarded a PT boat and escaped in the night from Bataan and Corregidor, leaving General Jonathan Wainwright for the final defense and surrender of American and Filipino forces of April 9, 1942.

After the fall of Java, Admiral Yamamoto, to demonstrate the vulnerability of Australia, sent Admiral Nagumo's Pearl Harbor task force to launch a devastating air attack on the port city of Darwin. From carriers off the Indonesian island of Timor, about three hundred miles from Darwin (calculated as the same distance from Port Moresby to Darwin, in the event bombers from Port Moresby were needed to provide air cover for a future Japanese landing), Nagumo's airmen struck at Australia. Japanese planes sunk a U.S. destroyer, four U.S. transports, one British tanker, and four Australian freighters in Darwin harbor. They knocked out twenty-three Allied planes, demolished several of Darwin's best buildings, killed 238 Australians, and wounded another 300. They lost four aircraft, the other 184 returning safely to their carriers off Timor.

Following that raid, Admiral Yamamoto wanted to land an expeditionary force from his ships on the north coast of Australia. With a division or two, he felt sure, he could terrorize this subcontinent. General Yamashita, who had captured Singapore, agreed with the plan and said he would lead the invasion. But General Tojo disagreed, saying a spectacular air raid was one thing, but that a full-scale invasion required more thought. Once ashore, he reasoned, a Japanese force would have to depend for supplies on freighters to the rear, and these freighters were already stretched to the limit. Another consideration was that the Americans would be capable of moving B-17 bombers and fighter planes into Australia, thus eliminating Japanese air superiority.

But by early summer Tojo believed it was time to move on Australia. He earmarked the divisions and the tank units that would land. From his intelligence reports he knew that the force of seven thousand Australian regulars he would fight had been strengthened: divisions from the Middle East and U.S. Marines and soldiers coming ashore would resist strongly. Yet the quality of Japanese soldiers he was prepared to throw into battle was excellent, and he believed that once ashore they could not be stopped. He was certain that with tanks spearheading these divisions, they could encircle the Allied troops and defeat them.

MacArthur was thinking along the same lines. With the troops and armaments he had on hand, he would be no match for the hard-driving Japanese who would be maneuvering over vast areas of open spaces, from Darwin on the north coast to Melbourne, Brisbane, and Sydney on the south and east coasts.

To invade Australia, Tojo first had to capture Port Moresby at the lower tip of New Guinea. His navy had failed to take this critical port and had been driven back on May 7 and 8 in the Battle of the Coral Sea. The alternative now was a land invasion. On the twenty-first of July, 1942, he sent a force of eight thousand to New Guinea. They landed at Buna on the west coast and then moved inland, slowly climbing the seven-thousand-foot passes that crossed the Owen Stanley range. Australian scouts radioed back reports to General MacArthur about these movements. MacArthur moved quickly, knowing that the rain forests of the New Guinea terrain would be a force in his favor. He dispatched two divisions—the U.S. Thirty-second Infantry and the Australian Seventh Division (the same division that had fought Erwin Rommel's Afrika Korps to a standstill at Tobruk)—across the Coral Sea to Port Moresby. Upon reaching Port Moresby, the two divisions pushed inland against difficult fighting conditions: deep, fast-moving rivers, high cliffs, blood-sucking leeches, poisonous snakes, treacherous swamps, and grass six feet in height.

They met the Japanese in this hellhole and stopped

them cold, pushing them back into a retreat over the same passes and mountains they had traversed on their way to the lowlands. The Japanese soldiers who fought were not elated about the conditions either. One colonel who led his men back to Buna recorded in his diary at the time: "It was a most terrible experience. We were existing on one handful of rice a day per man and my troops could barely drag themselves up over the mountains. It was a retreat of great losses."

MacArthur had moved his advance headquarters to Port Moresby. He listened to reports from his field commanders and planned strategy on his battle maps. But his divisions up ahead, as exhausted as the Japanese soldiers, were moving slowly, and as they came down to the coastal plain of Buna where the final battle for New Guinea would take place, they formed a defense mentality. Waiting for them ahead they could see seventy-five hundred Japanese troops, commanded by Lt. General Hatachi Adachi. The Japanese were protected now by coconut-log bunkers and Nambu machine guns emplaced with interlocking fields of fire. They were being reinforced at night by regiments of fresh soldiers being landed from destroyers. And by day, Zero fighter planes swept down from Rabaul, gunning the American-Australian positions and then returning to the safety of their own airfields.

As MacArthur paced the verandah of his headquarters at Port Moresby, he suddenly called out to his chief aide, "Sutherland, bring General Eichelberger up here from Australia." MacArthur wanted Eichelberger, his most aggressive general, to take charge of the stalled troops outside of Buna. Eichelberger arrived shortly after by plane and was taken immediately to MacArthur's headquarters, where, on the verandah, MacArthur immediately ordered him to take over field command.

Looking directly at Eichelberger, MacArthur promised: "If you capture Buna, I'll award you the Distinguished Service Cross." He then paced back and forth for a moment and added: "Bob, take Buna, or don't come back alive."

Buna was taken. The intensity of the fighting is underscored by the casualties. Fifteen thousand Japanese soldiers were killed. The cost to MacArthur was thirty-three hundred killed and fifty-five hundred wounded.

General MacArthur now had more on his mind than the victory at Buna. A delay there had stalled his plans for a forward thrust, the first steps that would move his forces up out of the South Pacific and away from Australia. He decided that taking Guadalcanal, a low-lying coral island about the size of Delaware, would be the diversion needed to thwart Tojo in his drive toward Australia and would spread Japanese forces into another theater of combat, thus preventing mobilization of an invasion force.

Guadalcanal was being occupied by twenty-five hundred Japanese; four hundred regular soldiers and the rest construction workers building an airstrip to assist in Tojo's planned invasion of Australia. On August 7, 1942, MacArthur landed eleven thousand U.S. Marines of the First Division on Guadalcanal. When the Americans landed, the Japanese fled back into the interior, reporting the new action by radio to their headquarters at Rabaul. Admiral Yamamoto sent aircraft carriers to bomb and strafe the new American beachhead. U.S. Navy pilots from the aircraft carriers *Saratoga*, *Wasp*, and *Enterprise* came up to meet these attacks and shot down twenty-seven Japanese bombers of the Bettie class and one Zero. They lost some of their own in the battle.

American navy pilots said the Japanese they encountered over Guadalcanal were skilled. They were, indeed, among the best in Japan; some had survived the battles in China, Singapore, and Midway. Their numbers would diminish as the war went on, but during those six months of war over Guadalcanal they matched the U.S. pilots' accomplishments. One of the great aces was Sakai Saburo. In a dogfight over the island one of his eyes was shot out and his plane was wrecked by gunfire. But, trailing his squadron, he managed to make it back to Rabaul, where he was flown to Tokyo for eye surgery. After his recovery he served as a training instructor for the new crop of airmen. He himself again took to the air during the battle for Iwo Jima and, as always, was a standout. He survived the war, and was credited with sixty-four victories over Chinese, British, Dutch, and U.S. combat aircraft and pilots.

Two other Japanese had high kill scores against Allied airmen. They were Nishizawa Hiroyoshi (104 kills) and Sugita Shoichi (80).

The top American ace in the Pacific was Richard Bong. He shot down forty Japanese aircraft in combat. Joe Foss of South Dakota was the top U.S. Marine ace over Guadalcanal. He shot down twenty-three Japanese Zeros.

Within weeks of the first American landings on Guadalcanal, Hirohito decided to make the island a decisive battle area in the South Pacific and to pump a counter-invasion force ashore. Vice Admiral Mikawa Gunichi, the naval commander at Rabaul, carried out the task in stages. First he sent soldiers south to Guadalcanal aboard six transports. A U.S. submarine, the S-38, waylaid the transports, sinking the largest. The other five turned back to Rabaul.

The next night Admiral Mikawa arrived off Guadalcanal with five heavy cruisers, two light cruisers, and a destroyer. He encountered a force of U.S. cruisers and destroyers, equipped with radar, which the Japanese did not have. But the Japanese naval gunners were better at night fighting; they fired at the flash that followed the shell launching. During the course of this battle for Savo Island, four Allied cruisers and a destroyer went to the bottom. Another U.S. cruiser and two destroyers were crippled and sent back to the States for repair. Some sixteen hundred Allied sailors, most of them American, died in this action. Admiral Mikawa was able to land several hundred Japanese soldiers on Guadalcanal and return to Rabaul. Other battles and troop reinforcements would take place.

This was the beginning of a momentous struggle, for on its outcome would rest the future of the entire Pacific war. Not again, for the duration of World War II in the Pacific, would the fighting men of the United States and Japan meet on such equal terms. Both sides strained themselves to the limit during the six months of the Guadalcanal campaign.

For U.S. Marines and Seabees stationed on Guadalcanal, there was a daily routine of survival. With predictable sameness, each night a squadron of Japanese destroyers would come down from Rabaul, stand off the island, and for one hour shell the American defenses, including Henderson Field, which had been built under fire by the Seabees. They would land reinforcements ashore at their end of the island, then turn and steam back to Rabaul at full speed. Once at the halfway mark they were assured of air cover from their fighter planes, necessary to their welfare because U.S. fighters would be racing from Henderson Field to engage in aerial dogfights and bombing of Japanese destroyers. While this was going on the shell holes on Henderson Field would be covered over by bulldozers and destroyed planes would be shoved aside. And all the while control tower officers would await the return of their air squadrons.

American and Japanese military leaders each tried to break the will of the other in this night-and-day routine of attack and counterattack. What eventually turned the tide were the continuing air battles; the Japanese pilots were tiring badly and their ranks were being decimated. The plane they flew, the Zero, was a superb fighter plane, but it suffered from inadequate attention from poorly trained ground crews and mechanics. Replacement pilots, who had been rushed through training in Japan and sent to this fighting zone, were second-rate. The Americans, on the other hand, had an edge of youth, good training, and continually improving aircraft. Soon control of the air at any given moment was in U.S. hands.

To Emperor Hirohito in the war room of the Imperial Palace, the battle for Guadalcanal had reached a stalemate. He thus ordered reinforcements sent to the Japanese garrison. On August 28, the Japanese landed their Twenty-eighth Division, and later the same month sent their Thirty-fifth Brigade of the Eighteenth Division from the Philippines and Palau. The Japanese now conducted bayonet charges nearly every night. On September 12 and 13, during one such attack, fifty-nine marines were killed, though the Japanese casualty toll was 708.

Out over the ocean U.S. Marine fighter pilots were taking aim on Japanese ships. On one mission the destroyer *Asagiri*, part of a squadron dubbed the "Tokyo Express," came down the slot for its nightly shelling of the American end of the island, and was sunk.

But about daybreak a Japanese submarine lined up its periscope on the U.S. aircraft carrier *Saratoga* and let go with a full discharge of torpedoes, scoring a direct hit.

Other Japanese submarines moved into the fighting area like sharks and also scored heavily on U.S. warships. They damaged the battleship *North Carolina,* and sunk the destroyer *O'Brien* and the carrier *Wasp.* But U.S. Admiral Fletcher, who was Commanding Admiral, then sent a convoy from Australia to Guadalcanal, landing the entire U.S. Seventh Marine Division and all supplies before the Japanese knew what was going on.

On October 24, under prodding from Tokyo and Rabaul, Lt. General Maruyama Masao launched an attack against U.S. positions, preceded by a tank foray. Two thousand Japanese infantrymen armed with bayonets just could not breach the marine defenses, and they all died. A banzai charge was likewise unsuccessful, and another two thousand Japanese died in the effort.

While this land action was taking place a sea battle began raging off nearby Santa Cruz island. The Japanese ships *Zuiho, Shokaku,* and *Chikuma* were damaged, and the *Yura* was sunk. The U.S. fleet lost the destroyer *Porter* and the carrier *Hornet.* The carrier *Enterprise* remained operative but damaged.

Meanwhile, Winston Churchill was prodding General Montgomery to launch an attack at El Alemain against the Afrika Korps. General Rommel, who had returned to Germany for a meeting with Hitler and for a rest, was suddenly asked by the Fuehrer to return to North Africa to take personal command of the German divisions, which now numbered only fifty thousand and were badly undersupplied. Churchill was still dealing with the demands of General Marshall, General Eisenhower, and President Roosevelt for an immediate landing on the European continent to assist Russia, now reeling under a German onslaught that had taken a toll of two hundred and fifty thousand Soviet troops in the Caucasus Mountains. Stalin had sent Molotov to London and Washington demanding the immediate establishment of a second front. The British knew this was not possible considering the forces at their disposal and the slow buildup of an American army in Britain. Eisenhower, who had never commanded a division in battle, had recently been raised to Supreme Commander in Europe, and continued to argue for Operation Sledgehammer on the French coast. He finally settled for a landing in North Africa.

In Tokyo, Emperor Hirohito faced similar decisions. He had achieved amazing military and naval successes during the year, despite losses at Midway. Now, having been driven out of New Guinea, his forces were locked in mortal combat on the small coral island of Guadalcanal. Unless they could defeat the Americans and General MacArthur here—on both land and sea—it would be a long war indeed.

In Washington, President Roosevelt was as nervous about the Guadalcanal battles as was Emperor Hirohito. When he learned that the *Hornet* had been lost, he cabled CINCPAC, attention naval chief of staff for the Pacific: "Make sure every possible weapon gets into the area to hold Guadalcanal."

But the Japanese were pushing just as hard for control of the island. They finally landed the Thirty-eighth Division, seventeen thousand men, from Rabaul, though it was a struggle getting these soldiers ashore. That action had been preceded by a naval engagement between Japanese and U.S. naval forces, during which the United States lost seven destroyers and two cruisers and suffered one badly damaged battleship. The Japanese, on their part, lost two battleships and two destroyers. Eleven troop transports carrying more than a tenth of their reinforcements were sunk.

On Guadalcanal both sides were now about equal in

manpower; MacArthur had two divisions, as did the Japanese. But the thirty-two thousand Nippon soldiers were short of ammunition, food, and medical supplies. They were now living on roots and rotting dried fish. By the end of November the Japanese soldiers could barely walk, and many were suffering from beriberi. The Emperor, getting reports regularly in the Imperial war room, was distressed and asked that all efforts be made to alleviate this situation.

Japanese destroyers came in by night and attempted time and again to land drums of supplies. Submarines even came in close to shore and sent torpedoes landward that were loaded not with warheads but with packages of rice and soy sauce. Nevertheless, U.S. PT boats intercepted most of these food torpedoes and blew them out of the water. Still, though Magic intercepts told continuously of the desperate plight of the enemy, and Admiral Halsey kept a constant patrol going, some supplies and Japanese reinforcements did slip through the U.S. Navy ships surrounding the island.

Japanese headquarters at Rabaul were equally determined to breach the U.S. naval defensive net. When they sent down supply ships and reinforcements they did so with the protection of pocket battleships and cruisers of the Rabaul naval command. In one engagement Halsey lost his heavy cruiser *Northampton,* and three other heavy cruisers were badly damaged: the *New Orleans*, the *Minneapolis*, and the *Pensacola*. The *Pensacola* was racked with fire for twelve hours during this naval engagement before being brought under control.

This was a naval victory of sorts for the Japanese, but it did not ease Hirohito's concern for his troops on the island. Occasional landings had increased the number of Japanese soldiers there to 37,680, but constant pressure by the U.S. Marines along with hunger and malnutrition kept whittling down their numbers.

Individual marine bravery in this Guadalcanal campaign was conspicuous and widespread, but the role of the commanding officer who led these men in battle, Major General Alexander Archer Vandegrift of Charlottesville, Virginia, should not be overlooked. As commanding officer of the First Marine Division he continued in a battle situation from August 7 to December 9, 1942. He demonstrated tenacity, courage, and resourcefulness against a strong, determined, and experienced enemy. General Vandegrift's citation noted that "his inspired leadership enabled his marines to withstand aerial, land, and sea bombardment, to surmount all obstacles and leave a disorganized and ravaged enemy."

Toward the end of November the troops on both sides were barely hanging on. Although the U.S. forces did not suffer from hunger and malnutrition as did the Japanese, they had simply been there too long and were greatly fatigued. On December 7, the first anniversary of the Pearl Harbor attack, General Vandegrift and his marines were replaced by Major General Alexander Patch and a contingent of soldiers. Marine casualties had totaled 9,788; another 3,070 had been wounded in action. The marine survivors who now left Guadalcanal could barely make it up the rope nets to the decks of the transports that would take them to Australia and rest and recreation.

The Japanese, on Hirohito's command, withdrew also. Hirohito told his chief of staff, Sugiyama: "Our withdrawal from Guadalcanal is regrettable. From now on the army and navy must cooperate better to accomplish our war objectives . . ."

Tokyo government propaganda officials described the withdrawal as a great victory, an "advance by turning." But civilians in Tokyo sardonically called the move "advancing backwards."

Over nine thousand Japanese soldiers made it to their ships to leave Guadalcanal forever. The two U.S. Army forces in the final days of the operation met little resistance as they advanced on Japanese departure positions around Kamimbo Bay. But where the battles had taken place during the six months they counted twenty-one thousand Japanese corpses. The United States Marine Corps report *The Japanese Campaign in the Guadalcanal Area* estimated Japanese losses on Guadalcanal at 28,580, a figure that included those who never made it to shore from sinking troop transports.

In the Imperial Palace, Hirohito assessed Japan's strategic situation and discussed with Lord Privy Seal Kido the future of the war. He remembered the statement made by Admiral Yamamoto, who, when presented with an Imperial command to lead the Japanese navy to victory, said to the Emperor: "I will run wild for the first year and a half, and if total victory has not been achieved by then it will be all downhill." After the Pearl Harbor attack Yamamoto had also remarked to Hirohito, "It is my desire to dictate peace terms to the United States in the White House."

The Emperor also wanted a quick victory. He thought that Hitler might succeed in his war enterprises, and even at this time, the beginning of 1943, it seemed possible that he could reach an accommodation with President Roosevelt despite the losses at Midway and Guadalcanal. Much depended, surely, on the German forces repelling the efforts of America and Britain to land in France, and also on the strength of his own island defenses against General MacArthur. If his positions held and the Germans proved impregnable, then a tenable peace could be arranged. Japan would keep Manchuria and Formosa, and share with the United States the resources of the Philippines. And both nations would share in the oil, tin, and tungsten of the Dutch East Indies. Further, England could have the great trading center of Hong Kong; but Singapore would be shared. While Hirohito was looking at the future in these terms, General MacArthur was planning the strategy that would move his forces north, eventually to return to the Philippines.

Five

Japan's Fifth Column and War by "Magic"

 During this time period, Magic (the U.S. cryptographic intercepts of the Japanese military and diplomatic codes) picked up the following message from the Vice Chief of the General Staff to all Japanese spies in Europe and North and South America:

> Intelligence reports to the effect that America has four hundred thousand troops concentrated in California ready for transport to the Pacific. We would like to have you gather and report all possible information of intelligence value in this matter, and whatever related information useful to the General Staff.

Espionage was another aspect of war in the Pacific that the Japanese pursued with great intensity. It had been a major factor in the conquest of Manchuria and China, expanding as far south as Australia and as far north as Iran. (European embassies had already been blanketed in the 1920s with an inordinate number of Japanese military attachés.) In Berlin, Ambassador Baron Oshima represented Hirohito and Japan throughout World War II and had access to Hitler and other Nazi leaders. Intelligence concerning the United States that flowed to Berlin was made available to him for transmission by Purple Code to Tokyo.

By 1940, the Japanese spy network had operatives in every major city of North and South America. The spearhead of this infiltration of the United States was the *Hokubei Kutoku Kai* (North American Military Virtue Society), which had its origin in Kyoto, the ancient capital of Japan (there it was known simply as *Kutoku Kai* [Military Virtue Society]). Even before the attack on Pearl Harbor, the spy network on America's West Coast, all Japanese army reservists, had infiltrated Japanese communities, calling on fellow countrymen to help them gather detailed information on American military and naval bases, aircraft production, and ship movements. This network stretched from San Diego to Los Angeles, and northward to San Francisco and Seattle. Some responded to the call of Japanese nationalism and assisted; many did not.

The Japanese army and navy intelligence departments and the various semiautonomous organizations that contributed information to the spy service studied the espionage techniques then being used by Germany in the United States. Of course, German embassies and consulates fed strategic data back to Berlin. But it was business, cultural, and news organizations that were the backbone of this German sweep of information. I. G. Farben had its N.W.7 department, which compiled military and economic data on all countries. From Chemnyco, Inc., a German business front in the United States, Berlin received information ranging from photographs and blueprints—such as that of the Norden bomb sight—to detailed descriptions of entire industrial complexes and secret processes such as the new method of production of isooctane for aircraft fuel, without which the air war in Europe and the Pacific could not have taken place. A leading I. G. Farben scientist has stated that this important process originated "entirely with the Americans and became known to us in detail in its separate stages."

After careful study of the German espionage system, the Japanese concluded that more effort should go into their own spy activities as a means of aiding their military forces. So, like the Germans, they established front organizations for intelligence gathering, under the guise of promoting Japanese friendship for their host country. These organizations ran the gamut from cultural and military groups to scientific and business organizations. Following *Hokubei Kutoku Kai* came the expansion of *Toa Kaizai Chosa Kyoku*, the East Asia Economic Investigation Bureau, an offshoot of the Black Dragon Society, which had specialized in the murder of Japanese "liberals" and other nonconformists.

Zaibatsu, the business leadership of Japan, now had organizations overseas for their own interests and for all of Japan. *Nichiro Tsushin Shad*, the Japan-Russia News Agency, was backed by the Mitsubishi interests. *Nippon Tsusho Kyogi Kai*, the Japan-China Business Association, and *Nippon Boeki Shinko Kai*, the Japan Trade Promotion Society, operated as the principal cover for the Japanese intelligence service. Branches of these two agencies operated in Calcutta, Karachi, Singapore, Bangkok, Sydney, Alexandria, Baghdad, and elsewhere. To the south, the *Nanyo Kyokai*, the South Seas Associates, was backed by the Foreign Office and the Ministry of Commerce in Tokyo. They specialized in areas that included Malaya, the Dutch East Indies, and the Southwest Pacific

Islands. All employees were intelligence agents trained in preparing areas for later occupation by Japanese troops.

Dai Toa Senso Chosa Kai, the Greater East Asia War Investigation Society, was a unit whose purpose was strictly to spread propaganda about the war in both the United States and Britain, as well as to clarify the war aims of Japan. In September 1944, this group published a booklet for Japanese consumption along these lines. Through a merger of the *Shimbun Rengo Tsushin Sha* and the *Nippon Dempo Tsushin Sha, Domei Tsushin Sham*, the Domei News Agency, was formed in 1936, a confederation of over two hundred Japanese daily newspapers and the Broadcasting Corporation of Japan. This agency maintained bureaus throughout the world, with many of its special correspondents and bureau chiefs active as spies. *Kaigai Dobo Chuckai*, the Central Association of Overseas Japanese, was established in 1940 for the purpose of creating a better understanding between the people of Japan and Japanese overseas, particularly in the United States.

The Japanese government and the Imperial Palace left no stone unturned in the utilization of organizations to serve their purposes. Religious groups, women's associations, and science, trade, and travel groups pushed into the Philippines and Australia bearing messages of friendship from Japan and the Greater East Asia Co-Prosperity Sphere it was promoting.

While soldiers drilled and navy pilots practiced their torpedo and bombing runs and diplomats played games with Washington and London, directors of the spy services maintained a charade of cooperation throughout the United States, Canada, South America, and Asia. One spymaster, a prince of the royal family, sped on their way the men he inducted with these words:

The Japanese are the only divine people on earth; that is the reason why they never try to mix with other people. Our culture is sacred. . . . The people whom we have conquered or shall conquer . . . will simply disappear. The Koreans will be eaten by vices; the Chinese will be the victims of opium and other narcotics; the Russians will be ruined by vodka . . . The destiny of Japan has been outlined by the gods. Nothing can stop Japan from becoming the greatest empire on earth . . .

Even Japanese business representatives who went abroad were bound by oaths of loyalty, much as were the representatives of German business firms, whose loyalty to Hitler and the New Order was of paramount importance.

Is it any wonder that President Roosevelt would regard this Fifth Column as a clear and present danger to the United States following the attack on Pearl Harbor? A detailed listing of all the Japanese intelligence organizations operating in the United States had been prepared by Ralph M., who, on leave from his post at the U.S. Embassy in Tokyo, had returned to the Japan desk in the State Department. Soon after, he received a call from the White House asking if the Japanese in the United States were a danger. "Some are, some are not. But how can you separate the bad from the good?" was Ralph M.'s reply. The President then ordered the FBI and other government agencies to embark on a relocation of all Japanese along the West Coast to detention camps inland. The move seemed heartless to some, but President Roosevelt had concluded that in preparing for a two-front war he could not tolerate the distraction of a Fifth Column that had worked its way into Japanese communities on the West Coast.

With war declared, members of *Hokubei Kutoku Kai* traveled south to Mexico, where they could operate with greater freedom. They formed an immediate alliance with the Gestapo secret service, which had infiltrated every U.S. aircraft plant from Columbus to California and had managed to get its agents into the Manhattan Project at Los Alamos. Because this Gestapo service was spread thin, it welcomed the assistance of the Japanese agents in Mexico, thus attracting many other Japanese to Mexico as "tourists." Unable to operate effectively in North America because of FBI scrutiny and President Roosevelt's relocation dictum, the Japanese spies began to spread throughout South America as a backup to the Nazis. For this assistance they received, as a matter of course, all copies of the reports sent by the German agents back to Mexico City. They also were able to use German radio facilities. Any report of interest to Japanese intelligence in Tokyo was sent to the German radio transmitter in Valparaiso, Chile, and then beamed to Hamburg. There it was forwarded to Berlin, attention of Baron Oshima in the Japanese Embassy, who then had it encoded and sent by wireless to Tokyo.

But American intelligence was several steps ahead of the Japanese. The U.S. Army Signal Corps had constructed an electronic listening post on a mountaintop in Ethiopia, determining this to be the most suitable point to intercept Japanese wireless communication between Berlin and Tokyo. Every message sent by Baron Oshima in his supposedly breakproof Purple Code was intercepted by Magic. The President and the Joint Chiefs of Staff quickly learned what the Germans and Japanese were receiving about U.S. defense installations. But they also acquired an insight into German defense capabilities along the west coast of France and in the Low Countries, because the Germans had permitted Baron Oshima to make periodic inspection tours of the

West Wall, reports of which went to Tokyo via the wireless route. His assessments no doubt received greater attention at Supreme Allied Headquarters in London than they did in Tokyo.

But as the war went on in Europe and the Pacific and General MacArthur moved northward island by island, the President and top officials in the War Department became increasingly alarmed over one item that had been intercepted by Magic: the Japanese had learned about American efforts to build an atom bomb at Los Alamos. German agents who had infiltrated the secret project had provided the Japanese with the information. So despite all the security surrounding the development of this astonishing and revolutionary weapon in remote northern New Mexico, the secret was now known to Germany, Japan, and Russia. The Soviets had come by their information from Communist-inclined scientists, who filtered their data through Soviet Communist cells in the U.S.; the Rosenberg group in New York was one dominant Communist spy ring that forwarded information to Moscow.

In Tokyo, Emperor Hirohito was not concerned about who else had information on the bomb testing. He had it, and he knew its implications: total destruction of a widespread area by the most terrifying weapon in the history of the world. A scientist of sorts himself, he had, in October 1940, after listening to Admiral Yamamoto's exhortations, induced the Japanese scientific establishment to work on an atomic bomb.

So in October 1940, the Japanese scientific establishment began work on nuclear fission as they pushed for an atomic bomb. Hirohito listened to Admiral Yamamoto's suggestion that an A-bomb in their arsenal of weapons would provide the muscle Japan would need for victory if the war began to go downhill. Japan's initial research was carried out in university laboratories, and they possessed but a small amount of uranium in Japan for this beginning research. After the victory at Pearl Harbor and America's entry into war, research was stepped up. Search teams went to Korea looking for uranium, and they called on Germany, their Axis partner, for more as their needs increased.

Admiral Yamamoto knew that the Germans were advanced in their research on nuclear fission; in 1939 they had begun a vigorous program to build an atomic weapon. It was Hitler's hope that in time his V-2 rockets would carry atomic nose cones aimed at the total destruction of London and Moscow; this was ultimately to be the wish of Hirohito too as MacArthur advanced, island by island, toward Japan. But at this point in time the Germans were still groping for answers. German research was dependent upon the use of heavy water (deuterium oxide), which required enormous amounts of electrical power to make and was being produced only at the Vemork plant at Rjukan, a small town in southern Norway. With the conquest of Norway, the Germans had taken possession of the plant and gained easy access to its production of heavy water. When the request for assistance was made by the Japanese Ambassador in Berlin, General Hiroshi Baron Oshima, the Germans complied.

A shipment of heavy water and uranium oxide was sent by submarine from Norway to Japan. The heavy water was from the Vemork plant, and the uranium oxide came from the uranium mines in conquered Czechoslovakia. The shipment to Japan was no problem; both German and Japanese freighter submarines made regular trips between east and west with the strategic goods that both Germany and Japan needed. It was a long submarine trip but generally safer than using surface freighters, and it was facilitated by the establishment of a refueling depot in Penang, Malaya, which was manned by German administrators and technicians.

When the first shipment of uranium and heavy water reached Japan, scientists there pushed ahead with their research, assisted by German nuclear data. They continued to ask for more uranium oxide and heavy water, which was subsequently shipped. The last uranium shipment to leave German waters for Japan was carried aboard the submarine *U-234*. It left Norway on April 15, 1945, and by German estimates carried enough uranium and heavy water to make two atomic bombs. The Japanese were determined to achieve their goal of producing two atomic bombs, to be exploded over General MacArthur's invasion fleet, scheduled for November 1945, according to Operation Olympic.

On May 8, as *U-234* made its way through the North Atlantic and headed south, the crew received via radio the news that Germany had surrendered. On May 10, Grand Admiral Doenitz, who had succeeded to leadership of the Third Reich for the surrender period, radioed all U-boats at sea that they were to surrender to the Allies. The U-boats were to surface, display a large, dark flag, and make for the nearest Allied port. The captain of *U-234*, Lieutenant Johann Fehler, decided to make for a U.S. port (both the British and the Canadians had wanted his U-boat as a strategic prize). *U-234* made its slow way toward Newfoundland, then went down the Atlantic coastline toward New Hampshire. On May 14, it was boarded by an American crew from the destroyer USS *Sutton*. The prize crew guided *U-234* to the naval yard in Portsmouth, New Hampshire, where its valuable cargo of uranium oxide, heavy water, and nuclear data was quickly shipped to the War Department in Washington. Two Japanese officers aboard *U-234* had committed *hara-kiri* and were buried in Portsmouth. The German officers and crew were interned as prisoners of war after being interrogated.

At this time, General Groves and other leaders of

the Manhattan Project still did not know if they had a successful bomb. Two months later, when they exploded one in the deserts of New Mexico, they knew they had succeeded.

In Japan there was not to be an atomic bomb. Using the German approach, they made the same two fundamental mistakes as the Germans. In trying to separate uranium, they used heavy water instead of graphite, and utilized thermal diffusion instead of ultracentrifuge. The scientists working for General Groves on the Manhattan Project in Los Alamos went the graphite-and-ultracentrifuge route, and so, to Hirohito's despair, the United States won the race for the atomic bomb.

But in 1942, Emperor Hirohito did not know if U.S. scientists would succeed in their experiments with nuclear fission; nor did the Americans, for that matter. He knew that if America did win this race it could be his ultimate excuse for withdrawal from the war. But for now the quandary facing Emperor Hirohito was that the Japanese code of honor decreed that the war must go on and on; to suddenly withdraw from the struggle and seek peace would be an unthinkable insult to the soldiers who had already died for their Emperor, and to the widows and orphans who still placed their faith in the wisdom of the Emperor.

Meanwhile, the war in the South Pacific went on. From Guadalcanal and Buna, MacArthur now looked northward to the ports of Lae and Salamaua on the eastern coast of New Guinea. They pointed directly at Cape Gloucester on New Britain Island, the opposite end of which was Rabaul, a Japanese stronghold of four large airfields, one hundred thousand infantrymen armed to the teeth, and a great naval anchorage.

Hirohito also knew the importance of Lae and Salamaua. If taken by MacArthur the Japanese defenses of the Bismarck Sea, that great "inner sea," would be cracked open. The land and sea battle that would develop in and around the Bismarck Sea would be for control of Lae and Salamaua. Hirohito, assessing strategy for this area in his war room, told his War Minister, Hajime Sugiyama, "The fall of Buna is regrettable, but officers and men fought well. Give enough thought to your plans so Lae and Salamaua don't become another Guadalcanal."

Sugiyama decided to strengthen his defenses at Lae and Salamaua by sending three thousand troops to seize an airstrip at Wau, southwest of Salamaua. MacArthur promptly airlifted an Australian brigade, which routed the Japanese. Sugiyama then ordered a troop convoy to set course from Rabaul, but as it steamed across the Bismarck Sea toward Lae, a U.S. B-24 sighted it and radioed the direction the convoy was moving. In two days of precision bombing U.S. planes sunk four of the troop transports and four escort warships; other Japanese ships were engaged in battle by a U.S. naval force. This battle for the Bismarck Sea went on for days, with twenty Japanese ships lost. But it was the air force under General Kenney that stopped the reinforcement and resupply of Lae. MacArthur was now using the aircraft under his command to isolate battlefields. As he commented, "If I can control the seas north of New Guinea we need not plow through fifteen hundred miles of jungle and the staging areas for a successful return to the Philippines." In keeping with this strategy, he decided not to attack Rabaul but to isolate it. He knew the Japanese garrison there was dug in and would make the battle costly in lives. He was determined now to fight a war of maneuver, a war of island-hopping over vast distances. In describing how the Japanese fight, he said, "They fight a static defense, like the Germans I fought in World War One. Come at them head-on and they will fight viciously to the death. But hit them where they don't expect it and it's another story. It also saves precious lives."

In Tokyo at Imperial Army Headquarters, Colonel Matsuichi Jui, a senior intelligence officer whose duty was to interpret General MacArthur's strategy for the Imperial General Staff, said in one of his reports: "MacArthur employs the kind of strategy we don't like . . . Our strongpoints are gradually starved out by envelopment, and the Americans flow into our weaker points and submerge us, just as water seeks the weakest entry to sink a ship. I respect this type of strategy, although the Japanese army prefers direct frontal assault, after the German fashion. MacArthur gains the most while losing the least."

MacArthur, commenting further about his tactics, said, "I can take any Japanese strongpoint with frontal assault. But I won't! I have too great a responsibility to the mothers and wives in America to do that to their men. I will not take by sacrifice what I can achieve by strategy."

The increased use of aircraft as part of MacArthur's strategy of island seizure was described in a special report by the Vice Chief of the Japanese Army General Staff. Writing of U.S. air operations prior to landing operations, this Japanese general said:

a. About 20 days before the landing, the air attacks grow more severe and they attempt to smash our air power and immobilize our sea power. Airfields in the vicinity of the place where they intend to land are the principal targets.

b. During the first period (10 to 20 days), air attacks are carried out every day, principally by fighters, with about 100 planes a day participating. First they try to destroy our fighter planes. Attacks at sea, aimed at the destruction of shipping, are carried out principally by bombers.

c. The landing and advance are aimed chiefly at airfields or territory suitable for the establishment of airfields. They establish air supremacy, and try to cut off our supply lines in the rear and to isolate our ground units.

d. They are very fast in setting up airfields. With machinery and material at hand they can set up an airfield on level ground for partial use in 10 days. An operational airfield can be set up in approximately one month, and a base airfield completed in approximately three months.

e. Other aerial operations are as follows:

(1) Cutting off the rear: They place great emphasis on this. They hamper our sea transport with precision torpedo bombings in conjunction with submarine attacks.

(2) Hampering of railway transport.

(3) Bombing: Formerly the enemy concentrated on low-level bombing, but recently the tendency has been toward medium altitude precision bombing.

(4) Balloons: The enemy recently has taken to sending up barrage balloons and this hampers the activity of our planes.

By the spring of 1943, the Japanese advance had ebbed. Their defeats at Guadalcanal, Wau, Lae, Buna, Salamaua, Papua, and the Bismarck Sea had convinced the Imperial General Staff that they would do better shortening their defensive arc. Their shipping losses had been enormous and they could no longer supply their forward island bases. By early 1944, they abandoned Rabaul, after fourteen out of a twenty-ship convoy sent from Palau to Rabaul was sunk by U.S. submarines and bombers. When the commanding officer on Rabaul was informed that they would no longer be supplied and that they were on their own his reply was simply, "This news is almost more than we can bear."

Japanese Eighth Area Army headquarters on Rabaul also objected to a news dispatch by the Domei News Agency in Tokyo they had heard by radio. It had been an optimistic report that all was well in the South Pacific and victories were being scored by Japanese forces. They sent their own analysis of conditions:

> In the Admiralty Islands, as a matter of fact, 3,000 officers and men are dying with honor. In Torokina also, a hard-fought battle is being fought without the cooperation of a single airplane or a single naval vessel. Release of such reports by Domei is injurious to morale.

Hirohito read this report from Rabaul and sighed.

Japanese food supplies in the forward areas were also precarious. The commander on Ocean Island reported his garrison had enough food to last only days, "despite our attempts to grow potatoes and catch fish for food."

Other islands fell to MacArthur's advance. At Bougainville, marines killed 5,460 Japanese and lost 263 of their own men. The capture of Biak, Los Negros, and Hollandia brought MacArthur into easy reach of any number of lightly defended islands in his drive north, stepping stones to the reconquest of the Philippines. But the fall of Saipan was a defeat that rocked Japan and brought about the downfall of Tojo and his entire war Cabinet.

Admiral Nimitz's naval armada had advanced into the Mariana islands chain. At Eniwetok the transports for the invasion of Saipan made their rendezvous, part of the six-hundred-vessel force that constituted the Fifth Fleet. Admiral Raymond Spruance was the fleet commander. Heading toward Saipan was the U.S. Fast Carrier Task Force of fifteen carriers, seven battleships, twenty-one cruisers, and sixty-nine destroyers under command of Vice Admiral Marc Mitscher. They were to shield the invasion ships against Vice Admiral Jisaburo Ozawa's Mobile Fleet.

On June 15, 1944, 535 ships carrying one hundred and twenty-eight thousand marines, sailors, and soldiers went to Saipan. Robert Sherrod, who covered that landing as a war correspondent, wrote:

> Cleverly concealed machine guns, mortars and small arms took a heavy toll of the marines in the water and after they hit the beach. But they charged forward, securing two beachheads from which they would not be dislodged. By the end of the second day, they had suffered 4,000 casualties, and Lt. General Holland Smith called for the reserves, the Army's 27th Infantry Division. By the end of the battle, July 9, about 3,500 Americans lay dead; 13,000 more were wounded.
>
> Nearly all of Japan's defenders fought to the death; as a crowning horror, hundreds of Japanese civilians threw themselves and their children off cliffs at the northern tip of Saipan as our riflemen watched in bewilderment.

On July 6, organized resistance collapsed. It was then that Admiral Nagumo came to his end. He had personally directed the naval force that bombed Pearl Harbor on December 7, 1941. He had led Japanese forces at the Battle of Midway and had directed the naval attack on Darwin, Australia. Now, charged with the naval defenses of Saipan that failed, he squatted at the entrance to a cave and slit his stomach open. As instructed, an aide who stood behind Nagumo finished him off with a bullet in the back of his head. The remnants of the Japanese garrison then charged the U.S. Marine lines, and those who were not killed by machine guns and rifles took their own lives with their hand grenades.

Bloody Saipan accounted for about thirty thousand dead Japanese soldiers and fifteen thousand civilians; in addition, 921 soldiers surrendered along with the 10,258 civilians who remained, believing it better to live than to die. Of 67,451 U.S. combat troops, 3,426 died.

With Saipan secured, the United States Marines invaded Guam on July 21, and Tinian on July 24. The three islands were quickly to become launching centers to Japan for American B-29s. (It was from Tinian, a wedge off Saipan, that a B-29 was to carry the first atomic bomb to Hiroshima the following year.) Meanwhile, the Allied advance wended its way toward the Philippines, where massive sea and land battles would take place.

In Tokyo, the Emperor was associating his name more closely and frequently with the war. His name was used as an incentive for greater effort, and the people were reminded more frequently of the Emperor's "deep concern" with the progress of the war. After the fall of the Tojo cabinet as a result of the defeat at Saipan—Tojo had personally guaranteed the defense of the island—all cabinet meetings were held in the Imperial Palace. This was a departure from custom, for throughout modern

Japanese history the cabinet had gathered at the residence of the Premier or in the Diet building. As the war went downhill, Japanese propagandists for the military and naval cliques running the Emperor's war machine turned more and more to him for support in harnessing the will of the people. They asked the Emperor to issue more Imperial Rescripts, which would give greater veracity to their own claims of victory. In December of 1943, for example, they had the Emperor issue two Rescripts honoring the navy for completely fictitious "victories" off the Solomon and Gilbert islands. This was an unprecedented mortgaging of the Imperial dignity to regain popular faith in the conduct of the war.

The phrase "The Emperor's War" was also being used with increasing frequency in newspaper articles, a usage that was to make the position of the Throne and Hirohito shaky indeed when the war ended and American occupation began. The magazine *Fuji* published an article of advice to the people of Japan entitled "Revere the Emperor, Expel the Barbarian," the slogan of the Meiji reign and now of Hirohito's Showa Restoration. The article was written by Kazunobu Kanokogi, who had long been prominent in Japanese secret societies. Abandoning the usual public conception that the Emperor was one who assumes no responsibility for the actions of his government, this article declared specifically: "It is neither the State nor the People that declare war . . . the Emperor himself declares war . . . Accordingly the war will continue until the Emperor says, 'Cease!'"

The Emperor was presently concerned about Mac-Arthur's advance toward the Philippines. Lord Privy Seal Kido, in his diary entry for January 6, 1945, tells what took place when he and Hirohito talked about the approaching war for the Philippines:

> On this occasion his Majesty said: "It is reported that the United States forces have

penetrated into Lingayen Bay in an attempt to effect a landing on Luzon. The war situation in the Philippines has assumed a more serious proportion than ever, and it might be necessary to seek senior statesmen's advice according to its outcome. What do you think?"

I in reply said, "As Your Majesty has just said, the war situation in the Philippine Islands, I think, is extremely serious. According to the trends of the fighting there, things might come to pass when we will have to pay our utmost attention to the future guidance of war. After watching, for the time being, the progress of the war situation, I think it necessary that, first of all, Your Majesty confirm the true determination of the Chief of the Army General Staff, who are the central figures in the conduct of the war. Therefore, I think it advisable that Your Majesty call them at the same time for the purpose of holding frank and candid conversations. Thereupon, Your Majesty might just as well call the members of the Cabinet and put to them various questions until Your Majesty be truly convinced. When Your Majesty finds it necessary to decide upon the final policy, it will be most appropriate to hold a council in the Imperial presence, which may be called a conference of the senior statesmen and the Cabinet members, to cope with the present state of affairs. Above all, however, I wish Your Majesty would quietly observe the war progress for several days."

This excerpt from Kido's diary demonstrates the close attention paid to the war in all its details by Emperor Hirohito. Hirohito knew the outcome of General MacArthur's return to the Philippines in full attack force would be decisive to the future of the war.

The German military attaché in Tokyo sent a coded message to Kiel, Germany, giving his opinion on what the loss of the Philippines would mean to Japan. Magic intercepted his wireless message:

Subject: Effects of the Loss of the Philippines.
1. Because of the very unfavorable situation of the Japanese ground forces and especially the air combat forces, and because the Allies, unlike the Japanese, can carry on reinforcements and supplies practically unhindered, wide circles of the Japanese Navy already count on the loss of the Philippines. They are convinced, however, that they will succeed in holding the Americans there at least three months and thus prevent further advances.
2. The loss of the Philippines would have serious results:
In foreign politics,
  i. The final blow to the hope for an understanding with Chiang Kai-shek and Chungking.
  ii. A fundamental change in relations with Russia, even the possibility of Russia's entering the war.
  iii. The loss of Thailand, Burma and Indo-China.
In internal politics,
  i. A Cabinet change, and strengthening of the circles which have already worked long for a compromise peace with the U.S.
  ii. Further decline in the people's confidence in victory, which, moreover, has not been very strong.
3. From the military viewpoint the loss of the

Philippines would place U.S. Fleet and Air pressure on the middle of the Japanese lines of communications between the Northern and Southern Areas. The consequences would be as follows:

(a) Elimination of all Japanese surface traffic between the North and South, including that of Naval forces.

(b) Splitting up of remaining Japanese Naval forces into a major northern group, and a minor, almost insignificant southern group.

4. A similar Allied expansion southward will gradually paralyze inter-island Japanese traffic and eliminate military installations, dockyards and oil production centers. This will be followed by a step-by-step occupation of the entire Southern Area, with probably very slight Japanese counteraction.

5. Japan imported from the South Area nearly 90 percent of her consumption in liquid fuels, 80 percent of her bauxite and 60 percent of her iron ore. Data on fuel supplies in Japan cannot be obtained, but they are generally referred to as sufficient for one and a half to two years. It is said to be already possible to manufacture synthetically about 20 percent of the aviation gasoline needed. But it should be taken into account that the synthetic oil plants, and also a large part of the fuel stocks, are located above ground in the vicinity of large cities and are not specially camouflaged in any way. Only now, under the influence of the first air attacks, are energetic steps being taken to place them underground. Increased mining of aluminous shale on the continent is expected to provide a tolerably satisfactory compensation for the loss

of bauxite from the Southern Area. As to iron ore, a noticeable shortage soon should make itself felt, especially since higher imports from China are hardly conceivable in view of the increased danger to the shipping routes. That danger also should have an unfavorable effect on the imports of foodstuffs from Korea and Manchuria, and should cause a further lowering of performance on the part of an already badly undernourished people—especially since at the time the supply of about 200,000 tons of rice from Thailand and Indo-China has been discontinued. There is no shortage of rubber and non-ferrous metals, in my opinion.

6. To summarize: The possible loss of the Philippines would have such serious consequences for Japan that a continuance of the war for a considerable period—I have in mind one year—seems highly questionable. Attention is drawn to the clear utterances of leading statesmen who repeatedly and in unmistakable terms designate the outcome of the Philippine battles as decisive for the war.

On the island of Leyte itself, defeat of MacArthur was proving not at all likely, because General Krueger's Sixth Army of two hundred thousand troops was pouring ashore to begin their attack on Japanese forces. In forty days at Leyte thirty-four inches of rain had fallen, rendering the island a huge quagmire and making it impossible for General Kenney to dig out airfields for support tactics. But the American GIs pushed on, to be reinforced and replaced by General Eichelberger's Eighth Army; in the weeks ahead Eichelberger's men would kill over twenty-seven thousand enemy soldiers. Eichelberger was to declare later, "It was bitter, exhausting, physically the most terrible thing we were ever to know."

In the waters off Leyte, the U.S. and Japanese navies faced each other. It was the greatest naval engagement in history: Admiral Kincaid's carriers against the ships of Vice Admiral Kurita, who was rushing toward Leyte Gulf with seven battleships, thirteen heavy cruisers, and three light cruisers. Admiral Halsey had been decoyed away from San Bernadino Straits in a search for a Japanese battle segment. Kurita passed through the Straits and trained his guns on some of Kincaid's fleet: six escort carriers and a group of destroyers guarding Mac-Arthur's beachheads. Kincaid's forces attacked the Japanese naval armada and Kurita hesitated, believing that Halsey's force of six fast battleships and a carrier force was about to appear (they were, in fact, three hours away). This, in brief, was the Battle of Leyte Gulf, its 283 warships numerically bigger than the 1916 Battle of Jutland's 250 warships. The U.S. lost one light carrier, two escort carriers, and three destroyers. They had sunk four Japanese carriers, three battleships, six heavy cruisers, three light cruisers, and eight destroyers. But on earlier landings Kincaid's vessels had suffered heavily from kamikaze missions—forty U.S. ships sunk or damaged by this new Japanese weapon of suicide attacks.

Ashore, MacArthur kept urging his generals to "get to Manila." Yamashita, with two hundred and seventy-five thousand men, was lying in wait. Though he had thirty-six thousand men on the beaches, he withdrew them, knowing defense there was pointless. MacArthur sensed Yamashita would not defend Manila but would withdraw to better positions in the mountains beyond. This proved to be the case, and the GIs kept moving forward until Manila, now in rubble from bombs, shell-fire, and Japanese demolitions, was seized by Mac-Arthur's soldiers. The General's driving obsessions were to free the thousands of American and Filipino prisoners of war at Santo Tomas and to retake Corregidor and Bataan. By this time, Yamashita's Bataan garrison was isolated, and the peninsula that had cost the Allied forces so dearly (ten thousand had perished on the "death march" from Bataan earlier in the war) was regained in seven days. At Corregidor, fifty-two hundred enemy defenders, equipped with huge quantities of ammunition, committed suicide in Malinta Tunnel by means of an awesome explosion. It was their last *banzai* for their revered Emperor.

In the Imperial Palace, Emperor Hirohito was near despair. The war minister had assured him of a victory at Leyte. Instead, a huge number of Imperial warships had been sunk, and sixty-five thousand crack Nipponese troops had died under attack from the forces of General MacArthur.

The Emperor wished revenge, retribution for this national disaster. The instrument that came to his mind was a proposed V-2 rocket, possessing an atomic warhead, that could fly the 1,893 miles from Tokyo to Manila at fifteen hundred miles an hour and destroy at once General MacArthur's headquarters. For him, an atomic-coned V-2 would mark the ultimate turning of the war.

Nevertheless, there was not to be a V-2 for Japan. Hitler had refused the Emperor's request for assistance, and Japanese university-connected scientists working in government-subsidized laboratories on the development of the V-2 were far from success. Hirohito knew that only the Americans were within reach of achieving an atomic weapon breakthrough; this information was straight from Ambassador Oshima in Berlin. If the war went on badly for Japan, the Emperor calculated, then the detonation of an American atomic bomb on Japan could be his face-saving rationale for surrender. Nevertheless, it was a very vexing thought, and a situation over which he had no control. So, he waited to see what the course of events would now be, and he tended his bonsai plants.

As he did so, he wistfully looked back in time. He commented aloud to Kido that the happiest year of his life had been 1921, when he visited England and Europe as the Crown Prince. He had boarded the battleship *Katori* with his entourage and steamed from harbor to open sea followed by the escort battleship *Kajima*. It had been a twenty-five-day trip from Japan to the docks at Plymouth. In England, Hirohito maintained his composure on all occasions before press and public, and the Japanese officials who accompanied him were flushed with pride over his performance. He gave his short set speeches at receptions, committing to memory the names of all principals he met. He spent three days at Buckingham Palace as guest of King George V, an ally in the First World War. He spoke of the King's entrance into his bedroom suite one morning attired in suspenders, slippers, shirt, and pants. The King had sat down and told him of Ypres and the million and a half men the British had lost there, suggesting that Hirohito take the time to visit Belgium and the battlefields. It was really an indirect way of telling the young Japanese Crown Prince, Hirohito said, that his nation had not done enough in World War I as an ally of Great Britain.

Hirohito spoke of a week in Scotland shooting grouse, which was followed by receptions and dinners in London. He had reviewed British troops and had admired the ease and aplomb of Edward, Prince of Wales. Then he had visited Paris and personally shopped for gifts for his parents—Emperor Taisho, who was gravely ill, and Empress Sadako—and his future bride, Princess Nagako.

Now, in the Imperial Library as he waited for further news from Luzon, where the greatest naval battle since Jutland was taking place between the Japanese and American navies, he moved around his office. Kido remained politely silent. Hirohito walked with his Imperial shuffle to the windows overlooking the gardens of the palace and the nine-hole golf course that he had ordered built upon his return from Europe in 1921. Lord Privy Seal Kido observed that the Emperor glanced with pride at the bust of Napoleon, which stood in one corner. He had purchased it in Paris and brought it back with him that year. Along with Darwin and Lincoln, Napoleon was a personality from the past that he admired. But on this afternoon his final remark to Kido was *"Ah so, Ah so, deska"* ("It is so"). He had resigned himself to the loss of the Philippines.

Six

Planning for
the Invasion of Japan

The aerial pounding of Japan now dominated the war in the Pacific. From Guam, Saipan, and Tinian the big B-29s would lift up at dusk from their airfields and head for Japan. The round trip was about two thousand miles, so when the bombers returned to home base it was with a feeling of gratitude. The antiaircraft fire was not so bad; it was the Japanese Zeros that did the damage as they swept with unbelievable bravery through the U.S. bomber squadrons. These were not the semiskilled kamikaze suicide pilots, but the best airmen Japan had.

I flew as a nose gunner/war correspondent on some of these missions, and the run I still remember was the one we did on the night of May 25, 1945, from Guam. It was surely the mission best remembered in the Imperial Palace, for much of the Palace was destroyed by fire that night.

This was to be a firebombing raid. The big planes, a mammoth extension of the B-17, which performed so well over Germany, were overweight with gasoline and bomb loads as they moved slowly and smoothly from their parking bays to the takeoff runways. One by one each plane lifted up and headed out over the Pacific northward to Japan. We flew a loose formation at twelve thousand feet, and as time moved on we passed over Iwo Jima, a small volcanic island, which had been taken at great cost by the U.S. Marines. The intensity of that battle was indicated by the casualty figures: 25,851 U.S. Marines were killed, and 19,917 Japanese. Air force leaders said the island's capture was necessary to the bombing of Japan. Only hours after seizure and the raising of the U.S. flag on a high promontory, the Seabees were ashore with their bulldozers and scraping out ten-thousand-foot runways to accommodate crippled B-29s limping back from Japan. As we passed over Iwo Jima, I recalled a reporting trip I had made to the island after it became U.S. territory on March 16. Tyrone Power, a U.S. Marine pilot, had flown me up from Guam as a favor. The Hollywood star was a good pilot, and we landed on Iwo Jima smoothly. We wandered around talking to men of the Third, Fourth, and Fifth Marine Divisions, who had taken the island. There was still danger. The surviving Japanese had dug deep into caves and were coming out at night. One P-38 fighter squadron just arrived was sitting around a fire eating, when a squad of Japanese suddenly emerged out of its caves and staged a *banzai* charge. Six of the American pilots were killed before the marines could wipe out all the assailants.

Iwo Jima was well behind us now and Japan dead ahead. As we approached Honshu we closed formation. I gave a few bursts of my Browning 20-millimeter nose gun to make sure there was no malfunction and settled back to an alert wait. I could hear the turret and waist gunners shooting their guns; the ball turret and rear gunner had all reported no malfunctions. We came in over Yokohama and went straight for Tokyo, three hundred bombers in tight formation. The lead squadron had already unloaded its incendiary bombs and had turned for the return flight. Japanese Zeros were all over the sky, their attacks constant and unrelenting as they made their way into the formations against a wall of intense gunfire. I shot down two enemy fighters head-on, just as the bombardier was saying over the intercom to the pilot, "Bombs away!" When he had released the huge load our plane lifted a thousand feet. I could see two B-29s going down, spiraling masses of flame. One Zero came winging past in flames. Below, it seemed that all Tokyo was on fire. Like a Pittsburgh steel mill being stoked, the fires in the city would escalate as each squadron dumped more firebombs. The island of Honshu now behind us, the pilot asked for damage reports from everyone. We had been shrapneled and cannonaded, but the reports the pilot heard pleased him: we were serviceable and would make it back to Guam. So we kept homing southward until finally the welcoming lights of Guam appeared ahead. We landed gracefully. The pilot was jubilant; this was his last bombing mission in the Pacific. He had finished the required number and would head home. We climbed down from the aircraft and took a jeep to intelligence headquarters, where each man gave his report. My own estimate of damage that night to Tokyo was a quarter of the city burned and perhaps one hundred thousand killed. I did not see how more than a few people down there could have escaped the conflagration.

Two days later U.S. air intelligence officers showed me a set of aerial reconnaissance pictures taken of the damage to Tokyo. Eighteen square miles of the capital had been burned to the ground.

A more detailed assessment of the damage came from the Japanese themselves. Foreign Minister Togo had sent a wireless message to his embassies in Europe telling of the destruction. The message was intercepted by the codebreakers of Magic, and read as follows:

(1) On the night of 25–26 May more than 300 B-29's attacked Tokyo with incendiary and explosive bombs, concentrating on the central part of the city. The number of structures destroyed in Kojimachi, Akasaka, and Azacu [all wards in Central Tokyo] and in other sections is estimated at 130,000, while the number of persons left homeless is estimated at 510,000.

(2) The Palace of Prince Kanin, the Foreign Office, the Naval Ministry, the War Ministry and part of the Imperial Palace and the Palace of Prince Chichibu were all burned to the ground. All our transportation facilities suffered tremendous damage. However, we expect the casualties to be surprisingly low.

(3) In addition to the Foreign Office building, the official residences of the Minister and Vice Minister were destroyed, so that we had to move into the Finance Ministry building for the time being. However, we expect soon to move the Foreign Office departments into the Ministry of Education building.

Lord Privy Seal Kido wrote in his diary his own report of that night:

At 10:00 P.M. an air raid siren sounded. Fanned by the strong wind that prevailed at that time, the fire turned out to be a great calamity, beyond our expectations, destroying all but completely the higher sections of Tokyo. Beginning with the Imperial Palace, the Empress Dowager's Palace, the temporary palace for the Crown Prince, the Aoyama Palace, Prince Chichibu's Mansion, Prince Mikasa's Mansion, Prince Nashimoto's Mansion, Prince Kanin's Mansion, Prince Higashifushimi's Mansion, Prince Riken's and Prince Rigu's Mansion were all burned down.

Japan Broadcasting Corporation later announced in a news report that the homeless total in Tokyo was 2,726,000.

The air war against Japanese military establishments was also constant and unrelenting. The U.S. naval task force, supported by B-29s from China, destroyed more than five hundred of the Japanese planes stationed on Formosa. The bulk of Japan's navy and a fifth of their air navy had now been destroyed in the battle for the Philippines. The Tokyo General Staff termed the losses a major disaster. Aircraft from the U.S. naval task force also ranged over Okinawa bringing great destruction, a foretaste of the invasion of this island.

Okinawa, where Commodore Perry had put in for refueling on his way to Tokyo Bay in 1853, was the last great enemy bastion between the Philippines and Japan. It was invaded on April 1, 1945. The attack was a U.S. Navy and Marine show under the command of Admiral Nimitz and the Central Pacific command. In scope and ferocity the battle for Okinawa was monumental. The Japanese people had still thought they were winning the war, so this American invasion of an island only a thirty-knot, one-day steam by cruiser to Japan was devastating news to them. They held on to the belief that Japanese forces on Okinawa, once they had permitted

U.S. Marines to land, would soon drive the Americans back into the sea. Instead the fighting went on until June 21, when the island was secured by the United States and Japanese forces were defeated. The cost in lives was great: U.S. servicemen killed totaled 12,500; Japanese troops killed totaled 110,000, along with 75,000 civilians on the island. The U.S. Navy had suffered severe losses in the waters off Okinawa, especially from kamikaze suicide bombers. Field hospitals took care of 36,631 wounded Americans sent by hospital ships to rear areas, then moved them on to Pearl Harbor.

General MacArthur's criticism of this battle was succinct. He said Nimitz and his field commanders had shed lives senselessly: "The Central Pacific command just sacrificed thousands of American lives because they insisted on driving the Japanese off the island. In three or four days after the landing the American forces had all the area they needed, which was the area they needed for airplane bases. They should have had the troops go into a defensive position and just let the Japs come to them and kill them from a defensive position, which would have been much easier to do and would have cost less men."

Quiet now descended over the Pacific. A submarine commander I knew commented: "It is so quiet in the waters off Japan that even a sampan would be a welcome sight." For him the calm was so unlike his days on Guam, when he would put out for a thirty-day mission to sink ships and rescue American pilots who had been shot down over contested islands such as Iwo Jima. I had read about these rescue missions from a Magic intercept that had come from Imperial Navy Headquarters in Tokyo:

> On the occasion of an air strike, the enemy dispenses submarines to pick up crews of aircraft forced down, and it is necessary to devise

means of sighting and attacking these submarines.

I approached this submarine commander and asked
if I could accompany him on his next mission. When his
submarine slipped out of its berth at Guam, I was
aboard. His orders told him to go into Tokyo harbor and
stand by for the next U.S. carrier air attack on the docks
at Yokohama. We entered Tokyo harbor, an inlet stretching from the ocean thirty miles into east-central Honshu.
The commander dawdled around at slow speed until
several rapidly steaming ships headed into the harbor
and their berths inside. As the defense nets and booms
opened to let them pass, we followed below, and once
inside we went to the bottom until nightfall, when we
surfaced and cruised slowly at periscope depth, waiting
for the U.S. air strike. The strike came at midnight, a fast
in-and-out raid, and then it was over. One plane had
been hit and the pilot had bailed out, tumbling to the
waters below. He had inflated his float pad and bounced
around in the choppy harbor until we suddenly surfaced
and brought him aboard. Then we submerged again and
went to the bottom of the harbor to await daylight, when
we knew Japanese ships would be leaving for the open
ocean again. In about six hours we heard ship propellers
and we followed the noise through the booms out into
the ocean beyond. We surfaced and the sub commander
broke radio silence briefly to send a coded burst to U.S.
naval headquarters giving the size and direction of the
Japanese squadron heading south. The squadron would
soon be intercepted and a naval battle would ensue. The
airman rescued from Tokyo Bay was later given rest and
recreation in Pearl Harbor. He requested return to his
squadron.

I interviewed the rescued pilot once we reached
safe waters. The interview was broadcast from the

submarine to Guam, where naval transmitters there sent it to San Francisco and onto the network. The airman's family, so they wrote later, happened to hear the broadcast at their home on Long Island. It was the greatest thrill of the war for them. Their son, a brave young man, had survived a dangerous bombing mission and was safe.

George Bush (later to be President of the United States), a bomber pilot in this Pacific theater, related a similar experience when his plane was shot down over Iwo Jima and he was forced to bail out and float around in the water off the island. "A couple of hours later a submarine came and picked me up. I saw this thing coming out of the water and I said, 'Jeez, I hope it's one of ours.'"

Bush stayed on the submarine, the USS *Finback*, for thirty days and lived through some harrowing sea battles before finally reaching shore for some much needed rest. He recalled, "We got depth-charged, we got bombed. We were out there for thirty terrifying days. I thought I was scared a few times flying airplanes in combat, but in this submarine you couldn't do anything. You just sat there." Bush was given three weeks' rest in Pearl Harbor and was then asked if he wanted to return home on leave. "I returned to my squadron," he said. "We were gung-ho in those days," he added laughingly.

Though the Japanese were now losing heavily in the Pacific, their naval escorts would always fight back. Once their sonar had detected the enemy after, say, a troop ship sinking, they would pursue until stopped by sudden shellfire. Then it became a sea battle. At such moments, my sub commander would turn and proceed into attack position at periscope level. It was taut and terrifying.

But when all torpedoes had been fired he headed for Guam and rest in the officers' club on the hill overlooking the harbor of this island, the largest of the Marianas, that ten thousand Japanese died defending.

In Manila at his staff headquarters in the bombed-out city hall, General MacArthur was now focusing on two fronts: Japan and Washington. President Roosevelt, terminally ill, was still formulating grand strategy and had decided that the Pacific command would be shared between General MacArthur and Admiral Nimitz. Mac-Arthur would command the ground forces and Nimitz all naval units for the assault on Japan. The General believed that his enemies in Washington had maneuvered the President into this decision, especially General Marshall, who was assisting Roosevelt, even sending cables to Churchill and other world leaders in the President's name. (It had taken Prime Minister Churchill several weeks to learn that replies to his questions to the White House were in reality coming from Marshall.) General MacArthur was visibly upset over this turn of events because he knew, as the foremost battle strategist of the Pacific theater, that one man only could be the Supreme Commander for a successful invasion and occupation of Japan. But he maintained his temper and kept his mind on the business of war and the man he was opposing, Emperor Hirohito.

When Roosevelt died in April 1945, the new President, Harry S Truman, made MacArthur the Supreme Allied Commander, thus straightening out the jarring interservice rivalry that had begun to rip apart the Allied command in the Pacific. MacArthur could now concentrate on the task at hand.

In the Imperial war room in Tokyo, Emperor Hirohito studied his battle charts and pondered the defense of his country. He listened to his generals, but knew the final decisions would as always be his. His generals and admirals were grimly preparing for the massive enemy invasion they believed would come. They told Hirohito the situation was not as bad as it might seem. Islands had been lost, including strategic Okinawa, but most of their conquests, including China, were still firmly in their hands, and most of their armies remained undefeated. It was their opinion that any invasion of Japan would be suicidal for MacArthur. And judging from the courageous ferocity of the Japanese defense of Okinawa, Hirohito believed his generals had a valid point.

General MacArthur, in Manila, tended to hold the same view, particularly after a careful study of the invasion plan that had been drawn up by the Joint Chiefs of Staff and General Marshall in Washington. Code-named "Operation Olympic," the plan grossly underestimated the ground forces in Japan at seven hundred and fifty thousand troops. But MacArthur knew better. He had received a more accurate estimate from his OSS agent in Japan, who had been unerring to date:

Japanese have available 2,350,000 regular soldiers for ground defense, and two hundred and fifty thousand garrison troops backed by thirty-two million civilian militiamen. Do not overlook fact all men and women between ages of 15 and 60 have been conscripted for defense. All invasion beaches have tunnels packed with ammunition and food. There are 10,000 Kamikaze pilots ready to die for Emperor. Also the trained pilots held back from Okinawa are ready. Equally important to defense are German designed V-1 pilotless rocket bombs which have been manufactured in quantity by Japanese Army and Navy. They are being positioned along invasion areas. End of transmission.

MacArthur knew these V-1 rockets would take a heavy toll on Nimitz's ships as they made their slow way through the minefields that blocked the landing areas on Kyushu, South Kyushu, and Honshu. Squadrons of aircraft would also be flown down to Japan from Formosa, Korea, and China to take part in the defense of their homeland. The Japanese navy, notwithstanding its heavy losses off the Philippines, Okinawa, and the Central and South Pacific, remained a formidable defense force.

General MacArthur sent this estimate of Japanese defenses to Washington. The White House and the G-2 staff now knew, as did MacArthur, that adjustments would have to be made to the invasion plan if it was to succeed. (See Appendix A: Operation Olympic Invasion Plan.)

In Washington there was despair at the thought of having to invade Japan. A consensus in the War Department was that Japan could hold out for another two years. But in Tokyo the Zaibatsu industrialists knew this was not so, and they informed top Japanese military leaders: "Our production is finished. We can produce war materials for only a few days more. Many of our factories have been bombed out of existence. Our workers have fled to the hills. But the worst of all, we have no more raw materials from China and the outside territories."

Emperor Hirohito knew the real situation. In Manila, General MacArthur knew it, too. He was still getting radio reports from his star agent within Japan. Twice weekly at 10:00 P.M., Ralph M. would hunker down in the basement of a church, his safe house, and send MacArthur a crisp, accurate analysis of the situation in Japan. Both wartime leaders realized that a negotiated peace was the only logical step. To Hirohito, it was the only way to end his nation's agony. And MacArthur wanted peace before the slaughter of his troops, who would soon come pounding ashore on three invasion beaches in Kyushu. Military statesmanship at the highest level was required. MacArthur had told Secretary of War Stimson to expect one million American casualties from the invasion. The medical evacuation logistics for Operation Olympic and Downfall—the point of immediate penetration—gave an indication of the heavy casualties that were anticipated. Sixteen big hospital ships, numerous, LSTs, and special hospital aircraft were being set aside to bring the expected constant flow of casualties to newly established hospital facilities on Okinawa, the Philippines, Guam, and Hawaii. At this time, early July of 1945, General MacArthur knew of the efforts being made to produce an atomic bomb, but was not certain this wonder weapon would work. Even a successful test explosion was no guarantee the bomb could be transported to the Pacific and used as a battlefront weapon. MacArthur knew he could only depend on his existing weapons and make his plans accordingly.

MacArthur did believe that Hirohito would welcome overtures of peace, so he alerted the Joint Chiefs of Staff and the White House to watch for conciliatory gestures from the Emperor (which, incidentally, might be made through the Swedish government or the Vatican). But the White House felt that nothing of the sort would emanate from the Imperial Palace, and so kept pressure on the scientists working on the atomic bomb in Los Alamos. The bomb was finally tested successfully in the desert of northern New Mexico on July 16, 1945. Hirohito, having learned of the test's results from

Ambassador Baron Oshima in Berlin, promptly initiated a series of surrender maneuvers in Europe. President Truman, in Potsdam meeting with Winston Churchill, Joseph Stalin, and Chiang Kai-shek, was handed a telegram from his chief of staff which told of the success at New Mexico. Truman informed Stalin, who, having already heard it from his agents in New York and Los Alamos, merely shrugged.

On July 26, 1945, the Potsdam Declaration was signed by President Harry Truman, Prime Minister Winston Churchill, and Chiang Kai-shek, President of China. Stalin did not sign. He had been invited only as a participating observer. With the atomic bomb now at hand, President Truman was confident that he could back up the Potsdam Declaration with the strength necessary to force Japan to surrender. The Declaration demanded that Japan surrender unconditionally or face "prompt and utter destruction." It also stated "there must be eliminated for all time the authority and influence of those who have deceived and misled the people of Japan into embarking on world conquest . . ."

When MacArthur read the Declaration, he was shocked. He realized "elimination" meant doing away with Emperor Hirohito and the institution of the Throne, a circumstance to which he knew the Japanese would never consent. Without Hirohito, the icon of ageless stability in Japanese history and tradition, there could be no orderly transition to peace. MacArthur knew the country would surely disintegrate and fall into the hands of Soviet communism. Nobody in Washington had consulted MacArthur—the premier authority on Japan and all of Asia—as to the wording and thrust of the Potsdam Declaration. Harry Truman, new in office, was impressed by the worldliness of Under Secretary of State Dean Acheson, who had been responsible for the presence of the Communist agent Alger Hiss at the Yalta

Conference and later in San Francisco, when the charter of the United Nations was drawn up. Truman was swayed, in addition, by the literary skills of Archibald MacLeish, another advisor, who drafted the wording of the Potsdam Declaration, and by the supposedly high-level investigative abilities of Harry Hopkins. Truman did not know that the late President Roosevelt had cast Hopkins aside during the last year of his presidency for embarrassing misjudgments made in assessing delicate international matters. Once, when Winston Churchill, a guest at Hyde Park, noticed that Harry Hopkins was absent from the official proceedings, he remarked to an aide, "Hopkins has evidently fallen from grace."

Yet Harry Hopkins had been sent to Moscow to represent President Truman in the period during which the Potsdam Declaration was drawn up. Hopkins cabled Truman the exact message the Russians wanted him to send: "Unless Hirohito is dethroned, the war will have been in vain." The Kremlin knew, as did MacArthur, that the abolition of Hirohito would produce a state of social chaos on which communism could feed and take hold.

Seven

The Longest Month in Hirohito's Life

July 27, 1945, was a hot, muggy day in Manila. General MacArthur pondered the problems that would confront him in an invasion of Japan, as well he might. The war in Europe had ended with a German surrender at Reims on May 7–8, allowing the transfer of thirty divisions to the Philippines for Operation Olympic; another million men were expected by December. Courtney Hodges, commander of the U.S. First Army, had already arrived in Manila, but MacArthur, who felt the war in Europe had been mishandled, favored his own battle-tested commanders. "The ETO commanders made every mistake that supposedly intelligent men could make," MacArthur said in an interview. The North African operation, he said, was "absolutely useless," and he declared that "the European strategy was to hammer stupidly against the enemy's strongpoints." MacArthur also observed that if he had been given "just a portion of the force" sent to North Africa in 1942, he "could have retaken the Philippines in three months because at that time the

Japanese were spread thin and not ready for massive counterattacks."

There was a great deal to be said for MacArthur's views, for during the five months he spent opposing the Japanese in the mountains of the Philippines he had waged an excellent campaign with limited forces before being forced back to Corregidor and Bataan. The strategy he had employed for his long haul back from Australia to the Philippines prompted Field Marshal Lord Alanbrooke, chief of Britain's Imperial General Staff, to call MacArthur "the greatest general and the best strategist that World War II produced."

MacArthur said his assault on Japan would begin on November 1, 1945. A frontal assault on Kyushu by 766,700 Allied troops, the first phase, would be under the command of General Krueger, whose principal objective was the airfields that would provide air cover for the second phase, the main assault on Honshu. This phase, "Operation Coronet," would take place on March 1, 1946, if all went well on Kyushu. MacArthur planned to lead the assault, with General Eichelberger as his chief of staff. With the tanks he would be receiving from the European theater that would be off-loaded from an armada of LSTs onto the invasion beaches, he felt confident he could outmaneuver Japanese armor and defenses on the great Kanto Plain approach to Tokyo.

July 27 in Tokyo was just another wartime summer day. Heat and humidity were high and most people were weak and hungry. Morale was low from continued bombing and destruction of homes. On this day Hirohito toured the bombed-out areas of the city. The futility of going on with the war was soon to become apparent to him. Lord Privy Seal Kido recorded in his daily diary for this day: "Leaving the Imperial Palace at 9:00 A.M., with His Majesty. The Emperor toured the war-damaged areas accompanied by me."

As he walked through the massive destruction, dressed in his army uniform, Hirohito was reminded of the great Kanto earthquake of 1923, which had devastated three-quartersof Tokyo and Yokohama. He had been Prince Regent then and had been shocked by the destruction and the approximately one hundred and forty thousand deaths. The reception he had received on that day was spectacular, an indication that this popular Prince would develop into a monarch of enormous popularity. He had announced that he was contributing immediately ten million yen (two and a half million dollars) from his privy purse toward an emergency relief fund. His popularity on that day disturbed many of the Court people, who preferred an Emperor who would bend to their wishes. But behind the facade of this quiet Prince Regent was a man of steel who had been raised in the Spartan tradition of ancient warriors by a foster father, Vice Admiral Kawamura, and tutored by General Nogi, the hero of Port Arthur who had directed the storming of the Russian citadel in 1904. Now, on this day in 1945, he knew that the destruction was beyond any grant from the privy purse and that before the homeless could again be made comfortable peace must come for Japan. He was saddened by what he saw, but the people took pride in his appearance in their midst. War is a great equalizer, as the British in London had experienced during their ordeal by fire and bombs during 1941–42. At the height of the aerial siege of London by the Germans, crowds from the poorer classes of the East End had stood outside Buckingham Palace to receive spiritual strength from the thought that their king and queen were undergoing the same ordeal. Likewise, this morning in Tokyo after a B-29 bombing, crowds stood outside the Imperial Palace to receive the strength to carry on.

Upon his return to the Imperial Palace the same day, a grim Emperor Hirohito presided over a meeting of the Supreme Council for the Direction of the War, called together to discuss the Potsdam Declaration, issued to Japan the day before. This group, the "inner cabinet," consisted of fleet marshals and fleet admirals, the Minister of War, the Minister of the Navy, the Chief of the Army General Staff, the Chief of the Navy General Staff, and various special appointees termed "elder statesmen." The Council, which had been formed on August 5, 1944, following the fall of the Tojo Cabinet after the loss of Saipan, gave Emperor Hirohito greater working control over the machinery of war and peace. It was an instrument through which he could deal with Imperial General Headquarters and the Supreme Military Body in formulating and carrying out a fundamental policy for the course of the war.

Some of the men on the Japanese Supreme Council wanted to accept the terms of the Potsdam Declaration, but Foreign Minister Togo won a delay. Togo's advice was that, before replying, Japan ought to make one final effort to use the "good offices" of the Soviet Union to effect a more favorable peace offer, even though four months earlier the Soviets had officially broken the neutrality pact with Japan. He reasoned that this would save face for the Japanese army and would gain the Soviets' support. But Naotake Sato, the Japanese Ambassador to the Soviet Union, was insisting that "There is no chance whatever of winning the Soviet Union to our side . . ." Moreover, Togo did not know that President Roosevelt and Prime Minister Churchill, as signatories of a secret agreement at Yalta, had agreed to major concessions in the Far East if Stalin, within two or three months after the end of war in Europe, entered the war against Japan.

This secret segment of the Yalta agreement, which was signed February 11, 1945, reads as follows:

The leaders of the three Great Powers—the Soviet Union, the United States of America and Great Britain—have agreed that in two or three months after Germany has surrendered and the war in Europe has terminated the Soviet Union shall enter into war against Japan on the side of the Allies on condition that:

1. The status quo in Outer Mongolia (The Mongolian People's Republic) shall be preserved;
2. The former rights of Russia violated by the treacherous attack of Japan in 1904 shall be restored, viz:
   (a) the southern part of Sakhalin as well as all the islands adjacent to it shall be returned to the Soviet Union,
   (b) the commercial port of Dairen shall be internationalized, the preeminent interests of the Soviet Union in this port being safeguarded and the lease of Port Arthur as a naval base of the USSR restored,
   (c) the Chinese-Eastern Railroad and the South-Manchurian Railroad which provides an outlet to Dairen shall be jointly operated by the establishment of a joint Soviet-Chinese Company it being understood that the preeminent interests of the Soviet Union shall be safeguarded and that China shall retain full sovereignty in Manchuria.
3. The Kurile Islands shall be handed over to the Soviet Union.

It is understood, that the agreement concerning Outer Mongolia and the ports and railroads referred to above will require concurrence of Generalissimo Chiang Kai-shek. The President will take measures in order to obtain this concurrence on advice from Marshal Stalin.

The Heads of the three Great Powers have agreed that these claims of the Soviet Union shall be unquestionably fulfilled after Japan has been defeated.

On August 8, 1945, when the Soviet Union did enter the war against Japan, Winston Churchill was to grumble that Russia "was determined to claim her full rights as a belligerent." But the Soviets' attitude was a predictable consequence of the Yalta agreement. Both Churchill and Roosevelt, and their chiefs of staff (excepting MacArthur), had overestimated Japan's ability to stay the course against the United States and Britain and had given away too much for Soviet cooperation on the Eastern Front.

The Supreme Council conformed in the end with Togo's request. They were, however, faced with the problem of how to explain the Potsdam Declaration to the people of Japan. It was decided that news about the Declaration would be released vaguely. The newspapers were ordered to downgrade the story, and the plan was for the government to ignore the Declaration officially for a time. By Monday, July 30, newspapers around the world reported that Japan had not even bothered to reject the Declaration. U.S. Secretary of War Henry L. Stimson issued the following statement:

The United States could only proceed to demonstrate that the ultimatum had meant exactly what it said when it stated that if the Japanese continued the war, "The full application of our military power, backed by our resolve, will mean the inevitable and complete destruction of the Japanese armed forces and just as inevitably the utter devastation of the Japanese homeland."

The Supreme Council waited for a result of Togo's overture to the Soviet Union. In Moscow, Ambassador Sato had to deal with Vice Commissar Lozovsky instead of Foreign Commissar Molotov (who had gone to Potsdam with Joseph Stalin) and found him bafflingly noncommital regarding Russia's attitude. Sato wired Togo that further efforts were of no use. Togo replied, "We must attempt to negotiate through the Soviet Union because there seems to be no other way to terminate the war."

Japanese army leaders had all along had the opinion that it was not possible to come to an understanding with the Soviet Union. General Korechika Anami, Minister of War, had predicted as early as June that the Russians "would attack Japan just as the Americans were preparing to land their forces on our islands." Later, a few days before the surrender, he would also tell Home Minister Abe that if Japan held out a little longer and fought the American forces on Kyushu, the United States would become so apprehensive about Russian occupation of the Asian mainland and northern Japan that she would be eager to conclude a peace treaty and would therefore offer more advantageous terms.

In the meantime Emperor Hirohito and the Supreme Council waited for the Soviet reply. In Lord Privy Seal Kido's diary of that month are notes telling of the efforts made by the Emperor to use Russia either to end the war or at least to produce better terms for Japan than those required in the Potsdam Declaration:

At 3:00 P.M. (27 July) Prince Konoye was received in audience by His Majesty. Retiring from the Imperial Presence at 3:15 P.M. he called at my office. On this occasion he stated, in substance:

"Asked my opinion by the Throne regarding the termination of the current situation. I reported to His Majesty that I believe it necessary at the present moment to speedily put a close to the situation. His Majesty intimated to me that I should be prepared as I might be sent to Soviet Russia, and I respectfully accepted this assignment."

(From the same day:)

In response to a summons from the Throne, had an audience with His Majesty in the Imperial Library at 3:35 P.M. His Majesty was pleased to explain the Imperial audience with Prince Konoye as follows:

"When I asked Konoye about his opinion relating to the future outlook of war, after outlining my intentions, he opined that it was imperative to bring a close to the war at this juncture. As I told him that I might ask him to go to Soviet Russia on a mission, therefore, he accepted this proposal, speaking outright that he would endeavor his utmost at the risk of his life were it the Imperial command."

Two days previous to the issuance of the Potsdam Declaration, Kido had noted in his diary:

From 10:20 to 11:20 A.M. granted an audience with His Majesty at the Imperial Library. His Majesty on this occasion earnestly urged steps to conclude peace with the Allies, disapproving the Army's proposal for a war of decision.

But Russia refused to do anything about Prince Konoye's peace mission. July passed, and in August President Truman, exasperated by Japan's delay in responding to the Potsdam Declaration, ordered that an atomic bomb be dropped on Japan.

The effect of Hiroshima was stunning, devastating—on that city, on the nation of Japan, and on the Supreme Council. The Council met to discuss the catastrophe. Each member had before him the following report by the Japanese Navy Bureau of Military Affairs, detailing the effects of the atomic bomb on Hiroshima:

1. Two or three B-29s came in at a high altitude and dropped near the center of the city three of what appeared to be bombs attached to parachutes. Since all three were of identical structure, it is supposed that two of them were concerned with detonating apparatus. The bomb exploded at an altitude of 500 meters.
2. The whole city was illuminated by a yellowish light and people on the ground became aware of great heat in the atmosphere. At the same time residential buildings collapsed and subsequently caught on fire. Pine trees were split and some straw roofs were set on fire simultaneously with the explosion but, since most of the fires occurred several dozen minutes after the explosion, we believe the fires were also due to carelessness in the demolished buildings.
3. Effects of the bomb blast: Within 500 meters, human intestines were laid bare and eyeballs pulled out, even at 2,000 meters there were

deaths from the bomb concussions, but people in long, reinforced trenches were safe. Within two kilometers, bodies were stark naked, there were deaths from burns, and wooden constructions within four kilometers were half-destroyed.

4. Effects of the thermic rays: Almost everyone within four kilometers suffered burns, but even at seven kilometers slight burns were received. The majority of these occurred only on the side which was exposed to the flash of the explosion in the parts exposed to the high radiation temperature. The effect on vegetation was comparable to that on human beings. Even at seven kilometers, parts of the branches and leaves have withered.

5. There is practically no defense measure. Forty percent of the people of Hiroshima are dead or wounded.*

President Truman then made a broadcast from the White House warning Japan of the destruction to come from further atomic bombs. In his statement he said:

> . . . If the Japanese do not now accept our terms they may expect a rain of ruin from the air, the like of which has not been seen on this earth . . . The source from which the sun draws its power could now totally eclipse the Land of the Rising Sun, on whose throne sits a direct descendant of Amaterasu O-Mikami, the Goddess of the Sun.

---

*A Japanese army intelligence message subsequently advised: "It is necessary that shelter trenches be covered. Underground rooms are suitable. There were comparatively few shelters destroyed. Those in shelters two kilometers from the center were not seriously injured."

Truman was to explain later, and repeat many times, that he ordered the atomic bombs dropped on Japan simply to force Japan into rapid and unconditional surrender and to save countless Allied lives. He had studied the proposed invasion plans, and it was plain to him what the casualties might be if Operation Olympic took place.

Kazutoshi Hando was a member of the Pacific War Research Society, a group of Japanese historians who interviewed seventy-nine of the Japanese leaders who took part in the decision to surrender.

Hando wrote in a report of those days:

> The Japanese believed the Emperor to be not only of divine descent but divine himself and upon his continued existence the continued existence of Japan as it had always been since time immemorial depended. It is impossible to guess what would have happened if the Allied powers had, at that moment, offered assurances that the Japanese polity, in the person of the Emperor, would be maintained: the war might have ended, the army might have been forced to concede—and the Russians might not have been given the opportunity to enter Manchuria. But these speculations are idle; Japan, in her stunned state (even before the A-bomb) followed the only path that seemed open to her; and the first few days of August passed in idle, not quite hopeless, watchful waiting.

For Japan the only alternative to the Potsdam Declaration, not realizing the futility of pursuing such a maneuver, had been to use the good offices of Russia to get better surrender terms with the United States, China, and Great Britain. When the atomic bomb exploded over Hiroshima, Foreign Minister Togo, now under great pressure from the Supreme Council and the Emperor, dispatched the following "Very Urgent" message to his ambassador in Moscow:

> The situation is becoming more and more pressing, and we would like to know at once the explicit attitude of the Russians. So will you put forth still greater efforts to get a reply from them in haste?

Sato did get an appointment with Molotov, who had just come back from the Potsdam Conference. As they faced each other, Molotov handed Sato a document, a declaration of war by Russia against Japan, effective "as of tomorrow, 9 August." (Molotov remarked later to an aide that Sato "certainly studied the text of it carefully, and left in a state of shock.") Only two hours later Red Army divisions entered Manchuria and started annihilating Japan's Kwantung army. Molotov, as part of the Soviet hierarchy, might well have been responsible for the clause in the Potsdam Declaration demanding the casting out of Emperor Hirohito. Using Harry Hopkins as his messenger, Molotov's cable had triggered presidential advisors Acheson and MacLeish to selling the President on a tough declaration, allowing for no facesaving for Hirohito, who, as it turned out, became under the aegis of General MacArthur, America's most influential ally during and following the years of occupation.

As the exigencies of war tightened for Hirohito, the makeup of his Cabinet became a cause for concern. In April, Prime Minister Koiso and his entire Cabinet had resigned en masse. In this critical time it was vital that there be sworn in a war cabinet by Imperial mandate. How this mandate was formulated and the stratagem the

Emperor used to get the man he wanted as Premier—
Admiral Suzuki, and not Field Marshal Hata, a Tojo
minion—is told in the diary of Lord Privy Seal Kido.

First there were constant meetings between Cabinet members and various heads of government agencies
who talked about the necessity of putting together a
stronger War Cabinet, a *Dai Honyei*, or War Guidance
Cabinet, that would combine army and state affairs
under one authority. Lord Privy Seal Kido was the
center of these discussions. From Chief of Army General
Staff Umezu and Chief of Naval General Staff Oyokawa
he elicited opinions as to the course of the war and the
need for a single War Cabinet. It had a Gilbert and
Sullivan air to it, but the opinions of the army and navy
leaders on the course of the war was of interest to
Hirohito. Kido recorded in his diary his interview with
General Umezu:

> In my interview with Chief of Army Gen-
> eral Staff Umezu, I said, "Premier Koiso has
> tendered his resignation to the Throne this
> morning, and the reason quoted by him is that
> it is imperative, in view of the present war
> situation, to remodel and strengthen the struc-
> ture and character of the Cabinet. In other
> words, it is urged to have the so-called Dai
> Honyei Cabinet, or War Guidance Cabinet,
> formed. If you, as representative of the War
> Command, have any suggestions or requests to
> make in regard to this, please let me know
> them. I also would like to hear your views on
> the future outlook of war, especially on the
> enemy's prospective political offensive as re-
> sulting from the collapse of Germany and the
> holding of the San Francisco United Nations
> Conference.

General Umezu answered:

"As to the future outlook of the war, prospects can be said to be anything but good. We have to push on with such dispositions as to fight out the war at any cost, no matter whether we may be able to beat back the enemy or not. If we could give full scope to the best of our efforts, with the nation's fighting spirit properly heightened, this, to my thinking, would not be impossible, although not easy. The Army is steadily carrying out arrangements to attain this purpose. Therefore, we earnestly hope that such a Cabinet as to meet this demand will be organized."

Umezu mentioned an additional concern:

"Though we are most concerned about oil supply, we still have enough stock to hold out for several months. At present, with the Imperial approval, we have decided to form a special corps to increase oil output in this country."

Kido then interviewed Chief of Naval General Staff Oyokawa, and recorded this conversation:

When I was told about the resignation en masse of the Cabinet, frankly speaking, I was shocked, as something troublesome had occurred.

As regards the war prospect, we have somehow managed to conduct "orthodox" naval operations down as far as the Marianas line in spite of the considerable difference of strength between ourselves and the enemy; but, after that, we have only conducted just a series of guerilla warfare actions, so to speak. In this sense, therefore, the present war may be called a big gamble.

In the future, we will employ a balance of Navy enlisted men in plants in order to keep up the war strength and thereby secure the monthly production of around 1,200 aircraft and 20 submarines with the intention of giving full play to the guerilla strength.

Though we cannot be too optimistic, there is nothing to be too pessimistic about either. For this, however, there are some conditions. I mean to say that this effort on our part has to be supported by the Cabinet, which is established on a firm foundation and is well trusted by the people.

As regards oil, we have enough stock for six months; and, after that, we will depend on "pine root" oil.

Marquis Kido, to give full play to various opinions, held a senior statesmen's conference in the Imperial Audience Hall on April 5, 1945. Attending the meeting were Konoye, Hiranuma, Suzuki, Hirota, Kido, Wakatsuki, Okada, and Tojo. Kido's personal diary notes the following:

Chief Chamberlain to His Majesty delivered an opening address followed by an explanation by the Lord Keeper of the Privy Seal of the circumstances leading up to the recent Cabinet change. Premier Koiso's resignation was read and circulated among the conferees.

Tojo: The resignation urges that both the State affairs and the war command have to be rectified. What does it mean?

Kido: No specific explanation has been given by Premier Koiso.

Tojo: That the Cabinet changes occur so often during wartime is not proper. Especially April 25, which is slated for the opening of the San Francisco Conference, to my way of thinking marks a very important date. Next Cabinet must be the last Cabinet. Meanwhile, there are two confronting opinions prevailing in this country: the one insisting that we have to fight out the war to a finish in order to cut our way to the future fortune of the nation, and the other asserting that we should speedily bring about peace, even submitting to unconditional surrender. I suppose, therefore, settling these issues takes precedence over all others.

Okada: The forthcoming Cabinet must of necessity consider a great many things. This is the Cabinet shouldering the national fortunes until the last moment, the Cabinet coalescing the total strength of the nation. Regarding such questions as making preparations for both war and peace, we can never form an idea until later in the future. I guess we have to decide only after we have thoroughly studied the matter.

Hiranuma: As has been pointed out by Their Excellencies just now, today there are diverse opinions as the war situation has become very pressing. It is necessary to unify the differences of opinion. There is no other way but to fight at any price. The question, I think, is simple. As the recent Cabinet change took place too abruptly, frankly speaking, I have been rather embarrassed. Therefore, I wish to have it arranged that we do not have to submit our report to the Throne as promptly as in the past. If possible, I should also have liked to listen to the opinions of Premier Koiso and Navy Minister Yonai at full length, but it could not be helped as the resignation had already been sent in. To be frank with you, there is no room for debating just now since we are asked to express our opinions at a moment's notice. Meanwhile, I should like to have such points, as brought up by Their Excellencies, fully discussed.

Kido: I do perfectly agree with you. In fact, there were signs indicating the resignation en bloc of the Cabinet for some time, and later I was told that the proposed resignation was replaced by the policy of the Cabinet reorganization. In the meantime, however, it has been decided that Marshals Sugiyama and Hata be transferred to the posts of Overall Defense Commanders and, inasmuch as the change of the War Minister has subsequently been necessitated, the Army informed the Cabinet of its recommendation of General Nami as successor to the outgoing War Minister. On the ground that it should be double-crossing the Army (I do not understand exactly what he meant) if the Cabinet resigned en masse soon after effecting this reorganization of the Cabinet at that time, Premier Koiso said that he had all at once made up his mind to resign. Anyhow, indeed, this was all of a sudden, and I, myself, have been very much nonplussed, too.

Okada: Before nominating particular personages, how about discussing the matters pertaining to the coalescence of the nation's total strength and the formation of a stronger Cabinet?

Hiranuma: Formerly, it has been customary that the Premier be decided first and that he, in turn, recommend his colleagues to the Throne. Unless we decide as much as important members of the Cabinet this time, however, the Cabinet will not be made a powerful one. According to the instances in the past, we will never reach a conclusion as to the affairs concerning the Army, Navy and peace.

Tojo: In case we nominate the Cabinet members, does it not mean that His Majesty would have to take the responsibility following the formation of the Cabinet?

Hiranuma: You are perfectly right as far as the formality is concerned, but what I mean to say is that I should like to propose to have some more of our opinions also consulted before deciding the current issue.

Hirota: Through thick and thin we must win the war. Although there has been some pessimism expressed, it is interesting to recall that none of the countries participating in the present warfare have been winning all through from the very beginning, and every one of them has staged a comeback after having been on the verge of defeat. The next Cabinet must be the Cabinet to prosecute the war to a successful termination. I think it was an extremely appropriate step taken on the part of the Lord Keeper of the Privy Seal to have interviewed the Army and Navy leaders, but was it not also necessary to confirm more fully the intentions of the Army and Navy authorities?

Kido: I have asked them at all lengths, but no specific intentions have been made known then.

Hiranuma: To be frank with you, I think Koiso's information of the Cabinet was a failure. We should have been consulted more about it. Reorganization, frankly speaking, always is a failure. As regards the formalism, it is just as has been stated by His Excellency Tojo. But, in fact, I think it be far advisable if we were consulted more freely without being swayed by logic.

Kido: As Hiranuma-San has pointed out, the Lord Keeper of the Privy Seal is also supposed not to meddle with the formation of the Cabinet after once reporting the matter to the Throne. But the strange part of it is that his responsibility for the report to His Majesty will have to be talked about in case the formation of the Cabinet turns out unsatisfactory. I admit this usage also, as a system, is by no means right; but today it was practiced against my good intentions as there was no other way.

Hiranuma: It is too much to make the Lord Keeper alone responsible for everything, and I suppose we ought to share the same responsibility.

Kido: When the mainland is about to turn into a battlefield under today's circumstances, the internal condition is immensely deplorable. There is great tendency that the nation has not necessarily been cooperating with the government's administrative policies but has been what we call "looking aside." Even considering questions relative to the foodstuffs, increased production and the peace and order,

141

we must form a Cabinet worthwhile being trusted by the people. I also should like to call your particular attention to the fact that the antimilitary trend has become rather conspicuous lately.

Hiranuma: There are two confronting views in this country regarding the termination of war: At this moment our choice must be he who will fight out the war. We cannot recommend a person interested in the discontinuance of war and the heralding of peace. Therefore, this matter has very important bearings upon the selection of the Cabinet head. If you mean that finally we decide on the Premier and we entrust him with everything after that, I can give you no opinion. I am by all means opposed to any views favoring the discontinuance of war and the heralding of peace.

Suzuki: At the time of the Sino-Japanese War, Premier Ito was leading in the Cabinet. The Premier does not necessarily have to be a serviceman.

Hiranuma: As a matter of fact, he would not understand the conduct of the war unless he were from the service in the first or second reserve. Again, here, it is a premise that we do see the war through.

Okada: It seems to me that what has been said so far roughly clarifies the character of the Premier.

Suzuki: How about the present senior statesmen "putting forth their efforts"? We ought to be prepared to sacrifice ourselves for the State, to assume every responsibility, and to die in action for His Majesty. As for the Premier's office, I should like to ask Prince

Konoye, the youngest among us, to assume it as the assignment is physically most strenuous. After that, all of us do the rest. How about four of us making efforts first? I hear President Hara had also once suggested the same thing. I do well remember that I was greatly impressed as I personally heard the former President say so one week previous to his demise. How about enforcing this by all means?

Hiranuma: That the Premier should be a serviceman is understood. Prince Konoye has said that the person not affected by the past circumstances was preferable, and this is quite sensible. As things are, I hope Admiral Suzuki would accept the offered post with a view of securing the nation's confidence.

Konoye: I agree with you.

Wakatsuki: That is more than satisfactory. We cannot wish for any better.

Suzuki: As I have told His Excellency Okada once, I used to think that the participation of servicemen in politics would constitute a cause to ruin the country. This was the case with the fall of the Roman Empire. Also, the same was the case with the fate of the Kaiser and the end of the Romanoffs. Therefore, there are some difficult circumstances for me to take part in the political affairs in view of my principles. Besides, I am hard of hearing, and I would like to be excused.

Tojo: Admiral Suzuki's "mental attitude" is admirable indeed. To think of the progress of the war, however, it admits of no prediction. The enemy is desperate. He will launch "extraordinary" operations. It is likely that he may invade some part of our homeland. Since utmost importance attaches to the internal de-fense, such a structure, which will enable the State affairs and the War Command to act in unison, is called for. We must consider this problem centering around the Army. In this sense, our choice has to be a person in the active service, if possible. What has been his-torically referred to is quite reasonable; but, in this respect, Japan is different from Europe. In European countries war command is included in the national defense. The principle of war command in this country is unique in itself. From this point of view, I believe Marshal Hata is best qualified.

Kido: I, too, will give my opinion about this matter. As I have already stated, it is more important than ever to strengthen the admin-istration today when our homeland is about to turn into a battlefield, and it is imperative that a "weighty" Cabinet, worthy of the people's trust, be formed. In this sense, I think His Excellency Tojo's opinion also stands to reason. But, under the present circumstances, I per-sonally wish that His Excellency Suzuki would come forward.

Tojo: If you were not very careful, there is a possibility that the Army would turn away. Should the Army turn away, the Cabinet would have to be dissolved.

Kido: It is serious at this moment that the Army would turn away. But, are there any signs or presentiment in this regard?

Tojo: I would say there are.

Okada: What in the world do you mean by saying that the Army would turn away against any Cabinet to be formed by Imperial command in these extraordinary times—amidst this great national crisis? Who is responsible for home defense, anyway? Is it not the Army and Navy who are responsible?

Tojo: As there were some apprehensions for that, I just called it to your attention.

The meeting of the senior statesmen adjourned at 8:00 P.M. Then Kido recorded in his diary:

From 8:45 to 9:15 A.M. the next morning I was granted an interview with His Majesty at the Imperial Library on which occasion I reported in detail to the Throne about the views expressed by the senior statesmen, and stated in my address to the Throne that I thought it advisable to have an Imperial mandate to form a new ministry issued to Baron Kantaro Suzuki.

At 10:00 P.M. the Imperial mandate was issued to Admiral Suzuki.

April 6: The investiture of the Suzuki Cabinet was held, thereby a new Cabinet making a start.

Through this procedure of having senior statesmen meet and discuss a new Cabinet in a critical time, Emperor Hirohito, with his Lord Privy Seal Kido serving as moderator and guiding the course of the conference, could direct the selection of a new Premier. It was direction by remote control, but it worked to keep the reins of government firmly in the hands of the Throne. It also demonstrated how carefully Hirohito had to move to counter vigorous army opposition in his desire to push through his peace overtures with the Allies.

Now Togo advised the Emperor to accept promptly the terms of the Potsdam Declaration. Hirohito instructed the Foreign Minister to have Prime Minister Kantaro Suzuki strive to terminate the war, stating: "In view of the new type of weapon that has been used against Japan at Hiroshima, Japan is now powerless to continue the war." Marquis Kido, Lord Keeper of the Privy Seal, commented that day, "His Majesty said he considered his own personal safety secondary to the immediate termination of the war."

Suzuki's government agreed with the Emperor that the alternative to unconditional surrender was total annihilation. There are those who assert Truman should not have ordered the August 9 detonation of the second atomic bomb on Japan, and that the Japanese had already notified the Allies of their intention to surrender. This claim, however, is false. By August 9, the government of Japan had not yet issued any statement of intent to surrender to the United States. Indeed, before surrender was possible, the Emperor would have to make many maneuvers within his government. The Japanese army, for one, was determined to fight on. General Anami had declared to both Suzuki and Togo: "It is far too early to say that the war is lost. That we will inflict severe losses on the enemy when he invades Japan is certain, and it is by no means impossible that we may be able to reverse the situation in our favor, pulling victory out of defeat. Furthermore, our Army will not submit to demobilization. And since they know they are not permitted to surrender, since they know that a fighting man who surrenders is liable to extremely heavy punishment, there is really no alternative for us but to continue the war."

A meeting of the Supreme War Council on August 9 had ended in an impasse, with no clear-cut decision for peace. Both Suzuki and Togo then met secretly with Hirohito to plot the next move, both men fully aware that should their position leak out they would be vulnerable to assassination by army hit squads claiming to be acting "to protect the Emperor from traitorous advisors." Certain and violent death would also be their fate were they to sign a surrender document without approval of both the Supreme Council and the Supreme Military. At their conference with the Emperor it was agreed to call another session of the Supreme Council for the Direction of the War, to be convened at midnight in the underground bomb shelter of the Imperial Palace. The Emperor would preside.

Precisely at midnight the Emperor, accompanied by an aide, entered the small bomb shelter. The Supreme Councillors, with their aides and two invited guests of distinction, were waiting. The conference room in the shelter, a modest eighteen feet by thirty, was close on that hot, humid night in August. The members of the Council and their guests rose when the Emperor entered and took his seat in a plain, straight-backed chair at the head table.

Premier Suzuki asked the Chief Cabinet Secretary to read aloud to those present the Potsdam Declaration. Suzuki then called on his Foreign Minister, Togo, to comment. Togo urged that the Declaration be accepted without further delay, if assurance could be obtained that the position of the Emperor and the Throne would be respected. Suzuki turned to the Supreme Council and said he agreed with Togo.

But the War Minister, General Anami, leaped to his feet and stated that the nation should fight on. In any case, he said, if Japan were to surrender it would be on the basis of four conditions: respect for the integrity of the Imperial structure, and Japan's right to disarm her own soldiers, to conduct her own war trials, and to limit the forces of occupation.

General Umezu agreed with Anami, saying that Japan was still more than a match for the enemy, and that unconditional surrender now would only dishonor the heroic Japanese dead. In the event of surrender, he added, he would insist on the four conditions outlined by General Anami. Admiral Toyada, the navy chief of staff, also favored the continuation of the war.

Premier Suzuki then called on Baron Hiranuma, asked the various ministers to explain about Japan's unfortunate Soviet diplomatic experience in the past weeks, and requested the identity of the men most likely to be classified as war criminals.

All eleven men present had their chance to express opinions. Finally Suzuki turned to the Emperor for his opinion. At two o'clock in the morning, on Friday, August 10, the Voice of the Crane, the Emperor, was heard:

"Continuing the war," the Emperor said quietly, "can only result in the annihilation of the Japanese people and a prolongation of the suffering of all humanity. It seems obvious that the nation is no longer able to wage war, and its ability to defend its own shores is doubtful. That it is unbearable for me to see my loyal troops disarmed goes without saying . . . But the time has come to bear the unbearable. Nevertheless I give my sanction to the proposal to accept the Allied proclamation on the basis outlined by the Foreign Minister."

Emperor Hirohito rose and walked slowly from the underground bomb shelter. In the silence that followed his exit, the white handkerchief of each man appeared as they wiped sweat from their brows and tears from their faces. Premier Suzuki then said, "His Majesty's decision ought to be made the decision of this conference as well." No one disagreed.

The Councillors left the Palace and went to Suzuki's office, where they were to approve the exact wording of the official reply to the Potsdam Declaration, a draft having been prepared earlier by Premier Suzuki.

Later the draft was reviewed and agreed to. Foreign Minister Togo transmitted to his ambassadors in Bern, Switzerland, and Stockholm, Sweden, the following message to be passed to the United States, Great Britain, China, and Russia:

In obedience to the gracious command of His Majesty the Emperor who, ever anxious to enhance the cause of world peace, desires earnestly to bring about an absolute termination of hostilities with a view of saving mankind from the calamities to be imposed upon them by further continuation of the war. The Japanese Government asked several weeks ago the Soviet Government, with which neutral relations then prevailed, to render good offices in restoring peace vis-à-vis the enemy powers. Unfortunately, these efforts in the interest of peace having failed, the Japanese Government, in conformity with the august wish of His Majesty to restore the general peace and desiring to put an end to the untold suffering entailed by war as quickly as possible, have decided upon the following:

The Japanese Government are ready to accept the terms enumerated in the Joint Declaration which was issued at Potsdam on 26 July, 1945, by the heads of government of the United States, Great Britain, and China, and later subscribed by the Soviet Government, with the understanding that the said declaration does not comprise any demand which prejudices the prerogatives of His Majesty as a sovereign ruler.

The Japanese Government hope sincerely that this understanding is warranted and desire keenly that an explicit indication to that effect will be speedily forthcoming.

Three important conferences followed the transmission of the message of surrender by Togo:

1. Prime Minister Suzuki, War Minister General Anami, and Admiral Yonai, the Navy Minister, conferred and agreed that if the Allies did not retain Hirohito and the Throne, the war would be continued to the death.

2. General Anami repeated this decision to his army staff officers, meeting in the underground bomb shelter at the War Ministry. He said, "We have no alternative but to abide by the Emperor's decision. Whether we fight on or whether we surrender now depends on the enemy's reply to our note."

3. In Washington, in the White House's Oval Office, President Truman held a meeting on Hirohito's message of surrender, which had been made public through radio news broadcasts heard around the world. It was an early-morning meeting. Among those present were: James Byrnes, Secretary of State; James Forrestal, Secretary of the Navy; Henry L. Stimson, Secretary of War; and Admiral William Leahy, the President's chief of staff. What concerned the President was the clause: "With the understanding that the said declaration does not comprise any demand which prejudices the prerogatives of His Majesty as a sovereign ruler." Truman asked, "Does this mean unconditional surrender, or not, as we demanded at Potsdam?" The opinions varied, and Truman decided to accept the Japanese request that the Emperor be retained as a sovereign ruler, providing Japan accepted the following provision, prepared by the State Department:

From the moment of surrender the authority of the Emperor and the Japanese Government to rule the state shall be subject to the Supreme Commander of the Allied Powers who will take such steps as he deems proper to effectuate the surrender terms.

Truman also requested that the Emperor and the Japanese High Command be required to sign the surrender terms. Copies of the American proposal were sent to London, Moscow, and Chungking. The British leaders suggested that on the point of ordering the Emperor to sign the surrender document it would be better to have the instrument read: "The Emperor shall authorize and ensure the signature by the government of Japan and the Japanese General Headquarters of the surrender terms . . ."

Washington agreed, China acceded, but Moscow stalled. Evidently the Russian Communists were hoping to delay surrender in order that the fighting could continue and they could gain more territory. But on the eleventh of August all three nations had agreed, and the U.S. State Department sent the reply of concurrence to Japan via the Japanese Embassy in Bern, Switzerland:

> With regard to the Japanese Government's message accepting the terms of the Potsdam Proclamation but containing the statement— with the understanding that the said declaration does not comprise any demand which prejudices the prerogatives of His Majesty as a sovereign ruler—our position is as follows: From the moment of surrender the authority of the Japanese Government to rule the State shall be subject to the Supreme Commander of the Allied Powers who will take such steps as he deems proper to effectuate the surrender terms.

The Emperor will be required to authorize and ensure the signature by the Government of Japan and the Japanese Imperial General Headquarters of the surrender terms necessary to carry out the provisions of the Potsdam Declaration and shall issue his commands to the Japanese Military, Naval, and Air Authorities and to all the forces under their control wherever located to cease active operations and to surrender their arms and to issue such other orders as the Supreme Commander may require to give effect to the surrender terms.

Immediately upon the surrender of the Japanese Government they shall transport prisoners of war and civilian internees to places of safety as directed where they can quickly be placed aboard Allied transports.

The ultimate form of government of Japan shall in accordance with the Potsdam Declaration be established by the freely expressed will of the Japanese people.

The Armed Forces of the Allied Powers will remain in Japan until the purposes set forth in the Potsdam Declaration are achieved.

But at this point neither Togo nor the Supreme Council had the consent of the army and navy for acceptance of the Four Powers' reply to the Japanese surrender proposal. Togo knew surrender was inevitable but was stalling for precious time, hoping for an even better understanding as to the role of the Emperor in Japan's future.

The Ultra codebreakers in England and the Magic cryptographers in the Pacific picked up Japanese army messages the day after the Four Power reply was received in Tokyo. It demonstrated Hirohito's delicate approach to peace as a necessary part of his internal strategy and diplomacy. In his southern army staff order, Field Marshal Terauchi stated:

> The plans of the Southern Army have changed in no way whatever.
>
> Each Army under our command and jurisdiction, in no way confused and blinded by scheming propaganda, will establish a unified and firmly united military discipline, and will go ahead to strengthen its war preparations more and more.

The navy was equally determined to wage war. The Navy Vice Minister and the Vice Chief of the Navy General Staff issued a joint order that their forces should take part in this holy war. The following day, August 15, Hirohito made his surrender broadcast agreeing to the Potsdam Declaration. The Vice Chief of the Navy General Staff knew the Emperor's decision could not be superseded and so committed suicide in protest.

Eight

Surrender and
Occupation

From the moment Emperor Hirohito announced the Japanese surrender over the nation's radio network, the Foreign Office moved swiftly to tidy up some loose ends before the occupation army arrived.

Foreign Minister Togo ordered Minister Miroshima in Lisbon to "convert as much as possible of the deposit holdings in your office into ready cash, and take all necessary precautions in connection with its safekeeping."

For days there was a constant flow of messages between Tokyo and these ambassadorial outposts; both Ultra and Magic intercepted them all. Kase in Bern, Switzerland, informed Togo that he had received a diplomatic note from the American government. The note, handed to him by the Swiss Foreign Ministry, ordered the "Japanese government to immediately instruct its diplomatic and consular officials in neutral countries to surrender custody of all property and archives to representatives of the Allied powers."

Foreign Minister Togo then advised his representatives in Switzerland, Sweden, Portugal, Ireland, and Afghanistan as follows:

> Inasmuch as this demand is not covered by any of the stipulations of the Potsdam Declaration which we have accepted, the Imperial government cannot agree to this demand of the United States. . . ."

Okamoto in Stockholm wired Togo, "It would be foolish to allow the 1,500,000 yen in my account to pass into enemy hands, therefore concluded to make advance allowances to 20 of my staff and myself. The Naval attaché in this office announced he has already withdrawn half a million kronen [$115,000]."

The Yokohama Specie Bank representative in Switzerland withdrew five million Swiss francs—approximately $1,150,000—from a safe-deposit box of the Banque Nationale Suisse, placed it in a suitcase, and turned it over to a "Swiss citizen on the faculty of the University of Basel."

The Japanese Foreign Office then ordered its diplomatic representatives in Thailand and Indochina to transfer title of certain military supplies and foodstuffs to private Japanese companies, with the caution, "Please be extremely circumspect in your handling of these transactions in order that the enemy will not be able at some later date to call them into question."

The Japanese army and navy high commands issued orders that all papers relating to prisoners of war and interrogation of American pilots be immediately destroyed. The army command also ordered that the records of those who ran their concentration camps in Burma and elsewhere be destroyed. As a result, camp commanders and other guards who had carried on a program of systematic torture and degradation of prisoners of war eventually arrived back in Tokyo under new identities and resumed their places in civilian society.

Togo, uncomfortably aware that Dr. Junod of the International Red Cross was visiting Japanese-held territory to report on conditions in prison camps ("Appalling, unspeakable," he called them), sent a message to Minister Kase in Bern. The dispatch announced a donation of ten million Swiss francs from Yokohama Specie funds in Switzerland "in the name of the Imperial Government and the Royal Family for ordinary activities of the Red Cross." Togo thought this would improve world opinion of the Japanese.

Near Harbin in Manchuria, the buildings and laboratories of the 731-Corps, the world's largest and most notorious germ factory, were ordered destroyed. Under the supervision of General Shiro Ishii, here germs of cholera, plague, and typhoid were injected into thousands of Chinese prisoners. In the Pacific war many British, Australian, and American prisoners were sent to the Harbin laboratories to see if the results of these injections on Anglo-Saxons differed from those on Asiatics. Careful records of each human test were kept by General Ishii and his laboratory staff. But when surrender was announced, the destruction of Harbin was complete. The staff returned to Tokyo, some indifferent to the experiments they had conducted and the deaths they had caused, others with terrible memories that would stay with them for years. General Ishii surrendered personally to representatives of the U.S. Chemical Corps, and his test records were handed over. In exchange he was flown to Hawaii, and later to the U.S. Army chemical and biological headquarters on the United States mainland. He died a peaceful death in America, having reached old age.

Minister Okamoto sent a message of advice to the

Japanese government as to how they should conduct themselves during the occupation:

> Speech and behavior in Tokyo likely to irritate the British and Americans should be avoided. For example, the enemy has been violently aroused by Tokyo reports claiming that Japan has been defeated only temporarily, or that Japan is "morally" undefeated and will fight again for Greater East Asia. Moreover, and I say this with the greatest trepidation, even the Imperial Rescript included a great deal of reproach, and this seems to have aroused in the British and American opinion a passionate demand that the people of Japan be made to feel in their hearts the fact of defeat.
>
> I realize that public statements just now must be made with an eye to the problem of domestic tranquility, but I think it is vitally important that full and prudent consideration be given to repercussions in the outside world.

General MacArthur, in his headquarters at Manila, was quite satisfied with Hirohito's surrender. The transcript of the Emperor's broadcast, which had been translated and put before him, read beautifully, he said. It was fortunate that the Potsdam Declaration had been altered sufficiently in execution by Washington and London to allow Hirohito to remain on the Throne. It would ease the task of occupation.

The Japanese people generally would respect the wishes of the Emperor, who wanted a true peace with no guerilla warfare. Still, there were those who might block MacArthur's entry into Tokyo, and the steps he would now take to ensure a safe entry with his occupation forces were of major importance. He had received from

President Truman and Chief of Staff Marshall the authority he required to proceed with the disarmament of Japan's army, navy, and air force preparatory to the official surrender of Japan. Authorization came in a top-secret message from Washington, and stated in part:

> . . . In accordance with the agreement among the governments of the United States, Chinese Republic, United Kingdom, and the Union of the Soviet Socialist Republics to designate a Supreme Commander for the Allied Powers for the purpose of enforcing the surrender of Japan, you are hereby designated as the Supreme Commander for the Allied Powers . . .

The designation was vital, but MacArthur knew that there would be attempts to whittle down this authority. He intended, however, to share his Supreme Command with no one. All decisions regarding entry and occupation would be his, and his alone. He knew what was required to reshape Japan and bring it back from the depths of defeat to a position where it could become a strong ally of the United States. It was his idea to set Japan on a new course that would hold for generations to come. He stated in Manila what victory now meant: "Victory over Japan makes us the greatest political influence on the future of Asia. If we exert that influence in an imperialistic manner, or for the sole purpose of commercial advantage, then we shall lose our golden opportunity; but if our influence and our strength are expressed in terms of essential liberalism, we shall have the friendship and the cooperation of the Asiatic peoples far into the future."

With the authority to achieve this objective now his, he recalled his father's advice of many years past:

"Councils of war breed timidity and defeatism." Douglas MacArthur would have none of that. His philosophy paralleled that of Winston Churchill, who had been given the titles of Prime Minister and Minister of Defense by his King in 1940. "Why should I share my command with anyone, when I know best what should now be done?" said Churchill.

MacArthur now moved into high gear. He summoned Admiral Sherman to a meeting, and Sherman, in turn, sent this cable to Admiral Nimitz:

General MacArthur considers that as Supreme Allied Commander he is now fully responsible for and commands all phases of the occupation of Japan. He desires no communication with the Japanese authorities by forces in the Pacific except through *his* headquarters. He expects to summon Japanese representatives to Manila to make a preliminary arrangement for the surrender. He reiterated in most emphatic terms his disapproval of the use of a fleet landing force prior to the arrival of troops in strength and prior to the clearance of Japanese forces from the area under armistice arrangements. This disapproval is based on both military grounds and effect on service relationships. He repeated his full agreement with occupation of Japanese ports and coastal waters and complete blockade by the ships of the fleet. For the initial seizure of the Tokyo area he proposes a joint operation using the 11th Airborne and the 27th Infantry divisions, both airborne, and at the same time landing the 4th Marine Combat Team. This operation would not take place until conditions set at

Manila had been met. I expect to take off at midnight.

The thrust of the taking over of Japan thus spelled out and the ground rules in general clearly stated, MacArthur sent a lengthy set of instructions via radio to naval headquarters in Washington for transmission to the Japanese government "by any means available." It was addressed to "The Japanese Emperor, The Japanese Imperial Government, The Japanese Imperial General Headquarters," from "Supreme Commander for the Allied Powers," and stated:

> The Supreme Commander for the Allied Powers hereby directs the immediate cessation of hostilities by Japanese forces. The Supreme Commander for the Allied Powers is to be notified at once of the effective date and hour of such cessation of hostilities whereupon Allied forces will be directed to cease hostilities.
>
> The Supreme Commander of the Allied Powers further directs the Japanese Imperial Government to send to his headquarters at Manila, Philippine Islands, a competent representative empowered to receive in the name of the Emperor of Japan, the Japanese Imperial Government, and the Japanese Imperial General Headquarters certain requirements for carrying into effect the terms of surrender. The above representative will present to the Supreme Commander for the Allied Powers upon his arrival a document authenticated by the Emperor of Japan empowering him to receive the requirements of the Supreme Commander for the Allied Powers.
>
> The representative will be accompanied

by competent advisors representing the Japanese army, the Japanese navy, and the Japanese air force; the latter advisor will be thoroughly familiar with airborne facilities in the Tokyo area.

Procedure for transport of the above party under safe conduct is prescribed as follows: party will travel in a Japanese airplane to an airdrome on the island of Ie Shima, from which point they will by transported to Manila, Philippine Islands, in Able United States airplane. They will be returned to Japan in the same manner. Party will employ an unmarked airplane, type Zero model 22, Love two dog three. Such airplane will be painted all white and will bear upon the sides of the fuselage and top and bottom of each wing green crosses easily recognized at five hundred yards. The airplane will be capable of in-flight voice communications, in English, on Able frequency of 6970 kilocycles. Airplane will proceed to an airdrome on the island of Ie Shima, identified by two white crosses prominently displayed in the center of the runway. The exact date and hour this airplane will depart from Sata Misaki, on the southern tip of Kyushu, the route and altitude of flight and estimated time of arrival in Ie Shima, will be broadcast six hours in advance, in English, from Tokyo on a frequency of 16125 kilocycles. Acknowledgment by radio from this headquarters of the receipt of such broadcast is required prior to takeoff of the airplane. Weather permitting, the airplane will depart from Sata Misaki between the hours of 0800 and 1100 Tokyo time on the seventeenth day of August 1945. In communications regarding this flight, the code designation "Bataan" will be employed.

The airplane will approach Ie Shima on Able course of 180 degrees and circle landing field at 1000 feet or below the cloud layer until joined by an escort of United States Army P-38s which will lead it to Able landing. Such escort may join the airplane prior to arrival at Ie Shima. (signed) MacArthur.

Such attention to detail, typical of MacArthur, had characterized every attack from Guadalcanal to the Philippines. When the Nazis sent their surrender party to Reims, France, on May 7, 1945, which I covered and broadcast in detail to the United States immediately following President Truman's radio announcement from the White House, the party came under far less elaborate instructions, from General Eisenhower, who at one time served as MacArthur's prewar aide in Manila. The Germans were to fly along a designated air corridor from Admiral Doenitz's headquarters in Flanders to Reims, where they were to be picked up by U.S. Army staff cars and whisked to a red brick schoolhouse, where surrender in Europe would take place.

From the airfield outside Tokyo, the Japanese surrender party of sixteen made it to Manila after twelve hours of flying. Army Vice Chief of Staff Torashiro Kawabe led his surrender group down the steps from the C-54 that had picked them up on Ie Shima, a small island off Okinawa. They were met at Nichols Field, southwest of Manila, by Brigadier General Courtney Whitney and driven to comfortable temporary quarters at the Rosario Apartments, a two-story building two blocks from the Manila Hotel, which was in ruins. After dinner they went as a group to General MacArthur's headquarters in the shell-pocked city hall. They were met there by

General Sutherland and his staff, who would be conducting the surrender conference. MacArthur now considered himself Hirohito's vanquisher in war and equal in peace. He understood that this Japanese delegation also considered him in such terms, and he knew he would hence be more effective if he remained aloof.

For eight hours the discussions went on, Kawabe handing over detailed maps of Japanese army and navy installations, and locations of submarines, mines, and minefields. Sutherland submitted MacArthur's instructions in regard to disarmament and the reception and billeting of U.S. troops in Japan. The Americans wanted to land at the Atsugi air base on August 23, but Kawabe explained this was the kamikaze training field and that even in the wake of the Emperor's surrender broadcast there were diehards at this suicide air base who would relish bombing the first American aircraft to land. Kawabe said that a five-day grace period would allow him to move in troops and neutralize the place. Sutherland agreed. Next, the locations of prisoner-of-war camps throughout Indochina were pinpointed for him. Sutherland declared that U.S. aircraft would be dropping emergency medical supplies and food into these camps as soon as possible. Finally, the Japanese were told to make the New Grand Hotel in Yokohama ready for General MacArthur and his staff in anticipation of their arrival at the Atsugi air base. Because American means of transportation could not yet be unloaded at Yokohama, Sutherland asked for fifty chauffeur-driven cars to take MacArthur's staff from Atsugi to Yokohama. Kawabe, knowing that there was a shortage of cars and other vehicles in Tokyo caused by the destructive raids of American bombers, nodded hesitantly.

The conference did not end until early morning, when the Japanese representatives were driven back to their quarters, tired and overwhelmed by the details of the MacArthur demands. The Japanese flew back to Tokyo that very day, arriving weary, but determined for their Emperor's sake to carry out MacArthur's instructions to the letter and prepare for his arrival.

As a check on Japanese intentions, the codebreakers of Magic continued to read the Japanese military instructions to their units throughout Japan and the outside territories they still controlled. Both the Navy and Army General Staffs sent radio messages giving the background of the surrender and the reason to comply with all terms: It was the Emperor's wish. The Navy Minister sent the following message from Tokyo to "all naval establishments" on August 16:

I respectfully submit a report on the events which led to the Emperor's acceptance of the Potsdam Declaration.

With regard to this matter, several meetings were held by the Supreme Council for the Direction of the War. No agreement could be reached. Finally, it was brought to the Emperor's attention, for his decision. His, and only his, decision was to the effect that, from the standpoint of the Empire's future, the only thing to do was to accept the Potsdam Declaration on condition that the structure of the nation be left intact. The Emperor said that he fully realized that for the High Command to order the laying down of arms is a pill too bitter to swallow. However, this must be done in order to preserve our nation, he explained. He further said that he was ready to do anything and urged us to do our best.

We who were present fully realized the extent of his determination and could not hold back the tears that welled up. We advised him that we would assume the duty of controlling and maintaining order within our respective departments.

These are the events which led to the decision. At the same time—as the Emperor directed in his radio broadcast on the fifteenth—maintain order within all units so as to prevent our nation's being forced to go back to the very beginning of its history. These are the Emperor's wishes and the Emperor can best be served by obeying these orders.

The army message was similar, instructing all units to maintain discipline in the face of surrender. When MacArthur read these Magic intercepts he expressed relief. The Japanese, with a homeland army of over three million crack troops and another three million in China and Manchuria, Singapore, Burma, Hong Kong, and Formosa, could have turned on U.S. troops at any time in the first weeks of the occupation, and in a *banzai* attack could have decimated the American forces. But such rashness would have soon meant the end of Japan as it was, for President Truman would not have hesitated in ordering additional atomic bombs dropped. The prudence of Emperor Hirohito was evident in his decision not only to accept the terms of the Potsdam Declaration but also to instruct and cool down his generals and admirals for the sake of the future of Japan.

Of course, deceitful courses were followed by some bureaucratic leaders of Japan, but their actions did not involve shot and shell. Lord Privy Seal Kido, for example, directed an underground campaign that he thought would confuse the occupation army. Forty days before MacArthur landed in Japan, Kido had ordered the arrest of four hundred members of the Peace Faction, a group of business and government bureaucrats who had agreed to be conspicuously blamed for opposing the military activities of War Minister Tojo—a "resistance" or "peace" group. Kido and the secret police toiling in the Imperial Palace worked up "dossiers" for all four hundred men being held in Sugamo Prison, complete with personal histories indicating moderation of outlook and outright resistance to the war factions of government. For these outlooks and actions they had been jailed, Kido claimed, as each personal dossier pointedly indicated.

Prominent among those imprisoned was Yoshida Shigeru, a former ambassador to the Court of St. James, son-in-law of Kido, and a proponent of the Strike South offensive. When General Willoughby, MacArthur's chief of intelligence, began searching for likely leaders of a new Japanese government, he was pointed toward the imprisoned four hundred, including, of course, Shigeru. Willoughby consulted with Prime Minister Higashikuni as to an appropriate candidate for foreign minister, and Shigeru's name was put forward "because of his moderation and opposition to the military during the war." Shigeru was duly selected. As he was released from his cell by an officer and a sergeant, the latter was heard to exclaim, "That's the best-fed Jap I ever saw come out of prison." MacArthur approved Shigeru, but he remarked later in a private conversation with Emperor Hirohito, "I was aware of his entire background and his backing of the Strike South war policy. But I felt he was the best man for the job, in spite of Kido's stratagem." The Emperor replied, "I knew Kido could not fool you."

Shigeru went on to become Prime Minister, serving from 1946 to 1954, and there are few who will dispute that he served his Emperor well during those years of transition. Many others of the imprisoned Peace Faction found stature in the newly created government of Japan.

At dawn on August 28, an advance party of one hundred and fifty landed at the Atsugi air base. They were followed a day later by General Eichelberger and his staff, then on August 30 by MacArthur himself, flown there by his personal pilot of many years, Lieutenant Colonel Tony Story. No one aboard MacArthur's plane knew what was going to happen on the ground; but neither did the Japanese themselves. Prior to landing, some of MacArthur's staff started to strap on their guns, but MacArthur told them to disarm, remarking, "Nothing will impress them like a show of absolute fearlessness. If they don't know they're licked, this will convince them." Eichelberger, on the ground waiting for the approach of MacArthur's C-54, *Bataan*, was concerned that kamikaze pilots were about. When the aircraft landed and Mac-Arthur stepped to the ground, a modest American band gathered there played the National Anthem, and the General saluted and walked to a waiting Japanese car, commenting to Eichelberger, "Well, Bob, it's been a long road from Melbourne to Tokyo, but as they say in the movies, this is the payoff." They stepped into an ancient Lincoln while the remainder of the staff got into a procession of ragtag vehicles, all Kawabe could muster from bombed-out Yokohama. The long drive from Atsugi to Yokohama produced another surprise: the route was lined with thirty thousand Japanese infantrymen, bayonets fixed to their rifles, their backs to the roadway along which the American cavalcade passed. This was a sign of submission to and respect for the Supreme Commander; it served also to prevent any possible rash attack from a roaming group of soldiers wearing white headbands and calling themselves the *Sonno Joi Gigun*, the Righteous Group for Upholding Imperial Rule and Driving Out Foreigners.

It was a depressing route through the outskirts of Yokohama to the New Grand Hotel. High explosives and firebombs had taken their toll; as far as the eye could see there was destruction. Although other buildings still

stood, the hotel among them, the American firebomb-
ings had destroyed 80 percent of the city. The people
appeared emaciated, as had the residents of Tokyo. But
the owner of the New Grand Hotel, Yozo Nomura, had
managed to dress in formal attire, with winged collar and
striped trousers, and he stepped forward to greet Mac-
Arthur and express the wish to make him comfortable.

MacArthur took his meals in the main dining room
with his staff. On the second evening he heard a
commotion in the entryway, and he looked up to see
Lieutenant General Jonathan M. Wainwright, the man
he had left in command of Corregidor and Bataan when
he had been commanded by President Roosevelt to
depart from the Philippines for Australia. Wainwright
had aged greatly, appeared haggard—his hair was snow
white and his skin like parchment—after having survived a Japanese prison camp in Manchuria. He had
been liberated by the Russians, traveled to Mukden by
train, then by a C-47 to Chungking and on to Manila.
Now here he was again, a courageous officer who
doubted he would ever again command an army unit.
MacArthur embraced him, saying, "Jim, your old corps
is yours when you want it." MacArthur could eat no
more, so moved was he by the appearance of Wainwright, and soon got up and went to his room.

Two days after that incident, on September 2, 1945,
formal surrender of Japan took place aboard the USS
Missouri, soon followed by a private meeting between
General MacArthur and Emperor Hirohito. Both knew
this meeting would signify to the Japanese people the
Emperor's approval of MacArthur as a person he could
work with in rebuilding Japan. It was an obligatory
meeting; both men regarded it as a symbol of easing the
climate around the occupation forces in the reconstruction period that lay ahead.

General MacArthur moved his command head-quarters from Yokohama to Tokyo on September 18, and established his Supreme Command Allied Powers (SCAP) offices in the Dai Ichi building, formerly Japanese army headquarters for the Tokyo region.

From his offices on the sixth floor of the Dai Ichi building, MacArthur would gaze across at the Imperial Palace and visualize Emperor Hirohito at work on his plans for the Japan of the future. And here MacArthur was to institute many reforms himself: a new bill of rights for the people; a new constitution to be approved by popular vote in 1946 and become law in 1947; the emancipation of women; the right of labor to organize; the elimination of cant and mythology from school textbooks.

But in 1945, foremost on MacArthur's and Hirohito's minds was the economy. Factories had to be rebuilt so there could be employment; without jobs the people would move around in a veritable vacuum. There had to be direction and leadership, and the Zaibatsu families could provide it, but the tight control the twelve families had exercised on the economy and people of Japan was on MacArthur's elimination list. In fact, these families *were* the economy; they were the leaders of business, industry, and banking. And until the Supreme Allied Powers leader made his intentions toward them clear they would play a waiting game; the factories would remain idle, and the people, generally, jobless.

There was another aspect to this problem: in the months before surrender, when defeat was in the wind, the Zaibatsu had moved their liquid wealth from Japan to the safety of Switzerland. The Emperor had also been advised to do so. The Zaibatsu, including the Imperial Household Zaibatsu, were thus poor in Japan but rich in Switzerland. So while they waited, the Emperor pondered how soon this overseas wealth controlled by the influentials of Japan could again be used openly for the economic revival of the nation.

In 1945, the financial investigators of SCAP placed Hirohito's personal fortune at more than one hundred million dollars. The Imperial property amounted to one and a half million yen, excluding jewels, art objects, and gold and silver bullion. SCAP accounting stated Hirohito had three hundred thirty million yen in cash and securities; three hundred sixty million yen in land; five hundred ninety million yen in lumber and timber holdings; and two hundred ninety million yen in buildings. The term "land" included forests, farms, real estate upon which office buildings and other structures stood, duck-hunting grounds, railroad sites, storage yards, and the Shinjuki Gardens.

In a move to transfer most of these assets into the general mainstream economy, both General MacArthur and Ambassador George Atcheson, Jr., chief of the Diplomatic Section of the State Department and one of MacArthur's political advisors, approved, with Hirohito's consent, the following insertion as Article 84 in the new constitution drafted for Japan:

> All property of the Imperial Household, other than the hereditary estates, shall belong to the State. The income from all Imperial properties shall be paid into the national treasury, and allowances and expenses of the Imperial Household, as defined by law, shall be appropriated by the Diet [Japan's general legislative assembly] in the annual budget. The actual transfer of the property of the Imperial Household to the State is to be effected when the new constitution becomes effective.

Hirohito was permitted to make the announcement of the news contained in Article 84 from the Palace to the people as part of the MacArthur-Hirohito goodwill campaign.

But it was the personal wealth of the Emperor that the economic division of SCAP wanted to shake loose. A confidential report stated, in part:

> By virtue of his position as head of the state, the Emperor of Japan has direct control of a large fortune . . . This immense fortune presents special problems to the military government. The convertibility of a good part of the properties to cash makes them particularly susceptible to use in financing hostile political and military activities . . .

At the start of the occupation, U.S. investigators had gone through the vaults of the Imperial Household. They had come upon jewelry, gold bullion, silver bullion, and coins that totaled a mere 3,010,066 yen. As the yen at that time was worth about 360 to the U.S. dollar, the cache amounted to a mere two million dollars. Answers were hence wanted to a simple question: Where had the Hirohito liquid wealth vanished to? Seeking a source of reparations, the Joint Chiefs of Staff sent the following priority message to Supreme Headquarters in Tokyo on January 21, 1947:

> Imperial Family or his or her nominees have been placed beyond the effective control of the Diet. For this purpose the commission desires to have a detailed and complete schedule of all properties and possessions, except purely personal items of comparatively small value or objets d'art, of the Imperial House,

171

the Imperial Household, and all members of the Imperial Family and their nominees, as at the moment of surrender, showing against each item the manner in which it has been disposed of.

Looking through Hirohito's securities portfolio of the time, I found that securities owned by the Imperial Household fell into three categories: corporation stocks, corporate bonds, and government bonds. The Imperial Household Zaibatsu had bonds of the Nippon Yusen Kaisha (Japan Mail Steamship Company), and great quantities of national bonds bought during the Russo-Japanese war of 1905 that had grown in value in the ensuing years. The Emperor, through his chief of the Imperial Treasury Bureau—the *Haizo-to*—held impressive shares (1,062,674) in thirty banks and corporations, all blue-chip, including corporations established by the Zaibatsu in Manchuria after the army's conquest of that land. The heaviest concentration of crown investments, three-quarters of all the commercial stock held, was in banking institutions. Shipping companies were next, then mining, paper, railroads, sugar, and utilities. Stock was held also in insurance, trust, and colonialization companies in such locales as Manchuria and China, and later companies established in Singapore, Hong Kong, Formosa, and the Dutch East Indies.

Disposition of the Imperial money had a further pattern: it was always invested in safe or sure ventures. There were Imperial holdings, for instance, in the Nippon Yusen Kaisha (Japan Mail Steamship Company) and the Osaka Shosen Kaisha (Osaka Commercial Ship & Company), both of which participated in the shipping administration of all occupied territories. As the U.S. military intelligence stated: "It is clear that the Imperial Household is at least indirectly engaged, therefore, in financing the Pacific war." This SCAP report went on to state: "The Imperial Household indicates a community of interest with the older Zaibatsu (big business) concerns, such as the Mitsui, Mitsubishi, and Sumitomo trusts and the Tokyo Electric Light Company." For the most part Imperial Household stock holdings scattered through many large enterprises were acquired as investments rather than for the purpose of enterprise management.

The Imperial Household, through the *Haizo-to*, held 47 percent of the authorized shares of the Bank of Japan, the central bank and the most powerful financial institution in Japan. In addition to its general short-term paper, and purchase and sale of government bonds, by means of which it regulated the circulation of currency and the money market, the Bank of Japan could undertake directly the financing of industry and the purchase and sale of corporate debentures. By means of its note-issuance power and its fixing of the discount rate, in particular, it could go far toward determining the success or failure of an inflationary or anti-inflationary policy. And though compared to ordinary corporations the powers of the stockholders in the Bank of Japan were severely limited by law, Imperial Household holdings were sufficient to give implicit power above and beyond the 47 percent of their shares.

It was, however, the Emperor's stockholdings in the Yokohama Specie Bank, a private bank and not as rigidly controlled as the Bank of Japan, that gave him clout in European financial markets. With a 22-percent ownership of 224,912 shares, the Emperor was by far the most substantial stockholder; the next highest held but twenty-two thousand shares. And by virtue of its stockholder rights the Imperial Household always controlled the General Meeting of the Yokohama Specie Bank. After all, who would confront the Emperor and his fiscal aides when they planned to increase the profits of the bank and in so doing the wealth of all the shareholders? When, for example, the German Reichsbank transferred ten million Reichsmarks in a payment to the Yokohama Specie branch in Switzerland for war materials purchased by Germany from Japan, the profitability of the entire bank increased.

The Yokohama Specie Bank, under tight control by the government, was not as powerful an institution as the Bank of Japan, but as the official foreign exchange institution, it had been specifically empowered to discount, buy and sell, and deal in and collect payments on foreign and domestic bills of exchange, drafts, promissory notes, and other negotiable instruments. Thus it held considerable potential power over the direction and volume of foreign trade in general and specific export and import companies in particular. Unlike the procedure in the Bank of Japan, the General Meeting of Shareholders elected the board of directors, which in turn elected the officers of the bank (though the Minister of Finance had to approve the election of the directors). Where the government laid down Bank of Japan policy subject to veto by the shareholders, the shareholders laid down Yokohama Specie Bank policy subject to veto by the government. It was apparent, then, that by virtue of its property rights, if wielded skillfully, the Crown had great power over the foreign trade of Japan and its own profits.

U.S. fiscal investigators concentrated their efforts on getting a true accounting of Hirohito's liquid and easily transported wealth. There was little Hirohito could do to conceal forests and museums, so he did as MacArthur had suggested and took credit for assigning some of it to the State. But the stocks and bonds and the gold and sensitive records that were in vaults of the Bank of Japan had largely disappeared when SCAP went searching for them. Bank officials politely explained that records had been burned up in the American fire raids. As for any gold, they knew nothing about that, they said.

When the SCAP financial report was transmitted to the Joint Chiefs of Staff, it contained an appendage, an escape clause. "No representation as to accuracy is made by this Division," it proclaimed. Quite simply, the SCAP had been unable to penetrate the mazes and thickets of concealment that had been erected around the Emperor's movable wealth. It had been discovered that bankers and financiers who customarily handled the business affairs of the Emperor and the Imperial Treasury, as well as those who took care of such matters for other Zaibatsu groups, were the most skilled and sophisticated investment bankers in the Far East.

In January 1944, when Hirohito had received reports from his chiefs of the army and navy that war in the Pacific could not be won after all, he had instructed Lord Privy Seal Kido to make plans for peace. Kido quite understandably took this to mean he should preserve the Imperial Treasury first, then prepare a plan that would move Japan into a peacetime mode. It was too soon to effect the second circumstance, but the first could get under way at once. Kido called a meeting of Japan's leading bankers, who were also financial advisors to the Throne. On their recommendation funds were transferred from Tokyo to Switzerland by bank wire, on a bank-to-bank basis, thus virtually emptying out the Emperor's cash reserves in Tokyo while sharply augmenting balances in his Swiss numbered accounts. Yokohama Specie then drew into Hirohito's Swiss bank-masked investment credits from the Greater Third Reich, which added further to his liquidity. Other Zaibatsu big-business leaders, aware of the money outflow, likewise began transferring their liquid assets to accounts in Switzerland, drawing on cash deposited in Afghanistan,

Turkey, Spain, Portugal, Sweden, Korea, Hong Kong, Manchuria, France, and Germany. They also added to their corporate and personal accounts in Buenos Aires.

Yokohama Specie Bank was to be taken over during the occupation by the Central Bank of Japan. This ensured the continued financial secrecy of the Imperial fortune.

The next problem that confronted Kido was how to shift gold kilo bars from the Imperial Treasury in the Palace to accounts in Switzerland.

U.S. military intelligence officers in Tokyo had gone through the Emperor's accounts, both in the Palace itself and in the fourteen banks in which he held shares. They were convinced that Lord Privy Seal Kido, anticipating the defeat of his country, had shifted the Imperial gold reserves to some foreign location in 1944. It seemed only logical and sensible that these gold reserves, a national asset, should be transported to safety.

Of course, all warring nations have fallback positions when defeat looms. In 1940, just after Dunkirk, when England stood alone and unarmed except for the Royal Air Force, Winston Churchill and his government had their fallback position. If Hitler dropped parachute divisions on England, and followed it up with an invasion force, Churchill and his cabinet planned to escape to Canada and set up their Government in Exile in Ottawa. Gold and other treasure from the Bank of England had already been shipped under great secrecy to Canada in the summer of 1940.

While it was strongly suspected that Hirohito's gold had been moved to a foreign safe haven, there were two theories as to precisely where it had been placed. Some U.S. financial intelligence officers were of the belief that Kido had had the Imperial gold flown to Hong Kong in several trips of special courier aircraft protected by squadrons of Japanese Zeros, plausible because the Japanese still controlled the air space over the northwest Pacific. Refueling was possible at Formosa, before going on to Hong Kong, where the gold could have been put up for sale on the Asiatic markets—gold is highly valued in wartime—and the currencies paid for it transferred to Zurich by bank wireless (from the Yokohama Specie Bank branch in this British crown colony, which had been under firm control of the Japanese army since early 1942).

Other intelligence officers thought that the transfer had been to South America by Japanese submarines. The gold need not have been sold; rather it could have been sequestered in a Deutsche Bank or Swiss bank depository in Buenos Aires. The Japanese navy, these proponents said, certainly was capable of getting the gold bullion out of about-to-be-defeated Japan, even in 1944. After all, their submarine squadrons had made it with ease to Pearl Harbor in 1941, and those that had escaped U.S. retaliation had returned safely to Japan. And in 1943 and 1944, Japanese freighter submarines of the I-52 class had made frequent trips from Japan to Kiel, Germany, returning with such weaponry as the famed and dreaded V-1 rocket bombs that Hirohito hoped would help defend Japan. Although a South American destination for gold shipments meant a long ocean trip, freighter submarines could well have refueled at Rabaul, an island still controlled by Japan. The submarines could have then proceeded through the South Pacific to one of several ports friendly to Japan and Germany (in Chile, for example) for fuel and food. Then, by going down along the west coast of South America and rounding the tip of the continent by traversing the Strait of Magellan, any Japanese submarines would have clear traveling up the east coast of South America to the River Plate, the estuary leading to Buenos Aires, where Evita and Juan Perón ruled supreme.

Perón in 1944 still believed the Axis would win the war. He was planning a haven and all possible assistance to Martin Bormann and others of the Nazi leadership and their Japanese allies. The Argentine leader so admired Hitler that he had learned German in order to read *Mein Kampf* in the original; Perón's own aide was the son of a prominent Nazi. A payment by Bormann of one hundred million dollars to Perón's account in Switzerland had helped cement their friendship, as had a joint account that Bormann and Perón held in Deutsche Bank of Buenos Aires, an account consisting of several solid currencies and such valuables as diamonds and platinum, with a total value exceeding four hundred million dollars. A footnote to this fiscal history is that once Perón had fled to exile in Panama and subsequently in Madrid, he was unable to touch his secret account in Switzerland. Bormann had blocked it, holding that Perón had been amply paid for services rendered up to that time. So Perón, denied the five hundred million dollars he had deposited in this "retirement" account over the years, had to be dependent on a relatively modest account in Madrid to sustain him and his new wife on his estate outside the Spanish capital. (After Isabel, successor to Evita, had assumed the presidency in Buenos Aires upon Perón's death, she felt compelled to loot the Argentinian treasury by the ruse of a check scam, for which she was caught and placed for more than a year under house arrest, until she was allowed to return to Madrid. The five hundred million dollars in Zurich still cannot be touched, and benefits no one but the Swiss bankers. There is a mystery here to tantalize an investigator.)

But did Lord Privy Seal Kido really ship the Emperor's gold to South America by submarine? Very likely. Kido performed for Hirohito as Bormann did for Hitler. In 1944, Kido learned from his ambassador in Berlin, General Hiroshi Oshima, that the Vice Fuehrer was moving the gold of the Reichsbank and other assets by U-boat from Kiel to South America. To Kido this was a clear signal that the Nazi leadership, in concert with German business leaders, believed the war in Europe was coming to a close. If this shipment method worked for Germany, it would also work for Japan, Kido believed.

Deutsche Bank in Buenos Aires would certainly have welcomed Japanese shipments of gold. So would the local depository of any Swiss bank, which as a matter of policy accepted gold bullion, telegraphing the credit to the client's account in Zurich. (Major Swiss banks have five such depositories around the world. They are referred to as "locos." Getting gold into a loco is as good as depositing it on Swiss soil.)

It was Kido's and Hirohito's belief that placing the Emperor's gold beyond the reach of the Allies would provide postwar stability for the Throne. Such a treasure, including the cash already on deposit in Zurich, would be of great assistance in the rebuilding of Japan. The Zaibatsu would need their own funds and loans from time to time from the Imperial treasure to rebuild factories and put people to work in the hard days of reconstruction. (As the occupation took hold, incidentally, the plan did work, Hirohito's own version of the Marshall Plan.) General MacArthur was aware of the Emperor's missing gold and transferred currencies, but chose to ignore it. He had other priorities, among them the revival of an industrial nation on which America's future security in the Pacific would depend.

While MacArthur looked at the big picture, he allowed his staff to continue their program of restructuring the Imperial Household. A force of three thousand civil servants made it no small operation, so SCAP began transferring many duties to the Diet. SCAP also ruled that all members of the Imperial Family give up their titles and become commoners, except for the Emperor and the Empress and Hirohito's immediate male relatives, his sons and brothers. The day this order went into effect, Hirohito presided over a sad ceremony in the Palace. Fifty-one "sisters, cousins, and aunts" gathered, and in a royal ceremony the Emperor walked from person to person, apologizing for their loss of royal status. With their loss of titles went their royal stipends, although each was granted a lump-sum gift and permanent ownership of their homes and villas. They would thereafter be on the tax rolls like everyone else.

With the transfer of Imperial lands and museums to the State now complete, the Diet was to be held responsible for the upkeep of the Imperial Family. In 1947 Hirohito was granted twenty-two thousand tax-free dollars a year. By the end of the occupation in 1952 this figure had been raised to eighty-three thousand, and has been increased substantially since. In addition, the Diet began a number of special building funds. In 1959, the villa of the Crown Prince was rebuilt, as was the Imperial Library. In 1967, construction was finished on a new palace that cost over thirty-six million dollars; it is a handsome edifice complete with an underground garage for one hundred twenty cars. Hirohito was to amass an official personal bankroll in Tokyo estimated at fifty million dollars from judicious investments in hi-tech electronic companies and hotels. These investments were made possible by the hidden Imperial fortune in Switzerland, estimated at three billion dollars. For lending some of this money to various commercial leadership families, he had been repaid with remarkable investment opportunities.

But in the 1945–46 period, an era of replanning by SCAP, first priority was given to the Imperial Household. Focus on the Zaibatsu would come later. Walter LeCount, Chief of the Finance Division of SCAP, sent a memorandum to the chief of the Economic and Scientific Section in which he outlined the following points of major importance in the transition of the Imperial Household to a government bureau. In this memorandum he said:

> The most significant change has been to subordinate the Emperor to the people's will, thus preventing his being used by special interests. To accomplish this, it has been necessary to:
> a. Completely change the emphasis of the constitution from one in which the Emperor was granting the people certain rights while reserving the ultimate authority himself to one which accords sovereign rights to the people as a whole;
> b. remove from the Emperor the private wealth which has given him an immense personal power and prestige quite apart from constitutional provisions; and
> c. eliminate as much as possible special treatment to the Imperial Household (e.g., the transformation of the Imperial Household Ministry into an ordinary government agency, taxation of the private wealth of the Imperial Family, etc.).

LeCount pointed out, however, that most of the "changes that have taken place up to now are paper changes and that continued surveillance by SCAP is necessary."

The editors of the big Tokyo daily newspapers were undergoing voluntary changes themselves. They were now operating with a freedom they had not known for more than a decade. The army and navy bureaus of propaganda, together with Hirohito's censorship czar, had until now exercised firm control over Japanese newspapers and radio. In addition, the Thought Control police could throw anyone in prison who did not think in a government-prescribed fashion. The buildup to the Pearl Harbor attack and the war against the United States and Great Britain had been preceded by a propaganda campaign to condition the Japanese people that Japan was sufficiently strong to win such a war. In fact, as Lord Privy Seal Kido testified to American interrogators during March 1946 in Sugamo Prison: "If someone was writing articles in opposition to the military program, they would be officially warned. And from behind the scenes they were intimidated and threatened. The Japanese press in those days was not a free press."

When the Tokyo press found new freedom after the war, great was the soul-searching as to who was responsible for the military defeat. Takasaki Masaki of Kyoto Imperial University, writing in the *Mainichi Shimbun*, ascribed the defeat of Japan to "Japanese subjectivity and inferior social morality, together with inferior material culture." This opinion was echoed in the newspapers *Asahi* and *Yomiuri-Hochi*.

There appeared only one statement in the Japanese newspapers that specifically placed the blame for defeat on the people's lack of political participation, their unquestioning following of army and navy and Imperial Palace leadership. *Asahi* published the statement that "extreme faith in military force also was responsible for a general ignorance and low level of political intelligence in the people."

Most Japanese press statements following surrender were ambiguous. There was no attempt to fix responsibility for Japan's downfall on individuals. From the Imperial Palace to the Prime Minister's office on down, there was an effort to generalize the responsibility for the war, to cancel the war as simply a bad job and direct the public's attention to the future.

Hirohito wanted the occupation to move forward smoothly. He wanted no firebrands and guerillas upsetting his surrender agreement. On September 4, he drove across the famous double moat bridge to address the Diet on the obligations of surrender. He had been told that some members were restless and might make trouble for Japan, that they were looking to Russia rather than to MacArthur, who represented the West and the best future for Japan, as he saw it. I was present when Hirohito gave this memorable address, his first public speech since he agreed to the Potsdam Declaration. Speaking in court Japanese, he stated:

> We issued some days ago a proclamation of the cessation of hostilities, and We dispatched Our plenipotentiaries and caused them to sign the documents relating thereto. It is Our desire that Our people will surmount the manifold hardships and trials which attend the termination of war, and make manifest the innate glory of Japan's national polity, win the confidence of the world, establish firmly a peaceful state and contribute to the progress of mankind. Our thoughts are constantly directed to that end. In the consummation of that great task, beware most strictly of any outburst of emotion which may engender needless complications, or any fraternal contention and strife which may create confusion, lead you astray and cause you to

lose the confidence of the world. At home, cultivate the ways of righteousness, foster nobility of the spirit, and work with resolution so you may enhance the innate glory of the Imperial State and keep pace with the progress of the world.

Hirohito also asked his audience to remember to assist the sick and wounded, and called for a united nation dedicated to a better future. When he had completed his address, Hirohito bowed stiffly and walked from the Diet Chamber and returned to the Palace. There were no cheers; in fact, there were some catcalls. Hirohito knew his prestige was at a low ebb, and alone in the Palace he wondered what steps he could take to burnish his image.

The people themselves adored the Emperor. An example of their feeling toward him was the reaction when news got around Japan in the first weeks of occupation that the Emperor was living in untidiness. The gardeners had been let go as part of Brigadier General Courtney Whitney's moves to trim the Imperial Household staff.

So the elders of village councils asked for volunteers to help clean up the Imperial Palace and its grounds; transportation would be paid for by village councils. Volunteers, mainly old men and women, soon began arriving with their own brooms. These sweeping parties grew to such numbers that lists were made as to which groups would sweep and in what order. What started out as a simple desire to help the Emperor soon became an honor, a veritable pilgrimage. The magnitude of these sweeping parties, which sometimes reached twenty thousand participants, was an indication to SCAP that the common people of Japan revered this diminutive and brilliant man.

Still, letters from Japanese citizens poured into MacArthur's headquarters urging that Hirohito be deposed, as punishment for his leadership in a war that had ended in disaster. During one of their many confidential talks, MacArthur suggested to Hirohito how he could improve his image among the general public. He urged Hirohito to get out among his people, "like our Presidents do, and court favor. Show you are a king among men, not a divine God." Hirohito nodded in agreement. If this American general thought it wise to eliminate divine pretensions publicly in the interests of preserving the Throne itself, then the Emperor would do so. The program to humanize his image started with his issuance of an Imperial Rescript on New Year's Day. The Rescript read:

> We stand by the people and we wish always to share with them in their moments of joy and sorrow. The ties between us and our people have always stood upon mutual trust and affection. They do not depend on mere legends and myths. They are not predicated on the false conception that the Emperor is divine and that the Japanese people are superior to other races, and fated to rule the world.

General MacArthur then issued these comments to the Japanese press on Hirohito's New Year's Day message:

> The Emperor's New Year's message pleases me very much. By it he undertakes a leading part in the democratization of his people. He squarely takes his stand for the future along liberal lines. His action reflects the irresistible influence of a sound idea. A sound idea cannot be stopped.

Edwin W. Pauley had been sent to Tokyo by President Truman to determine a program of reparations from Japan. In a message to the President dated December 18, 1945, a copy of which went to General MacArthur, Pauley said that after several months of studying Japan, China—excluding Manchuria—southern Korea, and the Philippines, he had come to the following conclusions:

a. In preparation for war against the United Nations, in aggression in China, and in war against the United Nations, Japan built up the most diversified and overexpanded industrial economy in Asia.

b. In spite of extensive destruction, especially in the closing phases of the war, Japan has left within her four main islands more industrial capacity than she needs or has ever used for her civilian economy.

c. The removal of the surplus, especially to neighboring Asiatic countries and also to other countries whose war effort and sacrifice entitle them to reparations, will help to raise their industrial standards and living standards without depressing the industrial standards and living standards of Japan, since only excess capacities are at the moment in question.

d. A program of interim removals should be announced to other claimant nations immediately, and the successive actions of seizure, inventory, packing and shipment should follow in the shortest possible time in order to make both the framework of policy and the course of action uncompromisingly clear. Interim removals will, in most cases, be below the total quantities that may eventually be allocated to reparations, but the sooner the interim removal program is made clear to the Japanese, the sooner they will see that they cannot rely definitely on certain things in order to build a peaceful, democratic Japan, and the better it will be for them as well as for us.

e. The immediate reparation program from Japan will deal only with capital goods, that is, with machinery and plants. At this stage it appears that any exportable current production will be required to meet costs of necessary imports and of occupation, which will be a first charge on exports ahead of reparations.

f. Japan should be deprived immediately of all industrial and financial interests outside her four main islands and such minor islands as may be left to Japan in accordance with the Potsdam Declaration.

g. Japan's gold and precious metals should be shipped to the United States to be held in custody. It should be made clear to the Japanese as soon as possible that they cannot rely on the use of this gold for her own purposes.

h. As an aid in opening up the road for the development of democracy in Japan, the whole reparations program should be administered in the manner best designed to break up the influence of the big holding companies, known as Zaibatsu, in the economic and political life of Japan.

Pauley went on to say that aside from gold held in Japan, there was practically no foreign exchange presently available to pay for costs of occupation or essential imports. "Unlike Germany, Japan has practically no assets in neutral countries, and Japan's gold holdings will probably approximate two hundred million dollars," he said, a grave factual error.

Japan was indeed a poor country by the time of surrender, a situation that prompted one Japanese witness to the surrender ceremonies aboard the USS *Missouri* to comment: "How was it that Japan, a poor country, had had the temerity to wage war against the combination of so many powerful nations? Indeed, it was Japan against the whole world." The poverty and devastation of Tokyo and the surrounding regions certainly illustrated the comments. The Japanese had accomplished what they had by decades of hard work, dedication to the Emperor and their nation, and skillful management by the business leaders of Japan.

Now the management groups of the nation were to be dissolved by order of the Supreme Commander, "to permit a wider distribution of income and of ownership of the means of production and trade," which, it was hoped, would encourage the development within Japan of economic ways and institutions of a type that would contribute to the growth of peaceful and democratic forces.

This move to outlaw the Zaibatsu economic structure was made after long and careful investigation by the appropriate economic and legal investigators within MacArthur's Supreme Command, who had concluded that the great monopolies that had expanded since the invasion of Manchuria and China in 1931 had vastly increased their power during the course of the Pacific war. So strong had these monopolies become that the government simply could not control their will. Rather, the government ruled on terms set by the Zaibatsu. A memorandum prepared by Solir Horwitz of the SCAP legal and trial staff concluded as follows:

> The predominance of the business group in Japan's ruling coalition . . . was, in fact, fully expressed in the Cabinets which both preceded and followed the Manchurian invasion of September 18, 1931, all the way down to Pearl Harbor. At that time Tojo was chosen by the monopolists, among others, as the most reliable and efficient instrument for the military conquest of Greater East Asia. Thereafter the forced growth of heavy industry and the still greater concentration of vested monopoly interests . . . merely confirmed and extended the dominant position by the Zaibatsu in the Japanese regime.

So on December 12, 1945, the order went out from MacArthur's headquarters to freeze the funds of the most powerful and important of the Zaibatsu families and 336 companies until such time as a mutually agreeable program could be put into effect. "Business will continue as usual and there will be no interference with management of these companies." But what was mutually agreeable would be hard to determine, for the Zaibatsu groups had been summarily outlawed by MacArthur.

Among those cited by MacArthur's order were the family corporations constituting the first team of Japanese industry:

1. House of Mitsui
   Baron Takakimi Mitsui, President
   Jihei Inoue, Chairman, Board of Directors

2. House of Mitsubishi (Mitsubishi is a trade name and is translated "Three Chestnuts." The surname of the controlling family is Iwasaki.)

> Baron Koyata Iwasaki, President and head of the family
> Hikoyata Iwasaki, Vice President
> Kiyoshi Goko, Chairman, Board of Directors of Mitsubishi Heavy Industries
> Shintaro Motora, President of Mitsubishi Heavy Industries

3. House of Sumitomo

> Baron Kichizaemon Sumitomo, Jr., head of family Shunosuke Furuta, Chairman, Board of Directors of Sumitomo Honsha
> Kiichi Mimura, President, Sumitomo Heavy Industries

4. Others

House of Yasuda	Hajime Yasuda
House of Okura	Baron Kishichiro Okura
House of Kawasaki	Hajime Kawasaki
House of Konoike	Baron Zenyemon (Zenuemon)
House of Nomura (Nomura Gomei)	Yoshitaro Nomura
House of Yamaguchi	Kichirobi Yamaguchi
House of Nezu	Kaichiro Nezu
House of Okawa	Tetsuo Okawa
House of Asano	Soichiro Asano
House of Kuhara	Fusanosuke Kuhara
House of Terada	Jinkichi Terada

| House of | Takeo Katakura |
| Katakura | |

MacArthur's financial officers noted that to determine actual economic power at a level below these family-controlled corporations was to enter a maze of financial interests—overlapping directorships, holding companies, exchange stock ownership, and similar complexities—through all the major industries of Japan. As for banking, in 1944 there were 1,299 family-name banks—for example, Mitsubishi, Yasuda, Nomura—and 3,695 local banks.

Simultaneous with dissolution of the Zaibatsu, the Economic Division of SCAP turned its attention to the financial institutions that had been operating under Japanese control outside the four main islands of Japan. Among these institutions were the central banks of Korea, Formosa, and Manchuria, as well as a vast network of corporations. Branches of these banks in Japan were closed down and the assets of central banks within other countries were taken over by the new governments of these countries. Regarding the overseas corporations, SCAP noted that "A large number of small creditors, principally depositors in the banking institutions and debenture holders, resided in Japan proper. Within Japan these companies held shares in and claims on many domestic Japanese concerns, and their interrelationships with other segments of the Japanese economy were close and with many ramifications . . . a major problem of the occupation authorities has been the stewardship of their Japanese assets, and the performance of managerial functions such as voting the stock held by the institutions in other Japanese concerns."

Handling this aspect of Japan's financial structure and attendant problems of liquidation could have been monumental, so SCAP delegated the task to the Bank of

Japan, at the same time referring the stewardship of other assets to a Committee of Conservators, an agency of the Japanese Ministry of Finance. SCAP recommended the "liquidation of the Japanese assets by sale to unobjectionable Japanese natural or juridical persons, payment of Japanese creditors senior in claim to shareholders, and the turning over of the residual assets to the Japanese Government against which foreign claims on the Japanese assets of the institutions would be made on a government to government level." It was an imperfect solution, since MacArthur had few Supreme Command finance professionals, but such major shifts as were made in the Japanese fiscal and economic situation did serve to ventilate and ease the economic vise of the Zaibatsu.

It was not MacArthur's intention to destroy economically the men who had developed these corporate institutions nor even the companies themselves. Rather, MacArthur wanted an easing of total control over the Japanese economy by the very few. MacArthur recognized that, as a fundamental measure to encourage competitive operation of the Japanese economy, the number of independent sources of credit should be increased substantially. The strengthening of local savings banks and of rural and urban credit cooperatives, as well as of independent local banks, was encouraged.

To speed this process of strong fiscal independence, the former owners of independent financial institutions that had been merged under duress with Zaibatsu concerns were likewise encouraged to reestablish their old enterprises through forced Zaibatsu divestiture, backed by SCAP. The SCAP spelled out a procedure through which former owners of merged banks, trust companies, or insurance companies had the opportunity for a limited period of time to compel the institutions to reshape into their former structures. But it was like attempting to put eggs back into their shells: it did not work out, although it had seemed like a good idea. As in Germany, where Allied occupation forces ordered the three main banks—Deutsche, Dresdner, and Commerzbank—to split into segments as a way of diffusing financial monopoly, so it was in Japan. When the occupation ended, the segments once again joined together, and the old monopolies resumed their places as the leading financial institutions.

One of the problems faced by businessmen and bankers in setting Japan back on its feet was the paucity of money available for business loans. To print currency in a random manner without gold backing would devalue the yen. Wild inflation would result, as had happened in Germany in the 1920s. Bankers therefore appealed to MacArthur for gold to be injected into the nation's financial mainstream to resolve fiscal problems. MacArthur was receptive to the idea, but questioned where such gold would come from. An answer would soon present itself. In early August, before the start of the occupation, two billion dollars in gold had been crated and flown in aircraft of the Japanese air force from vaults in Korea. The Japanese had mined it in Manchuria and elsewhere, and Korea had been the collection point for the refined product. The gold kilo bars had then been transferred to steel containers and sunk in Tokyo harbor. It was asked if this gold treasure could not be raised and placed in the central Bank of Japan for the common good of the Japanese people. Without hesitation, MacArthur approved. But having it shipped to a U.S. mint in San Francisco for storage—as Pauley had recommended to President Truman—was decided against. In San Francisco the gold wouldn't be of use to anyone.

MacArthur justified his decision by saying that his mission in Japan was to return the nation to solvency;

using the gold was a step in that direction. The treasure was dredged up from the bottom of Tokyo harbor in April 1946 and deposited in the central bank. The yen now had reliable gold backing and so regained international standing.

In all his decision making, MacArthur was guided by Article 5 of the SCAP financial report, which stated:

> Economic recovery should be made the prime objective of United States policy in Japan for the coming period. It should be sought through a combination of a long-term United States aid program envisaging shipments and/or credits on a declining scale over a number of years, and by a vigorous and concerted effort by all interested agencies and departments of the United States government to cut away existing obstacles to the revival of Japanese foreign trade, with provision for Japanese merchant shipping, and to facilitate restoration and development of Japan's exports. In developing Japan's internal and external trade and industry, private enterprise should be encouraged. Recommendations have been made concerning the implementation of the above points, formulated in the light of Japan's economic relationship with other Far Eastern Departments after consultation with other interested departments and agencies of the government. We should make it clear to the Japanese government that the success of the recovery program will in large part depend on Japanese efforts to raise production and to maintain high export levels through hard work,

a minimum of work stoppages, internal austerity measures and the stern combatting of inflationary trends including efforts to achieve a balanced budget as rapidly as possible.

Nine

Hirohito and MacArthur: Partners in Peace

Times were hard that first year of occupation for the people of Japan. But as the months went by, they started to emerge from the profound and catastrophic shock of defeat. They were relieved the war and the bombings had ended, but their outlook was one of sorrow, anger, and futility. When they became aware they were not fated to lead lives of slaves, as had been predicted by some army and government leaders, they brightened and turned to individual rehabilitation, the shoring up of their modest homes, and the tasks that would earn them a living. They quickly saw that U.S. military units that arrived were not looking for vengeance but rather a friendly accommodation in which both American and Japanese could go about their daily work without friction. (In MacArthur's headquarters one Japanese construction worker developed a code of hand signals with an American officer that enabled them to bypass the language gap and get on with putting up buildings.) Indeed, the longing for comprehension between the two peoples accounted for the success of a best-selling book, *A Japanese-American Conversation Handbook* (over three and a half million copies of the book were sold).

On the outskirts of Tokyo, one ex-soldier by the name of Honda poked through the rubble of his bicycle factory and put together a light bike that would run by a motor. Soon his brainchild dominated the city streets and countryside, and eventually the overseas markets. Other entrepreneurs went into production of cameras, radios, watches, and light factory equipment. The advice of the Americans in SCAP not to turn out any more junk, but rather to produce quality products, was taken seriously. Soon new industries were born and profitable exports flowed from Japan to foreign markets. No longer was Tojo's Greater East Asia Co-Prosperity Sphere the industrial framework; instead the catchphrase of the day, "export or perish," was emphasized. In Yokohama, a brewery dried hops on the street until it was able to rebuild. Free enterprise was the spirit of the times. Leaders of entertainment guilds, sensing prosperity was at hand with so many GIs in town, founded the Recreation and Amusement Association, capitalized it at two million dollars through a stock issue, and set up thirty-three entertainment establishments for U.S. enlisted men in Tokyo. An abandoned munitions factory was even converted into a hotel/brothel, known as Willow Run, until it was placed off-limits by the military police. There was many a brand-new identity, what with former prison guards and secret police changing names and personal data to keep their sense of security in a city now occupied by their former enemy.

To assist in the breaking down of American-Japanese language and social barriers, the Dowager Empress Sadako, Hirohito's aging mother, who had been a severe critic of the war and who had been on strained terms with her son ever since he launched the attack on Pearl Harbor, gathered together a group of princesses and marchionesses to hold social affairs for the entertainment of SCAP officers. Because these ladies had all served in Paris or London embassies with their husbands, they spoke beautiful English. The Japanese businessmen who had backed this venture thought it would pay dividends in improved business with SCAP.

In March 1946, with business and industry improving and employment on the upswing, the Emperor began the second phase of the image-improvement program suggested by General MacArthur by visiting a Kawasaki factory. He had been so removed from his people for so long that it was difficult for him to adjust to this role of a popular politician. (General Whitney, MacArthur's chief aide, had little regard for royalty and did not believe public visits by Hirohito would improve his popularity one bit. Whitney told the staff on the sixth floor of the Dai Ichi building that "One look at that myopic, apologetic little man will kill the emperor idea stone dead.") And in fact, Hirohito's first visit to a factory was not an instant success. He wandered around the factory floor, nodding and shaking hands shyly. Every time a worker ventured a few words of conversation his reply would be a meek "*Ah so, deska.*"

But this first factory visit excited Hirohito, and when he returned to the Palace he was in high spirits. He met with the Empress and remarked, "Do you see any difference in me? Do I look more human to you now?" They both laughed.

The Empress had her own experience to relate. On her first visit outside the Imperial Palace since the military surrender, she had gone calling on her mother-in-law, the Dowager Empress. Upon her return, she had heard shouting from a demonstration, organized by

Communists, so rumor had it, taking place just outside the Palace. She ordered her driver to proceed slowly, and as the car moved forward the crowd noticed the Imperial flag on the hood. Describing this experience in detail to her husband, the Empress, her eyes sparkling, told of the hush that came over the crowd, and of the fear that came over her. "And then," she exclaimed, "almost to a man, the crowd turned toward me and bowed." The royal limousine entered the grounds of the Palace, she continued, and the crowd went on with the demonstration. Both the Emperor and the Empress were elated and delighted by the day's happenings.

The Empress, the former Princess Nagako, granddaughter of Emperor Komei's advisor, Asahiko, had been Hirohito's personal choice, an unusual situation in a land where royal marriages were normally predetermined affairs. But Crown Prince Hirohito had had the support of his mother, who was determined her son would have a wife of his own choosing. The wedding took place on January 26, 1924, following Hirohito's return from a grand tour of Europe. Seven hundred guests were invited, including Black Dragon Toyama, the fourth power in Japan, who ruled over the now masterless samurai and those who lived and worked in the factory cities of Japan. A court official who was present at this wedding described the event as follows:

> All invited guests stood in attendance outside the Imperial Family shrine, in the forested area of the Palace garden. Clad in ancient court regalia, Nagako carried a fan, Hirohito a scepter, and the couple met before the assembled witnesses at the shrine entrance. The gates swung open and Hirohito, alone, entered the courtyard leading toward the Inner Shrine. The Chamberlain of Rituals chanted Shinto

prayers, in a high sing-song. The door of the Shrine opened, and Hirohito walked into his ancestors' Holy of Holies. Paying brief homage to the spirits, he returned to the outer gate, where Nagako was waiting. The two then drank alternately three times from a goblet of sanctified rice wine, and the ceremony was over. The ships of the fleet in Tokyo harbor boomed out a 101-gun salute.

The royal couple had fond memories of the past. Their lives had spanned the life of their nation, from the last of the samurai and the Knights of Bushido through the fanatics of Shintoism and Kodo to the democracy and neutralism of the occupation period. Together in the Palace they now looked to the future.

Hirohito became Emperor on Christmas day, 1926. His father, Emperor Taisho, had suffered a fatal stroke in the Summer Palace at Hayama. Crown Prince Hirohito, then twenty-six, had been told instantly by telephone of his father's death. After visiting Taisho's bedroom, saying prayers, and giving comfort to his mother, he went by car to the Imperial Palace in Tokyo and immediately to this family shrine. He walked across the white pebbles of the shrine courtyard into the Holy of Holies and there began the solemn private ceremony of declaring himself to the spirits as the new Emperor of Japan. When he emerged from the shrine, Hirohito was considered by all Japan as the Emperor, although he would be publicly crowned Emperor in an elaborate ceremony about a year later in Kyoto, the ancient capital, for benefit of the outer world. That night, he had decided on the name for his reign—Showa, Peace Made Manifest. And he had written the ceremonial purposes of his new regime: "Simplicity instead of vain display, originality instead of blind imitation, progress in view of this period of evolution, improvement to keep pace with the advancement of civilization, national harmony in purpose and in action."

Days later he would move from his own Akasaka compound into the main Palace. For his office he selected a large room with a low handsome ceiling. He had the walls stripped of the paintings preferred by Emperors Meiji and Taisho, and in their place hung photographs of himself in Europe with Petain, the Prince of Wales, and Crown Prince Leopold of Belgium.

He was an organized Emperor. He rose at 6:00 A.M., shaved and dressed, prayed to his ancestors, then went for a walk or horseback ride. He followed the same routine during the summer at Hayama. At seven o'clock he would sit down to a Western breakfast with Empress Nagako. He would then go to his study and read the Tokyo dailies, *Asahi* and *Mainichi*, and the English-language *Japan Advertiser*. He would then receive Lord Privy Seal Kido and begin his official day by calling in his chiefs of the army and navy to discuss military matters. From ten to two in the afternoon, he would see a steady stream of ministers and officials for their reports, frequently stopping them in midsentence and asking questions. At four o'clock he would retire to take a hot bath, wrap himself in a kimono, return to his study, and place his signature on official papers. Then he would retire to his apartment for dinner with the Empress.

But those were the good years, and during this occupation period Hirohito was determined, on MacArthur's advice, to improve his image with the people. He made more factory visits. The crumpled gray hat he wore on these tours was recognized in time as his political campaign badge. The questions posed to him were now answered in an easy, relaxed manner. He developed a sense of public personality that communicated itself to the people of Japan. Suddenly Hirohito, a newly democratic monarch, was vastly more popular than he had been as a mythical, traditional, and autocratic god-king.

In 1946, a public opinion poll showed that over ninety percent of the people favored Hirohito, and that all but four of the eighty-nine political parties now registered in Japan supported him, with only the Communists in opposition. On his birthday, three hundred eighty thousand citizens of Japan rushed into the opened Palace grounds and paid tribute to their Emperor. MacArthur had been right all along.

But a problem now loomed on the horizon. In early January 1946, Australia filed an official request with the War Crimes Commission in London that Hirohito be tried as a war criminal. U.S. Senator Richard Russell of Georgia had already introduced into the Senate proceedings a resolution demanding the same.

The Joint Chiefs of Staff sent a classified message to General MacArthur on January 21, 1946, that read:

> By direction of the President, the following message received by the Department of State from U.S. Ambassador in London:
> Message begins:
> Submitted by Australian representative on the War Crimes Commission is proposal that the Commission charge and list as a major war criminal Emperor Hirohito . . . wanted are instructions as to whether in accordance with Australian proposal Emperor should be listed and charged as a war criminal.

Though the war crimes trials had been on the mind of everyone in government and in the Imperial Palace, the people themselves did not particularly care about the issue. The popular attitude was the same as in Germany: the war had been lost and the leadership as a result no longer had credence. Though full support had been given to the leaders of their nation during the war, the men who had led Japan into war could now take their punishment.

The first trials were held in Manila in 1945 and early 1946. General Yamashita, the Tiger of Malaya who had captured Singapore and participated with Hirohito in planning the Strike South strategy, was tried for his responsibility in the rape of Manila and the death by incineration of one hundred fifty U.S. prisoners of war on Palawan Island. In both trials the prosecution did not have a good case. Palawan Island had been under the command of the Japanese air force and navy. In Manila, the Imperial marines had performed mass rapings and executions; and in the Batangas mountain area several thousand Filipino guerillas had been machine-gunned and bayoneted. In his defense Yamashita testified in part:

> . . . Nine days after my arrival in the Philippines I faced an overwhelming American tide moving on Leyte . . . I was forced to confront superior U.S. forces with subordinates whom I did not know and with whose character and ability I was unfamiliar. As a result of the inefficiency of the Japanese army system, I could not unify my command; my duties were very complicated. The troops were scattered and Japanese communications were very poor . . . I did not order any massacres . . . I put forth my best efforts to control my troops. If this was not enough, then I agree that somehow I should have done more . . .

Nevertheless Yamashita's death sentence was handed down in Manila on December 7, 1945, the fourth anniversary of the attack on Pearl Harbor. The defense, all volunteers from MacArthur's legal section, appealed to the U.S. Supreme Court. After a month of study the Court refused to overrule the military tribunal. In a five-to-two vote the Supreme Court Justices ruled that a military commander did have criminal responsibility for the misdeeds of his troops. Justice Frank Murphy wrote a dissenting opinion, saying ". . . Never before have we tried and convicted an enemy general for action taken during hostilities or otherwise in the course of military operations or duty—much less have we condemned one for failing to take action . . ."

General MacArthur, in a reply to Justice Murphy, issued his own thoughts on Yamashita:

> . . . The soldier, be he friend or foe, is charged with the protection of the weak or/and unarmed. It is the very essence and reason for his being. . . . Particularly callous and purposeless was the sack of the ancient city of Manila. . . . I approve the findings and sentence of the Commission and direct the Commanding General, Army Forces in the Western Pacific, to execute the judgment upon the defendant, stripped of uniform, decorations and other appurtenances signifying membership in the military profession.

On February 23, 1946, General Yamashita climbed up to the scaffold of New Biblical Prison outside Manila. He bowed north to the Palace of Emperor Hirohito, the trap was sprung, and he was hanged until death overtook him.

The Bataan Death March had left bitter memories

in the minds of all Americans. Of seventy thousand Americans and about fifty-eight thousand Filipinos under General Wainwright who had surrendered, only fifty-four thousand Americans and eight thousand Filipinos survived the march to prison camps. Those who lagged were shot and bayoneted, some decapitated. General Honma was tried and convicted for this war crime. Though he claimed that a cadre of officers from Tokyo had superseded his command and also that he had known nothing about the march, it was pointed out that the march, which lasted for one week, had passed within a mile of his headquarters.

Again the U.S. Supreme Court refused to reverse the decision of the military tribunal, and Justice Murphy again objected to the sentence. General MacArthur spoke of the character and moral fortitude necessary to high command and upheld the death verdict against Honma. Honma was shot by a U.S. firing squad on April 3, 1946.

In 1946, the war crimes trials moved from Manila to Tokyo. There were twenty-eight defendants. Two of the original thirty had committed suicide: General Matsui, who was held responsible for the rape of Nanking, and Matsuoka, who had led his delegation from the League of Nations when criticized for Japan's Manchurian invasion.

The twenty-eight defendants, alone to bear the guilt of Japan and go on trial for planning war and permitting atrocities, were held in Sugamo Prison for the duration of the trial. Ranging in age from seventy-nine to early sixties, about one-third were army and navy officers; the rest were bureaucrats, including Lord Privy Seal Kido and Lt. General Baron Oshima, wartime ambassador to Berlin. Prince Konoye, who had headed three cabinets, had committed suicide.

The Japanese people followed the war trials in their

newspapers but, too busy reshaping their lives, cared little for the defendants or the trial process. The families of all the defendants were everywhere shunned by their neighbors, as Tojo learned from his family when they visited him in prison. So during his trial he quickly ensured better treatment for his family. Tojo knew that Hirohito was reading the transcripts as they became available to the Imperial Palace. By claiming that he had ordered no crimes without Hirohito's authorization, thereby putting the Emperor under scrutiny, Tojo put the Emperor in the position of having to silence him with a favor. Tojo's family was quickly provided for. To be sure, his family was already living in a fine and costly house, which he had received as a merit gift from the Zaibatsu after the Pearl Harbor attack. But Mrs. Tojo had no coal or food, nor the means to buy them. Hirohito ordered a Zaibatsu group to obtain these things for her. The news quickly reached Tojo, and he publicly retracted his statements about Hirohito. Though his trial continued and he was sentenced to death, he took his secrets to the gallows.

Six others also received the death penalty. Lord Privy Seal Marquis Kido was sentenced to life imprisonment for having advised and voted for war against the United States and Britain. Kido was released on parole in 1955; he died in 1961. Foreign Minister Togo was sentenced to twenty years in prison. He died in prison in 1950.

When the trials neared an end, a Japanese newspaper reporter did a street poll and found this consensus among the people:

> If Japan had won the war we would be using slave labor from the territories we conquered to build bigger pyramids than the pharaohs. Instead we are erecting new facto-

ries with American bulldozers. As for Tojo and the others, they are a sample of the war guilty and could only be punished as a symbolic sacrifice to the angry spirits of those whom Japan had wronged.

General MacArthur was now faced with a monumental problem. His mandate from the President of the United States, to bring Japan back to economic parity, would be impossible if the Emperor was placed on trial as a war criminal. The country would come apart and the cooperation he had nurtured would end.

While MacArthur pondered his problem, the Research Unit of the Military Intelligence Service prepared a paper on the Japanese emperor, which went as a top-secret report to the Joint Chiefs of Staff in Washington. It said:

> The possibility of Hirohito's abdication has been discussed in Japan ever since surrender . . . The status of Hirohito with respect to "the issue of war responsibility" [is widespread]. A non-Communist Tokyo newspaper has stated that Hirohito "cannot evade the responsibility for bringing about the situation in which Japan finds itself today." Apparently, the belief that Hirohito will be named as an Allied war criminal is gaining support in Japan, and with a view to the effect on the future of the Imperial institution it is proposed arranging for the abdication of Hirohito before the action is taken. Abdication, in any event, is now a possibility. Meanwhile, Hirohito appears anxious to demonstrate that he is willing and able to adjust to the newly evolving Japan. In his New Year's Rescript he repudiated the

"false conception that the Emperor is divine and that the Japanese people are superior to other races and fated to rule the world."

This report further stated:

> The Japanese generally feel that the Russians and Chinese favor abolition of the Imperial institution, and that the Americans will uphold the Imperial institution if it is supported by the Japanese people . . . The two factors uppermost in the minds of the dominant groups on the subject are how to preserve the Imperial institution and how to prevent the Soviets and the Japanese Communists from gaining a dominant voice in the control of Japan.

In conclusion the report added:

> As chief of the Japanese State, Emperor Hirohito sanctioned the Japanese program and expansion, though his government had solemnly agreed to renounce war as an instrument of national policy by the Pact of Paris (1928) and was a party to the Washington Conference agreements guaranteeing the open doors and territorial integrity of China.

Hirohito was on insecure footing. Important Japanese groups were now more concerned about the retention of the Throne as an institution than they were about Hirohito himself. Emperors had been deposed in generations past by military chiefs called shoguns, but in modern times factional clans had lost their power to control the Throne, and Emperors had had an easier time retaining their position. Several dominant Japanese groups now felt that Hirohito should abdicate in favor of his minor son, Crown Prince Akihito. This would be an expeditious move, they said, because it would disassociate the Throne from any responsibility for the war. Hirohito was unsure. He told his intimates in the Imperial Palace he would consider suicide if given prior warning of his arrest, a move, he said, that would surely protect the Throne from the humiliation of a public trial.

But then public opinion hardened against such a trial for the Emperor, the result of the public-image campaign Hirohito had launched at MacArthur's urging. He had been helped along by Zaibatsu families, who had underwritten the expense of the skillful public-relations campaign. Royal retainers had toured Japan spreading word of the noble traits of the Emperor, blaming much of the war and its failures on former War Minister Tojo. The army had even been persuaded by the Palace to open their warehouses containing food, gasoline, tires, and clothing. These precious items had been distributed to the people as a gesture of Imperial compassion.

General MacArthur told members of his staff to leak the information that a war trial for Hirohito was in the wind, a rumor that reached Japanese newspapers and produced a ground swell of support for Hirohito. Editors wrote that the Allies were acting in bad faith, that a trial was contrary to the terms of the Potsdam Declaration. With such news being reported and reflected in U.S. correspondent reports from Tokyo to the American and world press, MacArthur believed the time was right for his own report to the Joint Chiefs of Staff. His top-secret cabled answer to Washington told why he thought Hirohito should not be placed on trial:

If he is to be tried great changes must be made in occupational plans and due preparation therefore should be initiated. His indictment will unquestionably cause a tremendous convulsion among the Japanese people, the repercussions of which cannot be overestimated. He is a symbol which unites all Japanese. Destroy him and the nation will disintegrate. Practically all Japanese venerate him as the social head of state and believe rightly or wrongly that the Potsdam Agreement was intended to maintain him as the Emperor of Japan. They will regard Allied action as betrayal of their history and the hatreds and resentments engendered by this thought will unquestionably last for all measurable time. A vendetta for revenge will thereby be initiated whose cycle may well not be completed for centuries if ever.

The whole of Japan can be expected, in my opinion, to resist the action either by passive or semi-active means. They are disarmed and therefore represent no special menace to trained and equipped troops; but it is conceivable that all government agencies will break down, the civilized practices will largely cease, and a condition of underground chaos and disorder amounting to guerilla warfare in the mountainous and outlying regions will result. I believe all hopes of introducing modern democratic methods would disappear and that when military control finally ceased some form of intense regimentation, probably along communistic lines, would arise from the mutilated masses.

This would represent an entirely different problem of occupation from those now prevalent. It would be absolutely essential to greatly increase the occupational forces. It is quite possible that a minimum of a million troops would be required which would have to be maintained for an indefinite number of years. In addition a complete civil service might have to be recruited and imported, possibly running into a size of several hundred thousand. An overseas supply service under such conditions would have to be set up on practically a war basis embracing an indigent civilian population of many millions. Many other such drastic results which I will not attempt to discuss should be anticipated and complete new plans should be carefully prepared by the Allied Powers along all lines to meet the new eventualities. Most careful consideration as to the national forces composing the occupation forces is essential. Certainly the U.S. should not be called on to bear unilaterally the terrific burden of manpower, economics, and other resultant responsibilities.

The decision as to whether the Emperor should not be tried as a war criminal involves a policy determination upon such a high level that I would not feel it appropriate for me to make a recommendation; but if the decision by the heads of state is in the affirmative, I recommend the above measures as imperative.

When MacArthur's message was read by President Truman, Secretary of State Byrnes, the Joint Chiefs of Staff, Senator Richard Russell of Georgia, and in England by Prime Minister Clement Atlee and members of the War Crimes Commission, it was decided to forgo any trial of Hirohito. MacArthur's forebodings had chilled Allied leaders. The very thought of a guerilla war, stretching out for years to come at a time when the

United States, the United Kingdom, and Australia were straining to disband, was a thought no political leader could bear. The temper of the times in these countries was reflected in the exhortation to "bring the boys home." Japan would be assisted in a return to equality with other nations of the world. A new beginning would follow. Emperor and Throne were secure.

One casualty of the decision not to try Hirohito was General Kuzma N. Derevyanko, chief of the Soviet mission in Tokyo. U.S. State Department intelligence officers in Japan had evaluated Derevyanko's efforts to rally anti-Emperor elements in Japan as "concealed aggression to deliver Japan into the Soviet orbit." Russia had been outmaneuvered by General MacArthur.

Emperor Hirohito was now freed from the ordeal of having to stand trial and testify to the world what he had stated in private to General MacArthur during their first meeting at the U.S. Embassy in 1945: "I bear sole responsibility for every political and military decision made and action taken by my people in the conduct of the war."

Hirohito certainly owed thanks to General Mac-Arthur. But first he would offer prayers and a report to his ancestors. On the afternoon he was informed of the favorable news from the War Crimes Commission in London, he walked to the Palace Shrine in the Fukiage Gardens and informed his honorable ancestors of the favorable turn of events.

Hirohito was now no longer the busy leader of previous years. There were no official ceremonies, and his evening dinners with the Empress were subdued. He simply read, studied his hobby, biology, and waited. The momentum was all MacArthur's. He met frequently with MacArthur in the Summer Palace at Hayama, where the Supreme Commander's mood was always circumspect. (MacArthur never even allowed the new

U.S. Ambassador to Japan to visit Hayama. This was MacArthur's territory, and his alone.)

At one of their meetings General MacArthur told the Emperor he was ordering the dissolution of the Black Dragon Society. Hirohito agreed, for this society, which had played an important role in Japan for many decades, had reached the end of its influence. The Black Dragon Society early on had dedicated itself to keeping Russia north of the Amur River—the Black River—on the Russian-Chinese border. When Hirohito had shifted Japan's war strategy from Strike North to Strike South the society's political influence had waned. The man who had led this society, Mitsuru Toyama, a fascinating character, had developed his organization into a subculture of political influence. He had gathered all the samurai who had become masterless after Emperor Meiji rejected them and had drifted to the slums of the big cities. There they had become members of the Black Dragon Society. They admired Toyama, and emulated his skills as a wrestler and swordsman. He became known as the master of the *ma*, the grunt that expresses the inexpressible. The Black Dragon Society would later carry out assassinations, blackmail politicians, and perform other acts of political consequence. But the society came to an end following MacArthur's directive.

As the occupation went on, the outlawed Zaibatsu emerged under another identity—Keiretsu, meaning "brotherhood," or "group." Although the ties of each group were much looser than before, the six big Keiretsus were to control absolutely the economy of Japan, as before. The six largest of the Keiretsus controlled 40 percent of the nation's corporate capital, and 30 percent of its corporate assets. The trading companies of these six groups held stock in more than fifty-four hundred companies in Japan. The Keiretsu-controlled banks owned even more. The Mitsubishi and Mitsui families became comfortably Keiretsu.

Sumitomo of Osaka, a Keiretsu, continues to be the third largest such group in Japan. Sumitomo and its sixteen core companies comprise the Sumitomo Keiretsu, with annual sales of fifty billion dollars. Sumitomo traces its history back to the seventeenth century, as does Mitsui, a company founded as a small shop by Takatoshi Mitsui, who had renounced his rank as a warrior-aristocrat to become a tradesman. Mitsui was part of the emergence of the Japanese merchant class. In 1876, eight years after the Meiji restoration, which marked Japan's opening to the West by Commodore Perry and its rush toward industrialization, this trading company was established to export coal and to import cotton-spinning machinery. The company has played a central role in the development of Japan as an industrial trading power for more than a century, trailing only the Mitsubishi Corporation. Both companies are middlemen in global transactions involving hundreds of commodities and finished goods ranging from iron ore to designer fashions.

Koji Kobayashi, president of Nippon Electric, a corporation within the Sumitomo brotherhood, tells about his links with others in the Keiretsu: "It is natural for me to feel kinship with Hotta of Sumitomo Bank, with Hosai Hyuga of Sumitomo Metal Industries, and other fellows. We were all in the old Sumitomo Zaibatsu together. After the war, after the Zaibatsu was dissolved, we rose together in our separate corporations. But we keep in close touch."

Just how close is shown in monthly meetings of an informal management council, *Hakasuiki*, or White Water Club, that discusses and plans corporate strategies of the sixteen basic companies of the Sumitomo Keiretsu. At these meetings, minutes are never taken; decisions are formalized with a nod of the head.

Goro Koyama, chairman of Mitsui Bank and Hotta's counterpart in the Mitsui Group, thinks that as Japan's expansion slows, more companies will gravitate toward the six big Keiretsus. "Capital is a coward. It tends to go toward stable companies," he asserts with a smile.

Just as General MacArthur visualized and as Emperor Hirohito acknowledged in one of their many private conversations, the private sector of the Japanese economy would be responsible for Japan's future success in world markets. The private sector was starting to achieve success toward the end of the occupation years. Japan soon gained economic dominance over nearly every island and area they had recently failed to win by war. China, South Korea, Singapore, Formosa, the Philippines, Thailand, Vietnam, and even the Dutch East Indies and Australia all became Japan's partners in trade. South Korea, Singapore, and Formosa even termed themselves "The Three Japans." Business leaders in those locations observed that Japan had the formula for international business success, and so decided to copy it.

In his final meeting with Hirohito at Hayama, MacArthur and Hirohito talked about the strategic future of Japan. They agreed that prosperity and peace were important, but that neither could be sustained without military strength. MacArthur then showed the Emperor a secret cable from President Truman stating the policy to be followed toward Japan. It was pleasing to them both:

The security of Japan is of such vital strategic importance to the United States position in the Far East that the United States cannot permit hostile forces to gain control of any part of the territory of Japan . . . The overriding requirement for the United States policy affecting all post-Treaty arrangements with Japan is the necessity for preserving and strengthening the voluntary and strong commitment of the Japanese government and people to a close association and to joint action with the United States and the free world . . . Japan has demonstrated its fighting abilities in war and defeat . . . The United States can attain its long-range security objectives in the Far East to the fullest extent only if Japan, in its own self-interest, fully recognizes its stakes in the free world, develops close political, military, and economic cooperation with the United States and other free nations, particularly in Asia, and assumes its fair share of the common burdens of the free world.

The Emperor nodded in concurrence with this statement. He remarked that Russia was their greatest problem to the continuing of peace and that thus it was essential that Japan's military buildup should go forward.

The people of Japan have not forgotten the islands seized by Russia in the closing month of World War II—Kunashiri, Etorofu, Shikotan, and Habomais. They all lie north of Hokkaido and south of the Kuriles. Japan would not go to war to recover these islands, and still hasn't. But they represent national pride besmirched, so February 7 is designated "Northern Territories Day," and rallies continue to be held calling for their return.

In Washington on June 15, 1949, a report by the

Secretary of Defense to the National Security Council centered on an agreement between the Emperor, MacArthur, and President Truman. It stated, in part:

> The ability of the Japanese to wage both aggressive and defensive war was proven in the last world conflict. It is almost inconceivable that the Japanese manpower potential would be permitted to continue in peaceful pursuits in the event of another global conflict. Under USSR control, Japan probably would provide both the arsenal and the manpower for aggressive military campaigns in the Pacific and to the southwest. If United States influence predominates, Japan can be expected, with planned initial United States assistance . . . to contribute importantly to military operations against the Soviets in Asia, thus forcing the USSR to fight on the Asiatic front as well as elsewhere.
>
> The ability of the United States . . . to deny Japan's ultimate exploitation by the USSR will depend largely on the course we follow from now on with respect to Japan. This course should, accordingly, take into account the essential objectives, from the military viewpoint, of denying Japan to the Soviets and of maintaining her orientation toward the Western Powers.

Change after change had swept Japan into an impressive new era. Voting rights for women, a new constitution that promised much, an outlawing of war, a destroying of the tyrannies of family life, and other new facets of Japanese life told these two leaders they had worked well together. MacArthur had moved this nation from despair to hope, and with Hirohito as the guiding mentor of his people, the future indeed held great promise for Japan. Two Allies now walked the road of peace and freedom. Japan had found its freedom under MacArthur, but Hirohito had found a personal freedom— as a democratic monarch. As he remarked to the great American general: "I am like a canary whose cage has been opened and someone says: 'Fly away!' Where would I fly to? If I have a song to sing, why should I waste it on places where the wind may blow it away?"

Epilogue

In 1952, when the occupation of Japan had come to an end, Emperor Hirohito resolved that his nation would never again go to war, certainly not without overwhelming economic strength. Japan has had that strength for many years now, but Hirohito came to accept that this strength had been accomplished by peaceful means and the territories with which Japan now did business outstripped in size and worth anything ever overrun by their armies at war.

Reflecting on the long view, the Emperor knew well that Japan's astonishing growth since World War II was no passing phenomenon. Between 1867 and Pearl Harbor Japan had surged ahead economically of every other country in Asia. Then came defeat in 1945, which left much of Japan an economic disaster, with factories as well as major cities in ruins. Yet Hirohito regarded this as a temporary setback in his lifelong quest to fulfill what "his ancestors required of him."

During the occupation, General MacArthur would often look down at the Imperial Palace from the windows of his office in the Dai Ichi building and wonder aloud, "What is that little man planning now?" The recovery of Japan was what Hirohito was planning. He pondered how to get Nippon's economic machinery going again.

His people badly needed work, but the employers who could provide it—the Zaibatsu leaders of business and banking—were keeping their wealth in Switzerland until they knew what General MacArthur had in mind for their country. MacArthur informed Hirohito he was going to dissolve the Zaibatsu but allow Japan's business leadership to have all the elbowroom they needed to rebuild the economy. Private enterprise would be respected, and the sooner the big mercantile families addressed themselves to rebuilding the economy—this meant returning their wealth to Tokyo—the more rapidly manufacturing and sales and employment would go forward. Hirohito, who also had most of his fortune in Switzerland and elsewhere in the final months of the war, was satisfied with MacArthur's stated intentions. Hirohito planned conferences with the Zaibatsu leaders like those he had had just previous to the start of the occupation, when he gave precise instructions to many military leaders and princes of the realm on how to conduct themselves during the occupation. To his war minister, General Anamu, he had allocated the task of controlling the army in defeat. To the princes he assigned the duty of effecting smooth relations among Japanese army and navy leaders and those officers under command of General MacArthur. Captain Takamatsu of the Imperial Navy, a brother of Hirohito's, described these meetings as simply a discussion of "How to be defeated gracefully."

In his later meetings with the Zaibatsu leaders, the Emperor persuaded the big money men to join him in bringing about a new Japan. Factories were rebuilt, and as a consequence employment rose. The per capita income was legally held at $500 annually until 1965, in order to keep goods shipped abroad competitively priced on world markets. "Export or perish" was the slogan moving industrial Japan, and the nation started to increase her wealth and potential more rapidly and more steadily than any other power. It was what we Americans call teamwork, although in Japan it was described as the "Family System."

Young Japanese showed great energy and initiative in the workplace, secure in the belief that high-flying financial activities and low-hitting commercial deeds would be sanctioned by the Emperor and the Japanese people in the interests of building a greater Japan. Those aging Japanese, who had worked together like brothers since youth, became once again brothers in commerce and banking. The long-entrenched Zaibatsu, the great cartels of Japan that had been sundered by General MacArthur, continued with business as usual, but under other names, as well-integrated units. They drew prosperity to Japan and to themselves. These were the keen-eyed bankers and industrialists who sat on Japan's Supreme Trade Council and determined national trade goals and how they would share world markets.

The three great cartels in twentieth-century Japan are Mitsui, belonging to the eleven branches of the Mitsui family; Mitsubishi, belonging to the Iwasakis; and Sumitomo, also named for the family itself. Taken together with the Imperial Household Ministry, which administered investments for the Throne, these were the control groups of Japan that steadfastly and absolutely held power over banking, industry, and foreign trade. These were the facts of Japanese business life both before and during World War II, when the Zaibatsu pressed Hirohito to, in his own business interests, "Strike South" and acquire by any means new territories and their raw materials that would aid Japan in its conquest of world markets. Surrender and occupation became only an unfortunate pause in the relentless forward movement of the cartels, once MacArthur, the Supreme Commander of the Allied Powers, made it known that he wanted an economically sound Japan based on political freedom and thriving private enterprise.

Emperor Hirohito's situation went through many changes in the seven years of the occupation. In 1946 Hirohito was forced by SCAP, Supreme Command Allied Powers, to dissolve the Imperial Family holding company and give most of his royal landholdings, buildings, and museums to the people of Japan. In 1947 he was compelled to demote his uncles and cousins to the status of commoner. The entire Imperial Household of three thousand employees was whittled down by SCAP until Hirohito was indeed that lonely little man in the Palace who devoted much of his time to his hobby, marine biology. This lifelong interest was carried out at his summer villa, overlooking Sagami Bay. Here the Emperor and his wife, Empress Nagako, spent the summer months with their children.

As to his need for a renewed public image, Hirohito let the professionals of business and industry handle that. Before large crowds in all the cities of Japan, distinguished notables lectured, in essence, that Emperor Hirohito had really been a benevolent and peace-loving emperor who abhorred the war and the aggressions that had preceded it. Tojo was the villain who had brought war and defeat to Japan, they declared. These speeches were covered by the Japanese press, and if the speaker happened to enjoy international stature, American and other foreign reporters were on hand to wire this material to the rest of the world.

Little known and seldom mentioned were the circumstances of Hirohito's boyhood. Taken at an early age to be raised in the home of a samurai warrior, General Nogi, his training was tough and rigorous and his education the best. Hirohito's most cherished ambition was to honor his ancestors and to exceed the consider-

able war exploits of his dashing and militaristic grandfather, Emperor Meiji, whose ships sank the Russian navy
and whose army defeated the Russian army, in 1905, in
the battle for Port Arthur. Crown Prince Hirohito was
entranced by the battle stories told by his guardian,
General Nogi, whose troops took the citadel in a charge
up a mountain overlooking Port Arthur that cost the lives
of twenty thousand Japanese soldiers, including sons of
General Nogi. When General Nogi had finished reshaping the young Hirohito in body and mind, he returned
him to his sick, dissolute father, who was no longer able
to reign. Hirohito was made Prince Regent, and upon
his father's death he ascended the Throne as Emperor.
This was the shaping of the low-key militant who was to
rule his country as the Empire of the Sun for so many
years.

It was Hirohito's practice in the early occupation
years to visit farms and factories, and anywhere else
people could be found, to ingratiate himself with Japanese citizens. By so doing he became quite popular, as
MacArthur had assured him he would. Still, there were
those in the Diet, the parliament, who wanted to keep
Hirohito at arm's length,

Hirohito managed, nevertheless, to retain his right
to place the Imperial seal on some ten thousand government documents every year. Finally in 1957 he demanded that as payment for this duty he receive weekly
briefings from the Prime Minister on the plans and
activities of the Diet and all government agencies. Now
he was drawn closer to the workings of government, no
longer isolated, as he had been during the occupation.
His questions to the Prime Minister and leaders of the
Diet on their conduct of state affairs were warmly
received and respected. He was Emperor in fact, once
again.

Hirohito's personal financial situation had been

shaky when MacArthur said that the Diet had the responsibility for paying the Emperor, not the Imperial Household treasurer. In 1947 the Diet voted Hirohito an annual stipend of $22,000. This placed the Emperor just about in the class of indigent world rulers. But there was no need to weep for this direct descendant of the Goddess of the Sun. He had over one billion dollars in gold and currencies hidden in Switzerland, and during the rebirth of Japan, when factories were being rebuilt, he was a source of investment money—at interest, of course—for those performing the reconstruction. In gratitude, these Tokyo financiers, who were thus able to receive "loan" money from the Swiss banks that served as Hirohito depositories, provided insider information to the Emperor. Assisted as well by advice from a score of investment counselors, Hirohito played the stock market like a virtuoso, and when the occupation ended, he was making forty-five to fifty million dollars annually, all aboveboard as far as SCAP was concerned, for this was private enterprise, just as MacArthur wanted. He had interests in major rebuilt factories now, and as they shifted from heavy-industry products to the more sophisticated items that began to dominate the markets of the West, his portfolio in SCAP intelligence files reflected large stock buys in electronics and hotels.

The Korean War of 1950–1953 proved to be a boon to Japan, and to Hirohito, for that matter. This war came on so suddenly that the United States military establishment found it needed weaponry of all kinds. Factories in America were not geared up to meet the demands of General MacArthur and his United Nations peacekeeping forces. They turned to the factories of Japan and West Germany, who were pleased indeed with the orders and the sudden prosperity they brought. The Emperor, with substantial investments in electronics and related technologies, found his stocks accelerating in value. When the Korean War came to an end in 1953, Japan had prospered so greatly it was able to reach out for new markets with the products they now could produce. The cartels accelerated their Family System of doing business; members of the Mitsui combine, for instance, all occupied the same building, consulted with each other over private telephone lines, and walked the corridors to each other's offices as they planned and schemed ways to subvert the United States in the world marketplace. For their contribution to manufacturing and export, the cartels—the superfamilies—received special treatment from the government: preferential credit, tax incentives, and insurance covering all their overseas investments. While the cartels are competitive with each other, they also cooperate jointly. Intercartel meetings of managers are held regularly under government auspices, where they agree on price fixing and the sales methods to be used in foreign markets.

A century ago, these great merchant families were, socially, nearly outsiders as far as the Throne was concerned. But in recent decades marked by prosperity, Hirohito changed all that. The families of these important cartels have been able to form ties of marriage with the Court nobility, and even with the Imperial Family. These banking and business leaders who sit on government trade councils consider themselves among the aristocrats of Japan, with the approval of the late Emperor Hirohito.

In recent times, the Diet as well has done better for the Emperor. The royal stipend of 1947 had been increased by 1971 to $83,000, and at the time of Hirohito's passing was well over $300,000 annually. But this was only the beginning. Each year the Diet made three appropriations that went toward the upkeep of the Imperial Palace and Imperial villas. The first item, $200,000, went to the support of Hirohito's daughters and brothers, each of whom receive a tax-free allowance of some $30,000 annually. The third annual grant to Hirohito and Crown Prince Akihito—the Emperor now—was over $300,000, all tax free. The government paid for the maintenance of grounds and buildings; the Imperial garages (120 cars), marinas, and stables; Imperial wardrobes, entertainment, and travel.

The Diet appropriated funds also for special building projects. In 1959 Akihito's villa was rebuilt; in 1962, Hirohito's wartime library (in which he had listened to accounts on naval radio of the Japanese defeat at Midway) was expanded, modernized, and refurbished. A new ceremonial palace was completed in 1967, which cost the government thirty-six million dollars, with another two million dollars set aside to rebuild Hirohito's summer villa overlooking the ocean, and to improve his marine biology facilities.

Time-tested practices are hard to cast aside. Hirohito had always directed armies on the basis of the intelligence he received and had shaped his strategies accordingly. When he became a player in the game of international business and finance, he felt it was time to establish his own postwar sources of information. The Mitsui, Mitsubishi, and Sumitomo groups all had their cadres of salesmen and managers in foreign markets feeding valuable data back to the home offices in Tokyo. But, the Emperor wondered, how much of it was really available to him. With this preying on him, Hirohito established the "Civilian Spy Service," a paramilitary espionage organization with links to army and navy intelligence departments of the General Staffs in Tokyo. The directors of this Civilian Spy Service had offices in the Imperial Palace, and its agents and informants worked through charitable and cultural organizations as fronts outside of Japan. Its agents infiltrated the marketing staffs of the big cartels of foreign trade and became part of the normal diplomatic corps of the Foreign

Ministry. As a network it blanketed Asia and spread to all major cities and markets in the United States and countries of Western Europe. Through the Civilian Spy Service, Emperor Hirohito became once again the best-informed man in Japan, as he was in former times. Lieutenant General (retired) Banzai Rochachiro served as director, but whether this unique spy service will be continued under Akihito is debatable.

In Tokyo, in government and corporate circles, there has long been the belief that if Japan can continue to infiltrate foreign markets and outstrip the United States, there will eventually come a time when it can confront the United States as an equal in trade.

That time has evidently arrived. When Japanese Prime Minister Noboru Takeshita met with President Bush and congressional leaders in 1989, he insisted on being treated as an equal. Takeshita told Bush that Japan wants to be more closely consulted as the United States carries on its relations with the Soviet Union. He also called on America to do more to reduce its federal trade deficit, because it affects Japan; the Japanese have a great amount of wealth invested in the United States and they do not want its value to diminish. The Prime Minister said also that Japan intends to take a more assertive political role around the world, including membership in the International Monetary Fund.

Citing a few statistics on Japan's race to the economic forefront tells why Takeshita could talk so assertively in Washington. He represented a nation that posted a record trade surplus of $10,932 billion in December of 1988. While the United States is running a fifty billion dollar trade deficit with Japan, Japan's economy averages a 2.5 percent unemployment rate, as of 1988. In 1990 Japan will be the world's largest provider of economic aid to developing Third World countries, and this is not out of altruism but for hardheaded business reasons. Once the Japanese arrive, they will stick with these economies forever.

Hirohito held the vision of his country's preeminence during his final years. He knew that in Japan there is a doctrinaire belief that the country must someday avenge herself for the defeats of World War II by somehow besting the United States. This feeling is expressed in recent remarks by many political leaders that Japan has no reason to feel remorse for its actions in Asia before and during World War II. This attitude distressed Hirohito, who viewed the influence of Japan in America as sufficient; retribution at a profit without the bloodshed of war, he remarked to his court.

He approved of the heavy spending by Japanese corporations to shape the American view of Japan. Immense sums have gone into American academia so that American educators from major universities will write and speak favorably regarding Japan and its years under Hirohito.

The West Germans were the first to use this sort of public relations. In 1947, when Chancellor Willy Brandt presented a forty-seven million dollar grant to Yale University from Ruhr industrialists, it was also noted that Ruhr industrialists had used slave labor in their factories in wartime. The grant, nevertheless, was effective, and there was nothing more said about wartime slave labor. The Japanese leadership observed this maneuver, and thought, if it worked for Germany, why not for Japan, and proceeded accordingly and with even more sophistication. Japan has poured millions of dollars into U.S. education from Ivy League colleges to inner city elementary schools to junior highs in rural Kentucky. Museums, public television stations, and think tanks are competing for, and getting, Japanese money. Japanese movers and shakers want influence and the ability to protect their broad interests in the United

States. "They've learned how to play us like a violin," comments Lester C. Thurow, dean of the Sloan School of Management at the Massachusetts Institute of Technology. "Japan's say in U.S. decision making will rise as their investments go from passive to active." It is estimated that Japan's government foundations and companies will spend at least $310 million this year on soft-side activities—lawyers, public relations advisors, academics, economists, journalists, political consultants, Washington lobbyists—which is relatively modest alongside their direct investments here of at least $35 billion, and exports of $85 billion, a year.

Many professionals who take advisory money from the Japanese say there are no strings attached; but some disagree. "Everyone who gets money from Japan has to worry about not offending Japan," says Ronald A. Morse, formerly head of the Asia program at the Woodrow Wilson International Center for Scholars in Washington. He is now development officer for the Library of Congress.

Universities such as Columbia, MIT, Johns Hopkins, Harvard, Stanford, University of California, all receive multimillion-dollar grants from Japanese corporations and believe that once the money is received the Japanese have no control over its use. But Japanese money carries with it more power than the universities admit. There are presently twenty-four thousand American students taking Japanese studies. Chalmers Johnson, Professor of International Relations, University of California at San Diego, states that many Japanese-funded scholars are "ready quickly and easily to express Japan's official points of view."

Despite its technological advances and its march from war-torn poverty to economic prominence in today's world, there is great hostility toward this one-dimensional nation that is without military, political, or ideological power. The posture of leadership and smugness that currently dominates Japan worries other Asian countries who remember well suffering under the yoke of Japan before and during World War II. "Japanese may feel patriotic sentiments when they see the rising sun on Japan's flag," observes Wu Ningkun, a professor at Beijing's Institute of International Relations. "But to the Chinese, it is just blood and murder," he continues, recalling Japan's ruthless invasion and conquest of China. Zhao Fusan, a vice president of the Chinese Academy of Social Sciences in Beijing, declares: "The Japanese are an aggressive people. They exploited us in the forties with force, and now with finance. They sell us inferior goods and deny us technology to try to keep China backward. But Asians have memories that can't be rubbed out with money."

The two largest economies in Asia are Japan and China, and memories of the Pacific war affect attitudes today. In the boardrooms of Wall Street, Japanese bankers and business leaders speak of a pan-Asian trading bloc, but such economic coherence is just not in the cards. Throughout Asia, trading experts laugh at such a Japanese concept. Ding Xinghao, director of American studies at Shanghai's Institute of International Study, observed, "Japan's view is always a flying geese formation, with Japan as the head goose. But our memories are long, so we aren't about to fly in Japan's formation." As Karen Elliott House reported in *The Wall Street Journal*, "It is America, not Japan, for which Asians cheer. That's not merely because they like America more, though many do, but because they need America more. America, not Japan, is Asia's major market. And it is America only that offers a counterweight to both Soviet and Japanese ambitions in Asia."

The United States still has a commanding lead on the frontiers of science. American companies are now working hard to protect their patents and to cooperate with each other in the development of new technologies. As Jiro Tokuyama of the Mitsui Research Center says, "We can sell cars and VCRs. We are winning the battle but losing the war."

From an American viewpoint, Emperor Hirohito's record is a mixed bag. He cannot escape the judgment of history for the part he played personally in Japan's military expansion in its war with America and its allies. On the other hand, he led his nation in a remarkable transition to peaceful ways and guided its surge toward world leadership in high technology and wealth.

When questioned by a reporter about possible changes from his father's reign to his own, the new Emperor, Hirohito's son Akihito, replied: "It seems to me a great majority of the people in Japan is in favor of the emperor's position as symbol of the state and of the unity of the people. Therefore, I don't think there will be a considerable change."

Appendix A

Operation Olympic Invasion Plan

JAPANESE GROUND DISPOSITIONS

. . . Seven (Japanese) active divisions and twelve depot divisions will be located in the main islands of Japan (Kyushu, Honshu, South Kyushu). These troops will be supported by at least three tank regiments, army, service, and A/A troops.

The active divisions maintained in Japan are intended for the defense of the homeland and will be as good as any other Japanese troops encountered so far. It is estimated that the activation program now under way will result in the conversion of eight to the present twelve depot divisions to an active status.

Three divisions (2 Depot and 1 Active) will be located in Kyushu. One or more of these divisions will probably have assigned a tank unit and medium artillery. Two divisions will be located north of the mountain mass which divides North from South Kyushu. Estimated locations follow:

Kurume Area	1 depot (depot divisions are considered to be nearly as strong as active divisions) division
Kumamoto Area	1 depot division
Kagoshima Area	1 active division

232

REACTIONS

It is estimated that small guard forces and patrols will guard the entire coast and that some field fortifications will be found at the important beaches.

Until the Japanese are convinced that the landing on South Kyushu is not a diversion coordinated with a main attack directed at some other point on the main islands, it is unlikely that they will set in motion any considerable number of troops toward Kyushu.

First landings on any beach south of the Kyushu-Summyaku range will be opposed by a regiment within 6–12 hours; by a full division within 3 or 4 days.

As soon as the Japanese recognize the Kyushu operation as a major attack they will start already alerted divisions from Honshu. First elements of reinforcements from Honshu probably would arrive in South Kyushu by rail and road on about D + 5 or 6. Successive reinforcements could arrive at the rate of one division per day. It is estimated that not more than four or five Jap divisions will be brought south of the mountain barrier by D + 12. It is presumed that we shall control the sea approaches to South Kyushu, otherwise the reinforcement rate and strength can be materially increased.

JAPANESE AIR DISPOSITIONS

It is estimated that at the time of the initial strike 2,500 first line combat aircraft will be in the Japanese main islands at an estimated serviceability of 70%, or a net of 1,750. Three hundred more combat aircraft can be brought in from Manchurian Area in 3 days and 400 more from China and Formosa in 8 days. Disregarding attrition and using a serviceability factor of 70%, we will face

Initially	1750
D + 3	1960
D + 8	2240

In addition to the above, approximately 500 carrier-based planes will be available with the Japanese Fleet.

JAPANESE NAVAL DISPOSITIONS

This committee has not attempted to estimate Japanese naval dispositions and intentions. Much will depend upon the FORAGER operation, possible subsequent strikes or feints against the Palaus and Japanese reactions thereto.

CONCEPT OF OPERATIONS

The concept of this operation envisages reduction of enemy air capabilities by a sudden and destructive carrier-based air preparation followed by amphibious assaults against southern Kyushu at Ariake Bay and Isaku Beach, supported by naval surface bombardment and carrier-based air. From the beachheads, ground operations will be directed at the early seizure of airfields and the harbor of Kagoshima followed by occupation of southern Kyushu to the general line Miyazaki-Minamoto, upon which will be based an active ground defense of the occupied area. At the earliest practicable time, land-based air will be established by fly-in from carriers and from the Marianas for the purpose of attacking strategic objectives in the heart of industrial Japan and supporting the ground lodgement.

TERRAIN

Kyushu forms a rough quadrangle 200 miles north-south by 125 miles east-west. The central section is mountainous and is passable only with great difficulty. The southern, northern, and western sections have many small, moderately flat coast plains and basins connected by narrow corridors and backed by irregular masses of hills and low rugged mountains. The lowlands are fairly easy to traverse except when the rice fields are flooded or soft (May–September). Southern lowlands are completely cut off from northern and western basins and plains by the central (northeast-southwest) mountain range. This range makes comparatively easy the establishment and defense of a beachhead on the southern tip of the island.

BEACHES

The most favorable beaches for large-scale landing operations and those which are accessible are found in southern Kyushu.

a. Miyazaki

Lying about midway off the eastern coast this sandy beach extends for thirty-four miles in a nearly straight line. Behind this beach is a coastal lowland varying in width from a few hundred yards in the north to six or seven miles in the south and made up of flat-topped terraces, low rounded hills, and broad steep-sided valleys. Exits from the plain toward Kagoshima (the only port in southern Kyushu) are through the narrow pass of the Oyodo valley and thence across a broad rolling plain to Kagoshima Bay.

b. Ariaka Bay

At the head of this bay is a stretch of about nine miles of sandy beach backed by gently sloping land with many low pine-covered hills and broad, flat river valleys. A highway and railroad run close to the beach and connect this area with the Miyakonojo Basin to the east, Kanoya to the south, and Kagoshima Bay to the west over relatively flat terrain routes.

c. Kagoshima

Within Kagoshima Bay are several small beaches with limited exits which can be used to supplement the port capacity of Kagoshima after we have secured the area. They are not suitable for assault.

d. Izaku

A long narrow beach about 20 miles in length lies on the western shore of Kyushu opposite Kagoshima. It is backed by rolling hilly country. From this area rail and road connections are made to the east with Kagoshima and to northern Kyushu by routes following the west coast.

PORTS

The only port in the area is that of Kagoshima. This has limited dockage, piers for 2 to 5 vessels of about 5000 tons, limited loading facilities, good lighterage and a good anchorage. Considerable development will be necessary.

COMMUNICATIONS

While not up to American standards, the roads and railroads of southern Kyushu satisfactorily cover the inhabited areas and appear adequate for the needs of troops established in a beachhead across the southern portion of the island.

AIRFIELDS

Information on airfields in Kyushu is out of date and cannot be firm until adequate photo reconnaissance can be made of the area. It is estimated that within the beachhead area there are at present six airfields and one landing ground. There appears to be plenty of area suitable for the construction of additional fields.

ESTIMATED AVAILABILITY OF FORCES

a. Ground

Considering the combined resources of Central and Southwest Pacific as of 1 September 1944, estimated availability of divisions for this operation is as follows:

(1) Allocated to
  SWPA   14 (inc. 1 Cav. Div.)
  Centpac   11 (inc. 5 Mar. Div.)
    Total   25
(2) Required for other purposes
  Solomons   1
  New Britain   2

New Guinea	4
Marianas-Marshalls	3
Total Required Elsewhere	10 Inf. or Mar.
(3) Available for Kyushu	15 Inf. or Mar.
(4) Required for Kyushu	8 Inf. or Mar.
(5) Indicated Surplus	7 Inf. or Mar.

The above computation takes into account employment of operationally available Australian and New Zealand Divisions in the Southwest Pacific Area in addition to U.S. Divisions shown above. The 7 Divisions indicated as surplus should be held available as a general reserve for the purpose of reinforcement or exploitation.

b. Air

It is considered that all aircraft allocated to the Southwest Pacific Area will be required to maintain that position and to continue neutralization of the Central Carolines. Accordingly only the 7th Air Force and land-based Navy Air of the Central Pacific will be available for installation in Kyushu, and to maintain Central Pacific positions. This will amount to:

	HB	MB	FTR	N FTR	RCN	TC		(GROUPS)
Army	3	1	3	1 Sq	2 Sq	2 Sq		
UE	(144)	(57)	(225)	(12)	(24)	(26)	=	(488)

	PB	PHOTO	B (T&D)	B (M)	FTR	N FTR	T	(SQUADRONS)
Navy	35	3	10	3	18	3	4	
UE	(420)	(36)	(180)	(36)	(324)	(36)	(48)	= (1080)

The proportion of this total which can be displaced forward to Kyushu and the timing of this displacement will depend upon a balancing of Kyushu airfield availabilities against requirements for continued neutralization of enemy positions in the Central Pacific and a security of our own line of communications.

c. Naval sea forces (less carrier) as assigned

d. Naval carriers

Overall availability in the Pacific will be as follows:

	VF	VSB and VTB
12 CVs =	432 A/C	648 A/C
9 CVLs =	216 "	81 "
54 CVEs =	972 "	486 "
	1620 "	1215 "

This cannot represent the total which can be employed in strikes against Japan since a portion of these carriers will be required for convoy escort and ferrying duties.

LOGISTIC IMPLICATIONS

Port Capacity:
Adequate if all ports from Miyazake to Akune (16 in all) are used. The force projected, 500,000 men, can be landed and maintained as follows:

	1ST MONTH	2ND MONTH	3RD MONTH
in area	—	250,000	400,000
landed	250,000	150,000	100,000
Total	250,000	400,000	500,000

The above is within the port capacity working 2-10 hour shifts. Considering the nature of the ports, normal capacity should be available shortly after capture. Some maintenance over-the-beach may be necessary during the first 30 days dependent on the rate of progress of the operation.

Roads:
Roads are adequate for port clearance.

Railroads:
Use of railroads is not essential.

Pipelines:
Provisions of pipelines (for AV, gas only) to HB fields should present no particular problem.

Service Troops:
There is an indicated shortage of service troops for the Formosa operation of at least 30,000 men. There is a general

shortage of service troops in the Pacific Theaters. While this shortage is not an insurmountable obstacle to the operation, in any final plan drastic measures will be necessary to roll up rear areas.

Assault Shipping and Craft:

The assault shipping and craft available will lift about 5 divisions with an excess availability of LSTs.

Cargo and Troop Shipping:

The following basic assumptions were used:

a. Navy support and maintenance provided for STALEMATE will provide for Navy requirements in Kyushu operation with shipping as set up for STALEMATE.

b. 80% of retentions provided for Halmahera and Mindanao operations in SWPAC will be withdrawn to provide necessary cargo shipping.

c. All forces will be provided from Pacific theaters, thus transferring maintenance requirements without increasing overall maintenance from U.S.

d. All Army initial movement from U.S. and all Navy initial movement except that provided for STALEMATE will be stopped.

e. Replacements of personnel will be allowed to the extent of 30,000 per month for Army and 20,000 per month for Navy for Pacific areas.

f. Div. in assault   —24,000 men
    Div. final strength   —35,000 men

ECHELON	UNITS
Assault	5 Div.
Immediate Follow-up	3 Div.
Buildup after D + 60	4 Div.
Air Force	8 Ftr. Gps.
	(4 on D + 5, rest after D + 15)
	8 H.B. Gps.

Under the above assumptions it is estimated that the following schedule could be supported by troop and cargo shipping:

a. Assault and immediate follow-up
    8 Divs.—212 Troops = 21,000 Vehicles
    4 Fighter Groups—(Includes 5 Divs. in assault shipping)

b. Buildup in first 30 days
67,000 troops (incl. 4 Fighter Groups)

c. Buildup in second 30 days
132,000 troops (completes full strength for 8 assault and follow-up divisions; includes 8 Heavy Bomb. groups and begins buildup of 4 additional divisions)

d. Buildup in third 30 days
89,000 troops (completes total force of 500,000 troops)

e. Total force can be supported in replacements and maintenance. Port and clearance capacities will support the Force.

It is emphasized that this uses up all shipping in the Pacific except for the movement of replacements and maintenance cargo to other Pacific areas.

Supply Implications:

T/O and T/E equipment for divisional units will present no great problem. Shortages of some special items and heavy equipment, particularly treadway bridging, are already indicated by accelerated Pacific operations.

General:

a. No estimate has been made of naval logistical requirements and availabilities.

b. If tonnage requirements for airfields are based on construction of new airfields rather than repair of existing ones, the rate of troop buildup will have to be reduced. The extent of reduction cannot be evaluated without a detailed airfield plan.

ADVANTAGES

Would attain maximum strategical surprise and capitalize on the Japanese buildup against our operations.

Would to a great extent blockade the other principal Japanese islands, because of Kyushu's strategical location, controlling the southern entrance to the Japan Sea, two of the three entrances to the Inland Sea, the Ryukyus approach, Tsushima Strait—shortest route for reinforcements and strategic materials from Asia—and to a lesser extent the Yellow Sea entrance.

The Sasebo naval base could be rendered useless to the Japanese.

Seizure can be limited to southern Kyushu: from this area it should be possible to restrict Japanese reinforcement, both by land and by sea, of the forces opposing us.

Sufficient airfields can be developed within the objective area to base our air forces.

Kagoshima and Ariake bays offer possibilities as naval anchorages.

The industrial, political, and military heart of Japan would be within range of medium bombers and fighters.

Should it prove necessary, furnishes a satisfactory base from which to conduct subsequent operations against the Tokyo plain.

Might hasten the entry of Russia in the war.

Might improve the situation on Chinese fronts by the diversion of Japanese forces.

DISADVANTAGES

Lodgement must be secured without land-based air support and cover.

An initial United States air superiority of somewhat less than 2 to 1 is indicated: because of the multitude of airfields within range of southern Kyushu on which the Japanese could disperse and shift their air forces, the knocking out of the Japanese air force by our carrier-based planes during the assault phase should not be counted on.

Fighter aircraft buildup and replacement must be brought in entirely by CVEs, thus further restricting the number of ship-based aircraft which can participate in the striking and covering forces for the assault.

Until the lodgement is secure and land-based air established in sufficient force, fleet elements must operate practically continuously at great distance from adequate bases.

Depends primarily on surprise to make up for the following preliminary operations hitherto considered necessary to reduce Japanese ability to wage war: further attrition of Japanese sea and air power and shipping; establishment of a sea and air blockade of Japan proper; preliminary land-based air bombardment of Japanese homeland installations. (The VHB operations would be limited to those possible from July through September from Chengtu—the Mariana VHB fields are not expected to be operational until November.)

Assault shipping limits assault force to 5 divisions.

Line of communication would be tenuous with few adequate intermediate bases, and subject to Japanese search and interdiction from the Ryukyus and Bonins.

Appendix B

The Potsdam Declaration

The Potsdam Declaration consisted of the following thirteen sections:

1. We, the President of the United States, the President of the national government of the Republic of China and the Prime Minister of Great Britain, representing hundreds of millions of our countrymen, have conferred and agreed that Japan shall be given the opportunity to end this war.

2. The prodigious land, sea and air forces of the United States and the British Empire and China, many times reinforced by their armies and air fleets from the west, are poised to strike the final blow at Japan. This military power is sustained and inspired by the determination of all Allied nations to prosecute the war against Japan until she ceases to resist.

3. The result of the futile and senseless German resistance to the might of the aroused free peoples of the world stand forth in awful clarity as an example to the people of Japan.

The might that now converges on Japan is immeasurably greater than that which, when applied to the resisting Nazis, necessarily laid waste to the land, the industry and the method of life of the whole German people.

The full application of our military power, backed by our resolve, *will* mean the inevitable and complete destruction of the

Japanese armed forces and just as inevitably the utter devastation of the Japanese homeland.

4. The time has come for Japan to decide whether she will continue to be controlled by these self-willed militaristic advisors whose unintelligent calculations have brought the empire of Japan to the threshold of annihilation, or whether she will follow the path of reason.

5. The following are our terms: We will not deviate from them: there are no alternatives: we shall brook no delay.

6. There must be *eliminated* for all time the authority and influence of those who have deceived and misled the people of Japan into embarking on world conquest, for we insist that a new order of peace, security and justice will be impossible until irresponsible militarism is driven from the world.

7. Until such a new order is established and until there is convincing proof that Japan's war-making power is destroyed, points in Japanese territory to be designated by the Allies shall be occupied to secure the achievement of the basic objectives we are here setting forth.

8. The terms of the Cairo Declaration shall be carried out and Japanese sovereignty shall be limited to the islands of Honshu, Hokkaido, Kyushu, Shikoku, and such minor islands as we determine.

9. Japanese military forces after being completely disarmed shall be permitted to return to their homes with the opportunity to lead peaceful and productive lives.

10. We do not intend that the Japanese shall be enslaved as a race or destroyed as a nation, but stern justice shall be meted out to all war criminals including those who have visited cruelties upon our prisoners.

The Japanese government shall remove all obstacles to the revival and strengthening of democratic tendencies among the Japanese people. Freedom of speech and religion and of thought, as well as respect for the fundamental human rights, shall be established.

11. Japan shall be permitted to maintain such industries as will sustain her economy and permit the payment of just reparations in kind, but not those industries which will enable her to re-arm for war.

12. The occupying forces of the Allies shall be withdrawn from Japan as soon as these objectives have been accomplished

and there has been established in accordance with the freely expressed will of the Japanese people a peacefully inclined and responsible government.

13. We call upon the government of Japan to proclaim now the unconditional surrender of their good faith in such action. The alternative for Japan is prompt and utter destruction.

Appendix C

Principal Individuals Surrounding Emperor Hirohito

1. Marquis Kido. Lord Keeper of the Privy Seal; confidant and advisor to the Emperor.
2. Hideki Tojo. Army General, War Minister, and former Prime Minister. He represented the Zaibatsu and pressed for war against the U.S. and Britain.
3. Prince Fumimaro Konoye. Former Prime Minister. He counseled against war with the U.S.; he wanted to meet with Roosevelt to arrange for a Roosevelt/Hirohito conference on a ship off Alaska. He was overridden by Tojo.
4. Kataro Suzuki. Prime Minister during the period when Hirohito was headed toward surrender. In 1941 he was army chief of staff.
5. Admiral Isoroku Yamamoto. Commander in Chief of the Combined Fleet. He planned the attack on Pearl Harbor. A Harvard graduate. Upon assuming command, he told Hirohito, "I will run wild for the first eighteen months, after that it will be all downhill." Hirohito replied, "By then Hitler will have won his war and I will reach an accommodation with Roosevelt." In 1941 events were going so well for Yamamoto that he boasted he would dictate peace terms to the U.S. in the White House.

6. Vice Admiral Tadaichi Nagumo. Commanded First Navy Air Fleet in Pearl Harbor attack.

7. Admiral Nagano. Navy chief of staff who also attended the September 6 meeting in the Imperial Palace.

8. Field Marshal Sugiyama. Commander of the First General Army, veteran of the conquest of Manchuria, and advocate of the Strike South war against the U.S. He attended the September 6 Imperial Conference to plan future moves. He was rebuked by Hirohito for his boastfulness.

9. Shigenori Togo. Minister of Foreign Affairs during the surrender period. He tried to enlist Russia's "good offices" to improve the terms of the Potsdam Declaration, but failed.

10. Naotake Sato. Japanese Ambassador to the Soviet Union.

11. General Korechika Anami. Minister of War who was determined to counter the expected invasion with military force. When Hirohito announced his decision to accept surrender he told all his officers at the War Ministry they must go along also. When one officer objected Anami slammed his riding crop on the table. It was like a rifle shot, and he exclaimed, "You will obey or it will be over my dead body." Later on, he committed suicide, and his last words were to urge his soldiers to live to rebuild Japan for the Emperor.

12. General Hiroshi Baron Oshima. Ambassador to Berlin, which was a clearinghouse of intelligence on Nazi-occupied Europe. Magic intercepts of his wireless messages to Tokyo revealed many secrets, including Westwall strength and the progress of atom bomb development at Los Alamos, material gathered by Gestapo agents in the United States. Oshima also arranged for Japan to receive design specifications of the German V-1 rocket bomb. He failed, however, to persuade Hitler to release the V-2, which Hirohito wanted in order to wipe out MacArthur's headquarters in Manila.

13. Baron Kuchiro Hiranuma. President of the Privy Council, he spoke for surrender during the fateful meeting of August 9 of the Supreme Council, held in the air-raid shelter of the Imperial Palace.

14. Prince Toshihiko Higashikuni. Hirohito's uncle, he was asked by the Emperor to form a government following the August 15 royal broadcast. It became known as the Peace Cabinet, despite the fact that Higashikuni had been an active planner of the war against Manchuria and later the United States. As

the new Prime Minister he was a signatory to the surrender document on the USS *Missouri*.

15. Ambassador Nomura. Ambassador to Washington prior to attack on Pearl Harbor. He had been instructed by his government to stall Cordell Hull and President Roosevelt until the attack on Pearl Harbor could be achieved.

16. Minister Kurusu. Assistant to Nomura in the stalling ploy.

17. Minister Kase. Japanese Minister in Bern, Switzerland, who handed Togo's surrender note to the Four Powers via Swiss diplomatic channels. Kase suggested to Togo that Swiss francs be contributed by Japan to the International Red Cross. This was in hopes of influencing the Red Cross report on conditions in Japanese prison camps, which were close to Auschwitz standards.

18. Suemasa Okamoto. Minister to Sweden, his messages of advice to Tokyo in regard to the surrender provide insights into the Japanese-European diplomatic structure.

19. Shigeru Yoshida. Became foreign minister with MacArthur's approval in 1946, serving until 1954. He posed as a member of the "Peace Faction," and thus was imprisoned just before the occupation by Kido. This was part of a stratagem to prove that there had been a bona fide "resistance" movement of which Shigeru was a part. Although MacArthur approved Shigeru as foreign minister in the occupation government based on Shigeru's experience as Ambassador to Britain from 1936 to 1938, he was aware of this Kido ploy and amused by it.

20. Mamori Shigemitsu. Led Japanese delegation to the surrender ceremony aboard the USS *Missouri*. He limped, due to a wooden leg resulting from a terrorist bomb some years before in Shanghai.

21. Yoshijiro Umezu. Chief of Imperial General Staff, he signed the surrender document on the USS *Missouri*.

22. Sadatoshi Tomioka. Imperial Navy Chief of Operations at the USS *Missouri* surrender ceremony. His chief, Admiral Toyoda, had refused to go to the surrender, despite the plea of Hirohito himself. Instead, he ordered Tomioka to go and sign in his place, saying, "You lost the war, so you go."

23. Empress Nagako. Hirohito's personal choice as a bride when a young prince. Nagako was a friendly, chubby girl at the time who tagged along with her brother, Prince Kuni Kunihisa, and her uncles Prince Higashikuni and Prince Asaka.

Hirohito as a young man always felt at home with the princess and her brother and uncles, and when it was time to select a bride his choice was Princess Nagako. Hirohito and her brother Prince Kuni shared interests in science. As Princess Nagako listened, they would talk at great length about the military future of Japan and the weapons that would be needed: the airplane, the tank, and bacteriological warfare.

Appendix D

Principal Individuals Surrounding General MacArthur

1. Admirals Chester W. Nimitz, William D. Leahy, Forrest P. Sherman, William F. Halsey, and Ernest J. King.
2. Army Generals: Robert L. Eichelberger (Eighth Army), Walter Krueger (Sixth Army), George C. Kenney (Chief of the Air Force in the Pacific), Jonathan M. Wainwright, who assumed command of troops on Corregidor/Bataan subsequent to MacArthur's ordered departure. Also, Carlos Romulo, Filipino army.
3. Mrs. Jean MacArthur, wife, and Arthur IV, son.
4. General Dwight D. Eisenhower, visiting in Tokyo, May 1946, with MacArthur during the occupation. A former colonel, and aide to MacArthur. When Eisenhower said to MacArthur, "I'm not running for the presidency," MacArthur retorted, "That's the way to play it, Ike."
5. Chief of Staff Richard K. Sutherland, until the occupation, when he returned to the U.S.
6. Brigadier General Courtney Whitney, the conniver who became chief of staff. MacArthur, criticized for the choice, said, "I know. Don't tell me. He's a son-of-a-bitch, but, by God, he's *my* son-of-a-bitch."

Principal Individuals Surrounding General MacArthur

7. Brigadier General Bonner Fellers, polished aide who first received the Emperor at the U.S. Embassy and took him to General MacArthur. He impressed Hirohito, who later wrote him a note.

8. Dr. Roger O. Egeberg, MacArthur's wartime physician and confidant.

9. General Charles Willoughby, MacArthur's Chief of Intelligence.

10. Colonel Lloyd "Larry" Lehrbas, aide to MacArthur.

11. Lieutenant Colonel Anthony F. Story, MacArthur's personal pilot.

12. Lieutenant General Curtis LeMay, Commander of B-29s in the Pacific.

13. Brigadier General Anderson, commander of B-29s on Guam.

14. George Atcheson, Jr., the General's chief political advisor.

15. Major Lawrence "Larry" E. Bunker, aide.

16. Major Faubion Bowers, aide.

17. Ralph M., America's premier spy in Japan. When occupation began he surfaced and became a member of General MacArthur's staff at Supreme Headquarters in Tokyo.

Index

253

Index

Index

Index

Index

Yonai, Admiral, 150
Yorktown, 66–67
Yoshihito, Crown Prince, 31
Yura, 78

Zaibatsu, ix, x–xi, 26, 30, 119, 221; economic expansion plans of, 17–18, 24, 27; and Hirohito's public-image campaign, 209; and the Keiretsus, 213–215; and the occupation, 169–170, 175–176, 179, 181, 188, 220; outlawing of, 186–193, 220, 221; overseas organizations of, 86, 172; and rise of Tojo, 22, 32, 206; SCAP report on, 173
Zaukaku, 52
Zuiho, 78